From

30119

D1322500

Brittany

with your family

by Rhonda Carrier

WILEY

A John Wiley and Sons, Ltd. Publication

UK Publisher: Sally Smith
Production Manager: Daniel Mersey
Commissioning Editor: Jill Emeny
Development Editor: Jill Emeny
Project Editor: Hannah Clement
Cartographer: Simonetta Giori
Photo Research: Jill Emeny

Wiley also publishes its books in a variety of electronic formats. Some content that appears in print may not be available in electronic books.

British Library Cataloguing in Publication Data

A catalogue record for this book is available from the British Library

ISBN: 978-0-470-68387-3 (pbk)
ISBN: 978-0-470-97998-3 (ebk)
ISBN: 978-1-119-97123-8 (ebk)
ISBN: 978-1-119-97124-5 (ebk)

Typeset by Wiley Indianapolis Composition Services

Printed and bound in China by RR Donnelley
5 4 3 2 1

Contents

List of Maps

About the Author

Rhonda Carrier (Brittany, France and Manchester, UK) was born in the Midlands but spent much of her teens wandering and lived in Hong Kong and Vienna before studying languages and literature at Cambridge and the Sorbonne in Paris. During the 1990s she lived in London where she worked as a writer and editor for local guides and listings maga-  zines, as well as publishing some award-winning short fiction. Since meeting her husband, the writer Conrad Williams, she has divided her time between Manchester in the UK and a crumbling old cognac farm in France, accompanied by their sons Ethan and Ripley.

Acknowledgements

As always, thanks to Conrad Williams for his support and companionship – and his great photos. Thanks too to the boys for allowing themselves to be dragged around the wilder shores of Brittany in the name of research.

Immense gratitude also goes to Daniel, Yolande and Sophie Amaglio, for long-ago summers that sparked my love affair with France and its language.

Friends, family and colleagues whose interest and encouragement are highly cherished by me are Holly McGrath and family; Fiona Dunscombe; Teresa Hardy; Barbara Dordi; Richard Dale; Heather Brice; Nick Royle; Gemma Hirst; Szilvi Naray-Davey; Paula Grainger and family; Liz Wyse; Judy Reynolds; Marie-Noel Brasset, Nicole Grimsdale and Judith Smith-Milne and their respective families; Christi Daugherty and all my former colleagues at Time Out; Dea Birkett, Lucy Ace, Georgina Allen and all my colleagues at TaketheFamily.com, and last but not least my parents Mary Freeman and David Carrier, my stepfather Tim, and my in-laws Leo and Grenville.

Sincères remerciements are also due to the many diligent tourist office and PR staff who helped in my research, particularly Elizabeth Thorold and Jenny Groutage, and of course to all the Frommer's staff who worked so hard on this book with me, especially Jill Emeny, Mark Henshall and Scott Totman.

Dedication

For Conrad, Ethan, Ripley and Zac: for adventures past and adventures to come.

An Additional Note

Please be advised that travel information is subject to change at any time and this is especially true of prices. We therefore suggest that you write or call ahead for confirmation when making your travel plans. The authors, editors and publisher cannot be held responsible for experiences of readers while travelling. Your safety is important to us however, so we encourage you to stay alert and be aware of your surroundings.

Star Ratings, Icons & Abbreviations

Hotels, restaurants and attraction listings in this guide have been ranked for quality, value, service, amenities and special features using a star-rating system. Hotels, restaurants, attractions, shopping and nightlife are rated on a scale of zero stars (recommended) to three (exceptional). In addition to the star rating system, we also use 5 feature icons that point you to the great deals, in-the-know advice and unique experiences, and amenities available. Throughout the book, look for:

FIND	Special finds – those places only insiders know about
MOMENT	Special moments – those experiences that memories are made of
VALUE	Great values – where to get the best deals
OVERRATED	Places or experiences not worth your time or money
GREEN	Attractions employing responsible tourism policies

The following **abbreviations** are used for credit cards:

AE	American Express
MC	MasterCard
V	Visa

A Note on Prices

In the Family-Friendly Accommodation section of this book we have used a price category system.

And the amenities:

A/C	Airconditioning		Jacuzzi/Hot Tub/Whirlpool
	Baby Changing		Laundry Facilities
	Babysitting		Lockers
	Bar		Microwave
BF	Breastfeeding		Minibar
	Buggy rental		Picnic Area
	Café		Play Area
P	Car Park		Pool - Children's
FREE	Car Park – Free		Pool - Indoor
£	Car Park - Paid		Pool - Outdoor
	Children's Club		Restaurant
	Children's Menu		Reservations
	Cinema		Safe
	Cots Available		Shop
	Cycle Hire		Shower
	DVD		Shuttle Bus
	Fitness Centre		Snack Bar
	Fridge		Spa Facilities
	Full Kitchen		Sports
	Games		Tennis Courts
	Garden		TV
	Garden Centre		Washer/Dryer
	Golf		Watersports Rental Equipment
	High Chairs		
@	Internet Access		Wheelchair Access
	iPod Docking		Wheelchair Rental

How to Contact Us

In researching this book, we discovered many wonderful places –
hotels, restaurants, shops and more. We're sure you'll find others.
Please tell us about them, so we can share the information with your
fellow travellers in upcoming editions. If you were disappointed
with a recommendation, we'd love to know that too. Please email:
frommers@wiley.co.uk or write to:

Frommer's Brittany With Your Family, 2nd Edition
John Wiley & Sons, Ltd
The Atrium
Southern Gate
Chichester
West Sussex, PO19 8SQ

Photo Credits

1 Family Highlights of Brittany

France has represented different things to me at various significant stages of my life: as a teenager spending long indolent summers in the country home of a French family; as a carefree student drunk on Gallic culture in Paris; as a thirty-something enjoying my first holiday with my husband-to-be; and as a house hunter while pregnant with my first baby nine years ago. But I've come to experience this wonderful country the most deeply as a mum, living in and exploring France with my three young sons, and learning to appreciate to the full its manifold charms: stunning landscapes, a laidback attitude to life, and superb food and drink.

I'm not alone—75 million foreign visitors to France each year make it the world's most popular holiday destination. A great many of these are British families, attracted by a number of factors—most notably, France's proximity to Britain and—despite the strength of the Euro—its lower living costs, which can make eating out and staying in interesting accommodation more affordable than in the UK, if you choose wisely.

Brittany, easily accessible from Britain and boasting kilometres of stunning coastline, has long been a favourite with visitors for its unspoilt beaches, untouristy inland sites bursting with authentic Breton culture, and child-friendly crêperies. This is also a region made magical by its myths and legends: countless sites are said to be linked with Merlin, Viviane, Sir Lancelot and other Arthurian figures, or with *korrigans*—shapeshifting Breton fairies with red flashing eyes, who like to substitute human children with changelings. Tales of these, and of mermaids and cities lost beneath the waves, are bound to enchant children of all ages.

Yet visiting France with children is not without its frustrations—for me, spoilt by having lived in central London with its round-the-clock facilities, the hardest aspect of French life has been the rigid and limited restaurant opening times and the tendency of shops, banks and businesses to shut down for two or three hours in the middle of the day. But once you've got your head around this and adjusted your routines, you'll find Brittany one of Europe's most delightful regions to visit with children. Just bear in mind that the weather can turn nasty on you whatever the season, so save some of those wonderful museums and aquariums for rainy days!

BRITTANY FAMILY HIGHLIGHTS

Best Family Events & Festivals

The 'festival of children in Brittany', **Bugale Breizh**, brings together most of the region's children's traditional dance groups—around 1,000 youngsters in all—in the Côtes d'Armor town of Guingamp, renowned for Breton dancing. See p. 156.

For one month in June, the hamlet of Nizon in Finistère hosts the quirky Fête des Cabanes featuring installation

St. Malo

pieces by modern artists placed in little huts that have been created from leaves, branches and other natural materials by local children. See p. 196.

Best Free Attraction There's street entertainment galore in the 17 'Stations Familles' that dot Brittany's coast as part of the school-holiday **Festival Place aux Mômes**. See p. 57.

Best Cities St. Malo in the Ille-et-Vilaine is a combination of ancient walled pirates' city and gorgeous seaside resort. It also offers some of the best shopping in Brittany, and has a fantastic aquarium. Also in the Ille-et-Vilaine, the buzzing Breton capital **Rennes** can't be beaten for eating and shopping, which go hand in hand with culture and amenities for the city's hip young families. See p. 61 and p. 60.

Finistère's naval port of **Brest** may not be the prettiest city but it has a cracking sealife centre—one of the world's best—and a stunning natural bay, the Rade de Brest. Similarly lacking in the looks department, **Lorient** in the Morbihan blends fascinating if dark history with state-of-the-art museums for an unbeatable family day out. See p. 196 and p. 106.

Best Natural Wonders The Côtes d'Armor's **Côte du Granit Rose**, with its pinky-brown rocks eroded into odd shapes resembling skulls, tortoises and piles of crêpes, is one of France's most famous stretches of coast. See p. 161.

The valley of **Huelgoat** in Finistère is strewn with as many legends as it is strangely shaped rocks. The best known, the Roche Tremblante or 'trembling rock', weighs about 100 tonnes but is balanced so precariously a child can make it move. See p. 202.

In the Morbihan, the inland sea of the **Golfe du Morbihan** has a magical landscape of tiny islands that you can see by boat or from a plane or hot-air balloon. See p. 112.

3

Cote du Granit Rose

Best Animal Attractions The Morbihan's **Ferme du Monde** is a remarkable farm with more than 400 domestic animals from around the world (including yaks, buffaloes and camels), created entirely by disabled workers. See p. 118.

The **Domaine de Ménez-Meur** in Finistère is a conservation park with farm, forest and country circuits where you can see wolves, boar and deer, and endangered Breton breeds. See p. 209.

Best Aquariums The **Grand Aquarium** in St. Malo in the Ille-et-Vilaine has an amazing **Nautibus** mini-submarine ride and a Bassin Ludique for young children, with a touchpool and funky interactive installations. See p. 72.

In Finistère, Brest's space-station-like **Océanopolis** is one of the world's best sealife centres, with a penguin colony, a multi-screen helicopter trip over Antarctica, a glass lift down past the shark tank and much, much more. See p. 210.

Best Beach Resorts Untouristy **St. Lunaire** in the Ille-et-Vilaine is a tranquil, low-key family resort with four lovely beaches, children's clubs and watersports, and lots of activities. See p. 74.

In the Morbihan, **Quiberon** has 'Famille Plus' status for its exceptional family-friendliness. Perched at the tip of its peninsula, it offers a superb beach, the Grande Plage, Festival Place aux Mômes events, (p. 57), a promenade lined by restaurants and ice cream parlours and boat trips galore. See p. 122.

Best Islands Wind-lashed **Ouessant** 20km (12.5 miles)

Océanopolis, Brest

off the Finistère coast is home to the world's most powerful lighthouse and a unique lighthouse museum. See p. 203.

Brittany's largest island, Belle-Ile off the Quiberon peninsula in the Morbihan, is a chic favourite among Parisians for its mild climate and idyllic beaches. Join local youngsters bodyboarding at Port Donnant. See p. 110.

Best Boat Trips The Nantes–Brest Canal, a chain of Napoléon-era canals and rivers, whose central junction is at Pontivy in the Morbihan. Now a thriving tourist waterway, it's best navigated by houseboat or canoe. See p. 130.

Trips in the Capitaine Némo, a catamaran with submarine viewing 'salons', allow you to get up close and personal with marine life around the Iles Glénan off the coast of Finistère, with guided commentary in French by a marine expert. See p. 200.

Best Outdoor Activities The annual countrywide Fête du Nautisme sees largely free tuition in and taster sessions of many of the watersports for which Brittany is famous, at locations around the coast. See p. 196.

The forest of Villecartier in the Ille-et-Vilaine is home to the Parc des Grands Chênes with its acrobatic routes through the trees. Bring a picnic for lunch by the lake with its Port Miniature, where you can ride replica ferries, tugs, steamboats and fishing boats amidst scale models of Breton landmarks. You can also

orienteer, walk and ride ponies. See p. 81.

For cyclists, Brittany has several traffic-free Voies Vertes or 'greenways', some of which link up to take you right across the region over the course of several days. See p. 82, p. 131, and p. 223. The Ille-et-Vilaine also has a Vélo Rail—a system of quirky two-person bikes, joined side-by-side, that you ride along old train tracks through the heart of nature. See p. 81.

The Fôret de Brocéliande (or Paimpont) in the Ille-et-Vilaine is a wonderland of Arthurian myths and atmospheric ancient monuments, as well as a scenic area for walking, riding and mountain biking. See p. 67.

Best Museums Rennes' Musée de Bretagne is a must-see for visitors to Brittany, tracing the region's history and identity through objects (including old toys), costumes, videos and more. It shares a building with the Espace des Sciences, a science museum with a planetarium and the Laboratoire de Merlin—a discovery zone with 30 hands-on installations. See p. 76.

On a coast bristling with majestic lighthouses, the Musée des Phares et Balises on Ouessant off Finistère is the world's only museum on the history of lighthouses and maritime signals. See p. 219.

Best Historical Sites The Abbaye Maritime de Beauport, a ruined Gothic abbey on the

Parc de Grands Chênes

Channel coast in the Côtes d'Armor, runs atmospheric Escales de Nuit night walks in July and August, with ethereal depictions of the monks' daily life—images of talking apples, a library illuminated by fireflies and other oddities—projected onto the abbey walls. There's also an apple festival including kids' workshops and storytelling. See p. 159.

Also in Côtes d'Armor, the fortified medieval **Fort la Latte** rises from jagged cliffs against a backdrop of blue sea, famous as a location for the final scenes of the 1958 film *The Vikings*. See p. 162.

Best Themepark The **Village Gaulois** in the Côtes d'Armor is a collection of Celtic-themed games in a setting out of an *Astérix* book, run by an association that channels profits into schools in Africa. See p. 166.

Best Markets Best known for its mysterious megaliths, Carnac in the Morbihan has a stylish beach resort that—in addition to

lots of children's activities—hosts **Nocturnes,** evening markets in July and August, with stalls full of local produce and crafts, Breton music and a *fest noz.* See p. 121.

Best Attraction for Teens The hip city of Rennes offers excellent parks and exciting festivals, including rollerblading **Rennes sur Roulettes** and the **Quartiers d'Ete**. See p. 56.

Best Attraction for Toddlers Watching marine life from the submarine 'salon' of **Capitaine Némo**. See p. 200.

Best Shops An unexpectedly great place for gifts and toys is **La Droguerie de Marine** in St. Malo in the Ille-et-Vilaine—a treasure trove of tin Pop Pop boats, games, ship's models, compasses, tin whistles, homewares, books, and local delicacies. See p. 64.

In Concarneau and a few other spots in Finistère, **Larnicol** has huge decorative chocolate

Fort la Latte

animals, colourful giant and mini meringues, slabs of chocolate, mouthwatering *kouignettes*, and *torchette* biscuits containing Breton seaweed. See p. 224.

BEST ACCOMMODATION

Best Family-Friendly Options

The Résidence Reine Marine in St. Malo in the Ille-et-Vilaine has pristine modern apartments with sea views and direct beach access. You pay a fraction of what you would at the résidence's big sister, the Grand Hôtel des Thermes, but can use its famous seawater therapy centre and children's beach clubs. See p. 92.

For those on a tighter budget, Pierre & Vacances' attractive Breton-stone holiday village at Port du Crouesty on the Golfe du Morbihan is a family paradise with a host of facilities including four pools and kids' clubs. See p. 144.

Best Grand Hotel

The Grand Hôtel Barrière—hotel of choice for French and foreign stars during Dinard's British film festival—is popular with well-to-do French families for its Club Diwi & Co kids' club, spa and hammam. See p. 90.

Best Seaside Hotels

Roscoff's Hôtel Le Temps de Vivre offers crisp modern rooms in an atmospheric old building, some with views towards the Ile de Batz (p. 200). See p. 223.

Unpretentious and relaxing, the Hôtel Bellevue in the super-family-friendly resort of Quiberon is a bargain given its lovely outdoor pool. Family rooms for three or four have a balcony or large decked terrace. See p. 142.

Most Stylish Hotel

Le Lodge Kerisper in the yachting town of La Trinité-sur-Mer in the Morbihan combines trendy 'beach hut' meets thrift-store décor with splashes of modern design. See p. 140.

Best B&B Le Char à Bancs near St-Brieuc in the Côtes d'Armor has five shabby-chic rooms for up to four people, filled with quirky objects, a charming inn, play equipment for children, Shetland ponies to pet (and ride in summer) and a river with pedalo hire in the warmer months. See p. 186.

Best Gîtes The chic *gîtes marins* at Les Maisons de Bricourt, part of superchef Olivier Roel-linger's empire at Cancale in the Ille-et-Vilaine, are in a league of their own—seaside cottages boasting log fires and cute sleeping nooks for children. A few steps away are a vegetable and herb garden where you can pick ingredients for dinner on your private terrace. See p. 90.

More affordably, **Le Rhun** on Finistère's Crozon peninsula comprises five tasteful gîtes in a former farmhouse and its out-buildings. Its owners, professional musicians, offer crash-courses in saxophone or clarinet. See p. 237.

Best Campsites If you love big campsites with plenty of activities and amenities, the vast **Domaine des Ormes** in parkland around a 16th–century château, handy for the ferry-port of St. Malo, offers everything from treehouses, 'nature lodges' and Russian-style log cabins to mobile homes and camping pitches. See p. 92.

Breton Stripes

No matter what the season's look is, there's room in every man, woman and child's wardrobe for at least one classic Breton sailor striped top—or marinière, as it's known in France. Along with its major virtues of being unisex, easy-to-wear whatever your shape, and relatively cheap, it's also perennially stylish—as evidenced by its popularity with the fashion elite, especially Jean Paul Gaultier, Karl Lagerfeld for Chanel, and the Japanese label Comme des Garçons. Indeed, it was Coco Chanel who transformed the humble marinière into a fashionista's staple, designing and wearing a striped top together with palazzo pants—a look adopted from French sailors. Other fans have included Brigitte Bardot, Jean Seberg, Jane Birkin and Debbie Harry, and, on the male side, everyone from James Dean and Pablo Picasso to Serge Gainsbourg and Kurt Cobain.

From punk to playground, the Breton shirt never looks out of place—and in Brittany, it's virtually de rigueur. And of course a holiday here is a great time to stock up on sailor stripes in a variety of incarnations, from classic tops to scarves and caps. Jersey is the fabric to look for, since it keeps its shape without being too clingy. One of the best places to find Breton tops is Comptoir de la Mer stores (p. 176) all over the region, but all seaside towns will have several shops selling them.

Domaine des Ormes

Also, but a totally different kettle of fish, the **Camping gîte de Loquéran** in Finistère offers a communal gîte reminiscent of a youth hostel and a basic but lovingly maintained 25-pitch campsite. See p. 238.

BEST DINING

Best Children-Friendly Restaurants On the busy Plage du Kélenn at the family resort of Carantec in Finistère, **Le Petit Relais** is a brasserie/pub/bar/*glacier* with a fine terrace, long opening hours and colouring sheets for children. See p. 227.

In the Ille-et-Vilaine, the **Auberge de la Cour Verte** offers country fare, grills and crêpes in an old stone farmhouse or on a flower-bedecked terrace beside a courtyard with kids' play equipment. See p. 84.

Best Seafood **Au Biniou** in the family resort of Le Val-André in the Côtes d'Armor is a stylish fish restaurant popular with locals for its shellfish platters, mussels from a nearby bay and fresh local fish. See p. 179.

La Corniche at Brignogan-Plages on the northern Finistère coast looks in part like a sailors' dive but serves incredible seafood against panoramic bay views. The children's creamy monkfish comes with some of the best *frites* they'll ever taste. See p. 226.

Best Crêperies The super-friendly **Crêperie des Grèves** at Langueux in the Côtes d'Armor uses local farm produce, much of it organic, in its faultless galettes and crêpes. Books for children are piled by the hearth, or they can wander out to the seaside play area as you enjoy a *bolée* of cider and keep an eye out from the window. See p. 182.

In the Morbihan, the **Crêperie Bara-Breizh** is another 'Crêperie Gourmande', that lures in families with its great galettes and crêpes together with an enclosed outdoor play area where junior diners can run off steam as their parents enjoy an aperitif on the terrace. See p. 137.

In the Ille-et-Vilaine, Rennes' **Crêperie La Rozell** is a delightful central spot that unfolds into a large rear garden. The wonderful galettes and crêpes include house specialities with black pudding and butter-cooked apples, and with marinated strawberries with violet ice cream. See p. 87.

Best Ethnic Restaurant Amid a sea of crêperies and seafood joints, the **Via Costa,** a camp Brazilian-themed 'lounge restaurant' by the beach at Etables-sur-Mer in the Côtes d'Armor, stands out. In a decor of fairy lights and exotic flowers, you can enjoy everything from chicken tagine with preserved lemon or creative Asian dishes to pizza or tapas dishes. See p. 181.

Best Outdoor Eating Le Surf at St.-Lunaire in the Ille-et-Vilaine masquerades as a humble snack bar but somehow produces an amazing variety of

Crêperie La Rozell, Rennes

wonderful dishes from its tiny kitchen, at bargain prices. See p. 85.

A great picnic spot is the **Fôret de Villecartier,** also in the Ille-et-Villaine. Work up an appetite on the treetop adventure course at **Parc de Grands Chênes,** or go out on the lake in a pedalo or a replica ferry or steamboat. See p. 81.

Best Views In Finistère, the **Restaurant Patrick Jeffroy** at Carantec has a panoramic dining room looking out over the yacht-filled Baie de Morlaix. See p. 226.

2 Planning a Family Trip to Brittany

BRITTANY

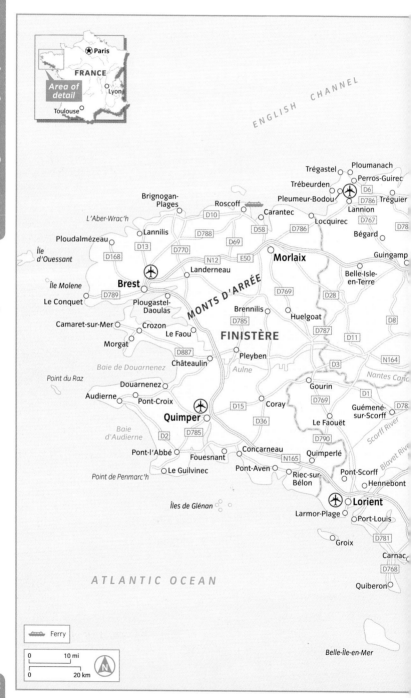

Paris

FRANCE

Area of detail

Lyon

Toulouse

ENGLISH CHANNEL

Trégastel
Ploumanach
Perros-Guirec
Trébeurden
D6
Pleumeur-Bodou
D786 Tréguier
Brignogan-
Plages
Roscoff
Lannion
D78
L'Aber-Wrac'h
D10
Carantec
Locquirec
D767
Bégard
Ploudalmézeau
Lannilis
D788
D69
Morlaix
Guingamp
Île
d'Ouessant
D168
D13
D770
N12
E50
Belle-Isle-
en-Terre
Landerneau
Brest
Le Conquet
D789
Plougastel-
Daoulas
D769
D28
D8
MONTS D'ARRÉE
Brennilis
Huelgoat
Camaret-sur-Mer
Crozon
D785
Morgat
Le Faou
FINISTÈRE
D787
D11
D887
Pleyben
Baie de Douarnenez
Châteaulin
D3
N164
Aulne
Point du Raz
Douarnenez
Gourin
Nantes Canal
Audierne
Pont-Croix
D1
D769
Quimper
D15
Coray
Guémené-
sur-Scorff
D78
Baie
d'Audierne
D2
D785
D36
Le Faouët
D790
Pont-l'Abbé
Fouesnant
Concarneau
Quimperlé
N165
Point de Penmarc'h
Le Guilvinec
Pont-Aven
Riec-sur-
Bélon
Pont-Scorff
Hennebont
Îles de Glénan
Lorient
Larmor-Plage
Port-Louis
ATLANTIC OCEAN
Groix
D781
Carnac
D768
Quiberon

Ferry

0   10 mi
0   20 km
N

Belle-Île-en-Mer

VISITOR INFORMATION

Family trips of any kind require you to find a happy medium between inflexible military-style advance plotting and being so *laissez-faire* that you may, when you're actually on holiday, make poor decisions because you don't know your options—and hence miss out on some of the best experiences. Be flexible enough to allow a place for the *unplanned*—unexpected events and encounters will constitute many of your most cherished memories.

It's also important that your children, as soon as they're old enough—are involved in the planning stages of your adventure, so spend some time discussing what every family member would like to see and do rather than making assumptions.

The Internet age has made researching and planning holidays a breeze while muddying the waters to some degree—it can be difficult to know that information is up to date, and it's all too easy for web-savvy tourism providers to make their accommodation, eatery or other attraction look far more alluring on-screen than it is in real life by masking its defects. Hence the need for a guide like this…

France's information-packed official tourist board website, *www.franceguide.com*, clicks through to separate sites for 30+ countries, including *http://uk. franceguide.com/* for the UK and *http://ie.franceguide.com* for Ireland. These individual sites have an interactive map that let you click through to fairly detailed information on the various regions, including Brittany, and provide links to the regional tourist board (Comité Régionale de Tourisme or CRT) and the *départmentale* tourist boards (Comite Départementales de Tourisme or CDTs). CRT sites then generally link to, or have contact details of, the tourist offices (*offices de tourisme*) for major towns and cities. Note that CRTs and CDTs aren't actual places you can visit. The CRT website for Brittany is *www.tourismebretagne.com*; the English-language version is *www. brittanytourism.com*.

I've listed CDT websites under 'Visitor Information' in the relevant sightseeing chapter; most are translated into English and some have pages on family holidays or children's activities. They usually list most tourist offices, *syndicats d'initiative* (small tourist office) or *mairies* (town hall) in the *département*. You may want to print out the page for any *département* you plan to visit. The French-only *www.tourisme.fr* also has an 'annuaire' or directory of tourist offices and *syndicats d'initiative*.

Child-Specific Websites

Brittany's regional tourist board website *www.brittanytourism.com* has an 'Ideas' bar with inspiration for families with children of various ages. Another useful

How this Book Works

Brittany is a vast area that subdivides into four administrative départements (similar to UK counties)—Ille-et-Vilaine, Morbihan, Côtes d'Armor and Finistère. For ease of planning, I've based the sightseeing chapters of this book (Chapters 3–6) on these départements.

While it's impossible to present a comprehensive survey of family holidays in the region in one book, I've strived to give an idea of the cream of what's on offer. Each of the four sightseeing chapters starts by focusing on the area's special qualities, its location and how to get there, and its family highlights. There follows a selection of attractions and accommodation, the latter ranging, for example, from a seaside campsite to self-catering cottages on a working farm or a five-star family-friendly hotel. And while most cafés and restaurants will accommodate children, I've tracked down those that are truly welcoming to families. Accommodation and eating places have been grouped according to average price; attractions show the suggested age range.

resource, *www.france4families.com*, has general information on France plus reasonably detailed information about family days out in regions including Brittany.

Famille Plus is an official label awarded to resorts judged to be particularly family-friendly, of which there were nine in Brittany at the time of writing; see *www.familleplus.fr* for information (French only). Sensations Bretagne (*www.sensation-bretagne.com*), restricted to Brittany, is a conglomeration of 19 child-friendly resorts; I've listed each resort in the Best Beaches section of each sightseeing chapter, but the website is a good place for detailed and current information.

More general family-oriented sites are *www.takethefamily.com*, with tips, destination guides (including lots on camping in France) and a discussion forum; and *www.babygoes2.com*, with general tips and location reports.

For route planning, the excellent *www.viamichelin.com* gives detailed directions (plus maps) from your home town to your destination in France, or between places in France, and also tells you how much you'll spend in tolls and petrol. Also useful is *http://maps.google.com*, with zoomable maps of just about anywhere, directions to and from places, and even detailed satellite images—look at Brest's Océanopolis from above, for instance, or even the hotel you're going to stay in!

Entry Requirements

Passports & Visas

Citizens of other European Union (EU) countries need an identity card to enter France—for

Knees-Up Breton Style

One festival you'll find all over Brittany, in just about every town and village, is the *fest noz*—an evening of traditional Celtic music and circle dances, often with a bonfire. You'll find one near you on any Saturday evening (look for flyers on town-hall noticeboards and in shop and supermarket windows), with visitors welcome to join in the dancing and general merrymaking for free; you pay for drinks and food.

the time being, this means a passport for UK citizens. Non-EU citizens need a passport but few nationalities require a visa— South Africans are among the few. However, stays of more than three months by non-EU citizens do require a visa. For French embassies/consulates round the world, see *www.expatries. diplomatie.gouv.fr*.

Customs

For the latest information on what you can and cannot bring out of France, see the English-language pages of the French customs website, *http://www. douane.gouv.fr/data/file/5461.pdf*.

Specialised Resources

For Single Parents

The best source of travel advice and destination guide for single parents is the US-based *www. singleparenttravel.net/*. See also *www.takethefamily.com/prepare/ singleparenttravel.php*.

Single parents get discounts with some tour operators, including **Eurocamp/Keycamp** (p. 38) and **Siblu** (p. 38), as

well as at most **youth hostels** (p. 33).

For Grandparents

Grandparents travelling with children are a rapidly growing market, but specialist operators in the field tend to be US-based, and there are no current tours that include Brittany.

Grandparents—many of whom may be retired and living in France—are most likely to holiday with their children and grandchildren in gîtes (p. 34). If you take your grandchildren on outings, remember that over-60s generally get **discounts** on travel tickets, museum and zoo entry, and so on.

For Families with Special Needs

Many of France's historic buildings, including museums and hotels, have limited or non-existent **wheelchair access**. Older town hotels, in particular, have tiny lifts or lack them altogether. That said, modern facilities are up-to-scratch, and most hotels have at least a couple of accessible or ground-floor rooms.

Tourism for All (*www.tourism forall.org.uk*) has holidays in purpose-built apartments in Brittany among their offerings, plus lots of useful information.

Although the Channel Tunnel is a long way from Brittany, if you come to the region via Normandy, it's within easy reach of the latter. Travelling on the **Eurotunnel** (p. 24) is easier than ferries for wheelchair users because you stay in your car. Alternatively, **Eurostar** (p. 24) offers first-class travel for second-class fares for disabled people.

Money

The Euro

France—in common with 15 other countries at the time of writing—has the Euro (€) as its currency. There are 100 cents in a Euro, with notes for 5€–500€ and coins for 1 cent–2€.

As of writing, the Eurosterling exchange rate was 1.19€ to £1 (83p to 1€), making holidays in France poorer value than in previous years. For current rates and a currency converter, see *www. xe.com*.

Credit & Debit Cards

Most French shops, restaurants and hotels take credit or debit cards, or at least **Visa** and **Mastercard**—**American Express** and **Diner's Club** are only really accepted in expensive hotels and restaurants. There is often a lower spending limit of 7€–15€ for cards. The only places unlikely to accept cards today are B&Bs, small campsites and inexpensive rural inns.

You use your **PIN** when making a purchase with your card as well as when using it at a cashpoint. You can now often use your card at automated pumps at petrol stations out of hours, but it's as well to have a backup option.

Before you leave, tell your credit card company you're going abroad, as they often put a **block on cards** that deviate from their normal spending pattern.

For **lost or stolen cards**, see p. 44.

Traveller's Cheques

These are becoming a thing of the past now that cities and most towns have 24-hour ATMs, and you need to show ID every time you cash one. If you do choose to take some traveller's cheques, perhaps as a backup, you can get them at some banks, building societies, travel agents and the Post Office, among other outlets. Keep a record of their serial numbers in case of loss or theft, and carry them separately from money and/or cards.

Cashpoints

There are 24-hour cashpoint machines or ATMs outside all French banks and in many supermarket lobbies—even relatively

What Things Cost in Brittany	€
1 litre unleaded 95 petrol	1.38€
Hire of medium-sized car (per week)	200€–550€
Taxi ride	2€ base fare; 1.10€ per km
City/town bus fare, adult	1.20€
City/town bus fare, child 5 or over	1.20€
Single train fare Quimper–Brest	15.80€ (75km/46 miles)
Single train fare child 4–11	7.80€ (75km/46 miles)
Single TGV fare, Rennes–Vannes	24€ (110km/69 miles)
Single TGV fare child 4–11	24€ (110km (69 miles)
Single Air France fare, Paris–Brest	62€–155€ (600km/375 miles) (inc taxes)
Single Air France fare, Paris–Brest	62€–155€ children over 2 (inc taxes)
Admission to zoo, adult	15€
Admission to zoo, child 3–12	8€
Cinema ticket, adult	8€
Cinema ticket, child	5.60€
British newspaper	0.55–2€
Local telephone call (per minute)	0.03€
European phone call (per minute)	0.22€
Fixed-price menu at mid-priced restaurant	11€–18€
Under-12s menu at mid-priced restaurant	8.50€
1 litre milk in supermarket	0.86€
1 litre apple juice in supermarket	0.86€
1.5 litre bottle still water in supermarket	0.30€
1kg bananas in supermarket	2.50€
Ham and cheese baguette from takeaway counter	3.50€
Packet of 20 small Pampers in supermarket	8.50€
330ml infant milk in supermarket	0.80€

small ones in out-of-the-way towns—and withdrawing cash is rarely a problem unless you've gone over your limit. You usually get a better rate at a cashpoint than at an exchange booth (which may also take a commission), but your bank will probably charge you a fee for using a foreign cashpoint, so don't withdraw small sums every day or two as you may at home.

Bring some cash into France as a backup, and have two or more cards in case of a hiccup—you can make withdrawals from cashpoints using credit cards, paying interest on the advance from the moment you receive the cash.

Weather & When to Go

The weather in Brittany is notoriously changeable, switching from glorious sunshine to pouring rain in the blink of an eye. As in the UK, winters are very cold and summers increasingly

Average Daytime Temperature & Rainfall in Brittany

	Jan	Feb	Mar	Apr	May	June	July	Aug	Sept	Oct	Nov	Dec
Temp. (degree C)	9.3	8.6	11.1	17.7	16	22.7	25.1	24.1	21.2	15.5	9.5	6.2
Rainfall (cm; St-Malo)	8.06	5.24	4.79	6.4	5.72	3.58	4.97	4.26	4.84	8.29	7.81	8.72

hot. Even late May can be a grey drizzle-fest, particularly on the west coast, and in summer you should still pack light sweaters, waterproof coats and hats, and Wellington boots alongside swimming gear (or buy some while you're in France). If you plan to eat in some of the fancier hotel restaurants during your stay, you also need to pack quite smart clothes.

INSIDER TIP

Men and boys travelling to France take note—many establishments won't let you wear swimming shorts but insist on Speedo-style fitted trunks.

A very helpful Internet/iPhone tool for planning days out is **www.meteofrance.com**; even with only basic French (you need to know the days of the week) you get a general idea of what to expect in your area from its click-on maps. A good English-language website is **http://weather.uk.msn.com**.

Since Brittany is most popular among tourists for its beaches and coastal resorts, it's at its busiest and most expensive in **July and August**. Remember too that the French holiday *en masse* in August, meaning congested roads and resorts, and crowding at big family attractions such as

Brest's Océanopolis. On the other hand, this is when most **festivals and events**, including **children's beach clubs**, take place. I've listed many of these beach clubs, often called 'Clubs Mickey', in the relevant sightseeing chapters; otherwise, they're generally detailed on tourist office websites or centrally on the national beach clubs federation's website, **www.fncp.fr**.

Otherwise, **spring, early or late summer** or **autumn** can be charming times to visit, when you have many animal parks and beaches virtually to yourself. But you'll need contingency plans for those days when the weather lets you down, and smaller attractions may not be open—so please look out for the Rainy Days boxes in each of the sightseeing chapters, listing softplay centres, cinemas and other wet-weather standbys. You're also best advised to save Brittany's wonderful museums, aquaria and other indoor attractions for rainy days.

INSIDER TIP

If you do visit at a busy period, note that the French tend to go out mid-afternoon, after the lunch break, so mornings can be good times to see the more popular attractions.

The Best of the Festivals

Festival Place aux Mômes, p. 67—Ille-et-Vilaine, Chapter 3
Breizh Sable Tour, p. 104—Morbihan, Chapter 4
Festival Interceltique, p. 105—Morbihan, Chapter 4
Bugale Breizh, p. 156—Côtes d'Armor, Chapter 5
Les Jeud'his de Guingamp, p. 157—Côtes d'Armor, Chapter 5
Festival de Cornouaille, p. 195—Finistère

Health, Insurance & Safety

Travel Insurance

Travellers to France from other EU countries need to carry their **European Health Insurance Card** (EHIC) as proof of entitlement to free/reduced-cost medical treatment abroad. The quickest way to apply for one is online (**www.ehic.org.uk**), or call 0845 606 2030, or get a form from a post office. You still pay upfront for treatment and related expenses; the doctor will give you a form you use to reclaim most of the money (about 70% of doctors' fees and 35–65% of medicines/prescription charges) when you get home.

The EHIC only covers '*necessary* medical treatment', and does not cover repatriation costs, lost money, baggage or cancellation, so is no replacement for **travel insurance**. But before you buy the latter, check whether your existing insurance policies, credit cards or bank account covers you for lost luggage, cancelled tickets or medical expenses. If they don't, an example of cover for a family of four travelling to France for 2 weeks,

without any adventure sports, with a reputable online insurer such as *www.travelinsuranceweb.com* is 25€; an annual (31-day) multi-trip policy costs 50€, so is well worth it if you make more than two trips a year. Make sure your package includes **trip-cancellation insurance** to help you get your money back if you have to back out of a trip or go home early (both more likely if you're travelling with youngsters), or if your travel supplier goes bust. Allowed reasons for cancellation can range from sickness to natural disasters or a destination being declared unsafe for travel.

You're unlikely to get stranded in Brittany, but if you do, your travel provider will almost certainly cover your accommodation and meals for the duration under EU regulations; those from outside the EU should check with their airline or travel provider, but special attention is usually afforded to those travelling with kids.

Other **non-EU nationals**—with the exception of Canadians, who have the same rights as EU citizens to medical treatment within France—need comprehensive travel insurance that covers medical treatment overseas. Even then, you pay bills upfront and apply for a refund at home.

Staying Healthy

There are no real health risks while travelling in France, and you don't need vaccinations. For general advice on travelling with children, read *Your Child Abroad: a Travel Health Guide*, by Dr Jane Wilson-Howarth and Dr Matthew Ellis (Bradt).

If You Fall Ill

For **emergency treatment, doctors and chemists,** see p. 42 and p. 44.

Bring along copies of **prescriptions** in case a family member loses their medication or runs out. Carry the generic name of prescription medicines in case a local pharmacist is unfamiliar with the brand name. Also bring along an extra pair of any contact lenses or prescription glasses.

When flying, pack any **prescription medicines** you'll need while in the air in your hand luggage in their original containers, with chemist's labels. At the time of writing, anti-terrorism precautions required some medicines to be verified by airport chemists.

If you or your child has an illness that may make explanation of what's happening impossible, and that needs swift and accurate treatment (such as epilepsy, diabetes, asthma or a food allergy), the charity **MedicAlert** (*www.medicalert.org.uk*) provides body-worn bracelets or necklets engraved with the wearer's medical condition(s)/vital details, ID number and a 24-hour emergency telephone number that accepts reverse charge calls so his or her medical details can be accessed from anywhere in more than 100 languages.

Travelling Safely

France—especially outside Paris and other major cities—is generally a very safe country. A traveller's main worry, as in most countries, is the risk of being targeted by **pickpockets and petty thieves,** so travel with your car doors locked as a precaution. As a parent, be especially wary of French drivers; some pay no heed to the speed limit, exceed the alcohol limit and drive aggressively. Virtually no one in France stops at **pedestrian crossings,** so tell your child to wait until vehicles are motionless before proceeding.

As everywhere, **hold hands with young children** and don't let them out of your sight unless someone you trust is supervising them—they can move faster than you think. Avoid situations where your child could get swept away in a **crowd,** and with older children, agree on **a place to meet** should you get parted— at the information desk at a museum, for instance. Make sure they have your mobile number and accommodation address on them, with instructions to ask for a member of the police force (*agent de police* or

Children's Kit

The following items can make travelling with babies or young children in Brittany easier or more relaxing:

Bébétel Baby Monitor Unlike battery-powered listening devices, this is not limited by range and suffers no interference, so you can use it in all hotel restaurants. You plug it into a standard phoneline (there are foreign adapter sets) and program in your mobile number (you may have to add the international code); if your child gets up or cries, the monitor calls you. It costs about 176€ (*www.bebetel.com*); a few hotels have them but none in Brittany. You can also now get Bluetooth versions and motion detectors for added peace of mind.

Littlelife Baby Carriers These backpacks-with-children-in, great if you're walking or hiking and don't want to be encumbered with a buggy, include 'Voyager', with a changing mat and a zip-off bag for drinks, snacks and wipes, for about 199€; lighter models start at half that. Littlelife is sold at *www.johnlewis.com* and outdoor pursuits shops.

Portable Highchairs Most French restaurants provide at least one highchair, but if they don't, or it's taken, or it's a weird old-style one without a front bar, you may be left trying to eat with one hand and hold a squirming baby or toddler with the other. Lightweight options you can carry around include the supremely compact Koo Di Pack It (a loop of fabric that secures your baby to the chair), the foldable Minui Handysitt toddler seat, and The First Years' inflatable booster seat. All are sold at *www.kiddicare.com*, with prices from around 14€ to 65€.

gendarme) should they not be able to find you. Their name should never be visible on their bag/clothing, and tell them the importance of **never divulging their name to a stranger**.

Beaches can be lethal: you lie back and close your eyes for what seems like a second, and when you open them your child is nowhere to be seen. With the sea close by, the potential for disaster is clear. The rule is to take it in turns to flake out while one parent keeps watch. If you're alone, you have no option but to stay hyper-alert. Try a set of walking reins if you have a toddler who likes to go walkabout.

ESSENTIALS

Getting There

By Car & Ferry Most families, especially those with younger kids, find bringing their own car across the Channel the best way to holiday in France, since they can simply pack up your car and drive, without worrying about luggage restrictions.

Brittany has ferry ports at **St. Malo** in the Ille-et-Vilaine and Roscoff in **Finistère**. For more details, including crossing times, see the 'Getting There' sections of the respective sightseeing chapters.

The major ferry operator between Britain/Ireland and northern France, **Brittany Ferries** (UK ☎ *0871 244 1400*/ France ☎ *0825 828 828*, *www.brittany ferries.com*), has crossings to St. Malo and Roscoff, as well as Caen-Ouistreham and Cherbourg in Normandy, both of which can be handy for eastern Brittany. All vessels have children's facilities, and some are positively luxurious—the *Pont-Aven*, for instance, which sails between Roscoff, Plymouth and Cork, has a swimming pool, cinemas and some plush accommodation, including Commodore Class rooms with a double bed and sofabed, TV/DVD player, balcony and free breakfast.

Although long sailings (as compared to the most popular routes from Dover to northeastern France; p. 24) are evidently the costliest, with small children in the car you'll probably be keen to reduce driving time—it doesn't make sense, for instance, to take a cheap ferry to Boulogne and then drive all the way across northern France to holiday on the western Breton coast, unless you're visiting other places en route. What you save in ferry fares, you lose in petrol money (especially with current prices), possible overnight stays in hotels, countless snack stops and general shredded nerves. Try to think of a long ferry crossing as part of the overall adventure of your holiday, not simply the act of getting there.

Prices vary widely according to whether you travel by day or night, the standard of accommodation you choose (it's obligatory on overnight sailings), the number of passengers, the size of your car and other details. However, as a rough guide, a return trip (overnight both ways, late Aug to mid-Sept) between Plymouth and Roscoff for two adults and two children aged 4 to 15 with a standard car, 4X4 or MPV without a roof load, trailer or bike carrier, in an outside four-berth cabin, costs about £530. An outside cabin (that is, with a window) is only slightly more expensive than an inside one but makes the experience all the more exciting for youngsters (and often for adults too!). The cheapest option is an inside couchette with shared facilities. The same journey with a **motorhome** is £560, with a car and the smallest model of **caravan** £640.

The **online booking system** is good; some people prefer the transparency of talking to an operator about the cheapest options, but Brittany Ferries' online system does give you a colour-coded guide to the scale of prices around your preferred date so you aren't trapped into the most expensive crossing. And make sure to play around with the buttons when getting an online quote: you may find, for instance, that a cabin with a TV is no more expensive than one without. Note that Brittany Ferries is also an award-winning **tour operator** (p. 37).

Other ferry firms operating to Brittany are **Condor Ferries** (Poole/Weymouth–St. Malo, plus Portsmouth–Cherbourg in Normandy; *0845 609 1024, www.condorferries.co.uk*), and **Irish Ferries** (Rosslare–Roscoff, or Rosslare–Cherbourg in Normandy; Ireland *0818 300400, www.irishferries.com*). Ships have children's amenities. Again, purely as a guide, in late Aug/ early Sept you might expect to pay £450 for a Poole–St. Malo return with Condor Ferries, for a family of four with a standard car and no trailer (there are no overnight crossings).

The shortest, cheapest and most popular Channel crossings are **Dover** to **Boulogne, Calais** and **Dunkerque,** which are on the other side of northern France from Brittany but may be useful if you're touring Normandy first. Normandy also has its own ferry ports: **Caen-Ouistreham, Cherbourg, Dieppe** and **Le Havre.**

You might save by booking ferries (and **Eurotunnel;** p. 24) through a 'one-stop shop' such as *www.ferrybooker.com*, but it's difficult to make direct price comparisons because its search facility may not throw up the same sailings and accommodation availability. Families who can be flexible about when they travel will nearly always find that fares are cheaper mid-week.

By Eurotunnel If you come to Brittany via Paris or Normandy, the **Eurotunnel** shuttle train service (*08705 353535, www.euro tunnel.com*), which takes cars through the Channel Tunnel between Folkestone and Calais, can be the least painful crossing option, since the journey takes just 35 minutes and you don't even need to get out of your car. The standard return fare is £98 but this can vary considerably, with the best prices available to those who travel early in the morning or late at night. More expensive Flexiplus fares allow you to get an earlier or later train from the one you're booked on, for free provided you arrive within two hours of your scheduled departure time, and you also get access to an Executive Lounge where free snacks and drinks, kids' lunchboxes and Wi-Fi access are available.

By Rail You can travel from London St. Pancras International or Ashford Kent to Calais, Lille or Paris on **Eurostar** (*08432 186186, www.eurostar.com*); London to Paris takes about 2 hours 15 minutes, with fares varying according to how far ahead you book and the degree of flexibility you require regarding exchanges or refunds—they can be as low as £69 per adult and £49 per child aged 4–11 for a return ticket in standard class.

Eurostar can also book **onward journeys** from Lille or

Paris to Rennes, Brest, Quimper, Lorient and Vannes in Brittany. Alternatively, *www.raileurope.co.uk* offers combined booking for Eurostar tickets and onward journeys.

By Air **Low-cost airlines** have opened up Brittany to air travellers; routes tend to come and go, but at the time of writing you could fly from points in the **UK and Ireland,** including the Channel Islands, to:

Dinard (Ille-et-Vilaine)

Rennes (Ille-et-Vilaine)

Brest (Finistère)

Lorient (Morbihan)

Companies that operate regular flights to destinations in Brittany from Britain and/or Ireland are **Ryanair** (UK ☎*0871 246 0000*, Ireland ☎*0818 303030*, France ☎*0892 780210, www.ryanair.com*); **Flybe** (UK ☎*0871 700 2000*, outside UK ☎*00 44 01392 268529, www.flybe.com*), **Aer Lingus** (Ireland ☎*0818 365000*, UK ☎*0871 718 5000, www.aerlingus.com*); **Aer Arann** (Ireland ☎*0818 210210*, UK ☎*0870 876 7676*, and rest of world ☎*00 353 818 210210, www.aerarann.com*).

For who flies where, see the 'Getting There' section of the relevant sightseeing chapters.

As a general rule, **under-2s fly free** if they sit on your knee; older than that, they pay the same fare. **Fares** can start as little as £0.01 depending on your destination and when you book, but often don't include **airport taxes and other charges** (everything from checked-in baggage to online check-in), which can add up to more than £200 for a family of four.

You can also fly to **Paris** from the UK or Ireland with a number of operators, including **British Airways** (UK ☎*0871 663 3777*, France ☎*+33 0825 825400, www.britishairways.com*) and **Air France** (UK ☎*0870 142 4343*, France ☎*36 54, www.airfrance.com*). From Paris, there are flights to **Rennes** (Ille-et-Vilaine), **Lannion** (Côtes d'Armor), **Brest** and **Quimper** (Finistère) and **Lorient** (Morbihan) with Air France (above).

Among airlines that fly regularly between the **USA** and Paris are: **American Airlines** (☎*800 433 7300, www.aa.com*), **British Airways** (☎*1-800-AIRWAYS*), **Continental Airlines** (☎*1-800 231 0856, www.continental.com*), and **Delta Air Lines** (☎ *1-800 221 1212, www.delta.com*). **Air France** (above) flies to Paris from the USA and Canada, and **Air Canada** (☎ *1-888 247 2262, www.aircanada.com*) flies there from Toronto and Montreal.

There are currently no direct flights from **Australia** to Paris; most people go to London and get a connecting flight. **South African Airways** (☎*0861 359722, www.flysaa.com*) flies to Paris from Cape Town and other cities in South Africa.

What can you take on flights: With regulations and increasingly heightened security measures in place, be sure to check with a reliable official source such as *www.direct.gov.uk*

for the latest guidelines on hand luggage rules.

By Bus This is your cheapest but slowest and least comfortable means of getting to the Continent, and with children in tow you may be asking for one long headache of a journey. It may be bearable with teenagers, if you bring the requisite iPods, game gadgets and books.

Eurolines (☎ *08717 818181*, *www.eurolines.co.uk*) runs from London–Victoria to Paris, taking between 7 hours 15 minutes and 13 hours, depending on how long you have to wait at the port. Some buses have extra leg room; all have air-con and toilets. Prices start at £12 one-way ('Funfares' for all ages from 0).

Getting Around

By Car Though far from environmentally friendly (or cheap, given today's petrol prices), having your own set of wheels allows you the necessary flexibility when it comes to exploring Brittany, especially more rural areas.

Most visitors from the UK bring their own cars on the ferry (p. 22) or—less handy for Brittany—the Eurotunnel (p. 24); if you're among them, you need to bring your **driving licence,** the original of the **vehicle registration document,** a current **insurance certificate** and, if the vehicle isn't registered in your name, a letter of authorisation from the owner. Your British insurance will give you the

minimum legal cover required in France, but it's advisable to ask your insurer for a **green card** (international insurance certificate)—these are no longer compulsory but provide fully comprehensive cover. Get yourself some extra peace of mind by arranging **24-hour breakdown assistance** too (p. 28). Note that if you break down on a motorway (of which there is only one in Brittany), however, you can only call the official breakdown service operating in that area; there are orange emergency telephones every two kilometres. They have a fixed fee of 113€ for repairing or towing a vehicle Monday to Friday, from 8am to 6pm, 169.50€ the rest of the time including public holidays. You can call your breakdown firm once towed off the motorway.

Those coming into France must display an international **sign plate** or sticker (i.e. 'GB') as near as possible to their rear registration plate. Carrying a **red warning triangle** is strongly advised even if your car has hazard warning lights because breakdown may affect your electrics (triangles are compulsory for cars towing a caravan or a trailer). You should also buy a complete **spare-bulb** kit before you go, as it's illegal to drive with faulty lights. You need to **adjust your beams** for right-hand drive, which means buying special stickers to affix on your headlights. All gear is available at shops at the ports.

The **French road system** is generally excellent, although Brittany has only one of its excellent **motorways,** a short stretch out into Normandy. The largest roads here are mostly *routes nationales* (RN or N)— main roads, usually single lane, that sometimes take you through scenic towns. They have fairly frequent parking/rest areas (*aires*) and petrol stations.

Driving rules and advice: Traffic rules in France resemble those in force in Britain—the key difference is that in France you *drive on the right*. Be wary of forgetting this for a moment when you come out of a petrol station or junction. In built-up areas, you must give way to anybody coming out of a side turning on the right (the infamous *priorité à droite*); this rule no longer applies at roundabouts, where you give way to cars that are already on the roundabout. Common signs you'll see are *chaussée déformée* ('uneven road/temporary surface'), *déviation* ('diversion') and *rappel* ('continuation of the restriction'). The official text of the **French Highway Code** is available in English at **www.legifrance.gouv.fr.** For **road signs,** see **www.permis-enligne.com,** or your road atlas will probably picture many of them. Note that you must be at least 18, not 17, to drive in France. For **child car seats,** see p. 28.

Don't **drink and drive** at all—apart from the safety implications, there are frequent random breath tests and the alcohol limit is just 0.05%. The **speed limits** are 130km/h (80mph) on toll motorways, 110km/h (68mph) on dual carriageways and motorways without tolls, and 90km/h (56mph) on other roads except in towns, where it's 50km/h (30mph). On wet roads it's 110km/h (68mph), 100km/h (62mph) and 80km/h (50mph) respectively; in fog with visibility of less than 50m, the speed limit is 50km/h (30mph) even on toll motorways. For cars towing a caravan, the limit is 65km/h (40mph) if the weight of the trailer exceeds that of the car by less than 30%, 45km/h (28mph) if the excess is more than 30%. Speeding is supposed to always result in fines *and* a court appearance, but it's not clear what this means for foreign drivers.

Car hire: The best way to hire a car in France is in advance, via the Internet, so you have **proof of your booking** when you arrive. When collecting your car, as well as your reservation printout, you need a **driving licence** for each driver, additional photo ID (your national identity card, or your British passport), your passport if you're a non-EU resident, and a credit card in the main driver's name (sometimes two cards for expensive models). Different hire firms have different **lower age limits for drivers;** it's generally 21–25, but it can depend on how expensive the model is, and you may have to pay a young drivers surcharge. For child seat hire, see p. 28.

Think of paying anything upwards of £175 for a week's

Tips for Travelling by Car

- When travelling long distances by car, it may be worth timing your trip to coincide with your child's naptime or even leaving after dinner and unloading youngsters into bed at your pre-booked accommodation or driving in shifts through the night.

- Think about investing in an in-car satellite navigation system—marriage-savers for many, they're particularly handy for parents who are trying to map-read and deal with the demands of children in the back. However, be vigilant about removing the system from your car when you leave it parked on the street, or someone else may do it for you.

Other desirables or essentials are:

- A fully charged mobile phone.

- Breakdown cover/roadside assistance. Europ Assistance (☎0844 338 5533, *www.europ-assistance.co.uk*) has fair prices and an excellent reputation. If you do break down, tell the operator you have children so they prioritise you; if you're where other cars could run into the back of you, such as the hard shoulder of the motorway, it's wise to get children out of the car. If you have a hire car, make sure the booking includes 24hr roadside assistance.

- Child seats. Under-10s must be seated in the back in France, except for babies in rear-facing safety seats, though the latter must not be used if the front passenger seat is fitted with an

hire of a compact 5-door car. **Prices** can vary enormously, even between cars of a similar size, so make sure you get a few quotations from different firms—and check that they include unlimited mileage, full insurance, tax and 24-hour breakdown assistance. With some cheaper deals, you may need to buy **damage excess liability waiver** so you're not liable for a considerable initial chunk of loss or damage to the car. This starts at around 5€ per day. Good deals are often available if you book via low-cost airline

websites (p. 25) at the same time as buying your air ticket. All of the major car hire companies operate in France, including the following. The websites will tell you which operates where.

Avis *www.avis.co.uk*

Easycar *www.easycar.com*

Europcar *www.europcar.com*

Hertz *www.hertz.co.uk*

National/Citer *www.citer.com*

If you bring a car hired in the UK into France (for instance if airbag. New laws that came into force in the UK in 2006 require children under 13 (or under 136cm in height) to use a specialist seat for their age, except in certain mitigating circumstances. There is no such law in France, and the types of car seat provided by car-hire companies vary. You need to reserve them when you book your car, but that can work out expensive; you might also bring your own seat or booster by plane—they just go in the hold with your other luggage (though may come out at a separate point in the baggage hall at the other end; ask staff at the airport if yours doesn't materialise). An inflatable booster such as the Bubblebum (available from ***http://kidstravel2.com***) can be invaluable. A good source of information on car seats both for the UK and abroad is ***www.childcarseats.org.uk***.

- Other miscellaneous equipment includes: a first-aid kit; window shades; children's travel pillows; a portable highchair (p. 22); a cooler box to replenish with drinks and snacks each time you set off; wipes, nappies and plastic bags (for nappies or motion sickness); blankets, sweaters and a change of clothes; audio-tapes/CDs of your children's favourite stories or songs; sticker books, crayons/paper or a magic slate, or a compact travel book with games and activities, such as *100 Things for Little Children to Do on a Journey* (Usborne, available from ***www.amazon.co.uk***).

your own car is involved in an accident just before your holiday), you must inform the hire firm that the car is being taken to France to ensure you're covered there. You might need to show the French police the rental agreement to prove you have this insurance.

Motorhomes Motorhomes are subject to the same road rules as cars. You can stop for a few hours in a motorway service area but note that toll tickets are only valid for a limited time. You're also not allowed to stop overnight at the roadside: to find out about the 1,700 places adapted for motorhomes (i.e. providing waste disposal and water) in France, including campsites, see the French-language *Camping-car Magazine* (from newspaper kiosks), or print out sites for your area from its website, ***www.campingcar-magazine.fr***, ahead of your trip).

If you're not bringing your own motorhome, you can hire one in Brittany from Rennes, or otherwise from five spots in northern France including Paris: the best firm is **Avis Car-Away** ***www.aviscaraway.com***. Expect to pay 147€ to 200€ per day for a four to five person motorhome with unlimited mileage in high season, with special rates for long-term rents (two months or longer). Damage excess liability waiver and 24-hour breakdown assistance are optional but highly advisable; you can also get child seats, bedding sets, bike racks, folding picnic tables and satellite navigation (with a hefty deposit).

By Air There are no low-cost airlines operating within France, but a single ticket between Paris and Brest can cost as little as 62€ with Air France (p. 25). Children pay the full fare from age 2; below that they can occupy your lap. When travelling with a baby, you may want to invest in a Baby B'Air Flight Safety Vest (*http://babybair.com*), which attaches to your seatbelt to protect lap-held children during turbulence, and allows you to sleep knowing your baby can't fall from your arms. But do check with your airline first; some loan baby-carriers for free.

The following domestic routes are operated by Air France (p. 25) to Brittany:

Paris (CDG/Orly)–Rennes (p. 54)

Paris (Orly)–Lannion (p. 155)

Paris (CDG/Orly)–Brest (p. 194)

Paris (Orly)–Quimper (p. 194)

Paris (Orly)–Lorient (p. 103)

Note that Paris's Charles de Gaulle (CDG) airport is sometimes referred to as Roissy.

By Rail France's national rail system, run by the SNCF (*www.voyages-sncf.com*, with versions in other languages), is efficient and inexpensive compared with the British network, and a very good way of getting between cities and larger towns, especially aboard its famously zippy TGV (train à grande vitesse or 'very fast train') network—see the English-language site *www.tgv.co.uk* (run by Rail Europe) for routes and booking.

Brittany is very well covered by the TGV. See 'Getting Around' in the sightseeing chapters for your options between the main cities and towns in each département, with journey times. Branch lines serve some smaller towns (see the SNCF website), though to explore Brittany properly you need your own wheels.

Expect to pay about 24€ for a single ticket from Rennes to Vannes (110km/69 miles), the same for a child 4–11, but do investigate your options on the website as family discounts may be offered on certain trains. Under-4s travel free on a parent's lap on all trains, unless you want to pay for an extra seat. The very clear online booking system will tell you if you need a seat reservation or not (on some trains they're compulsory, on others you can't reserve). Note that onward tickets within France can be bought at the same time as your Eurostar ticket to Lille or Paris, via Eurostar or Rail Europe (p. 24).

Getting Children Interested In Brittany

Involving children in planning your trip is the best way to get them interested. As well as using this book to show them what to look forward to in Brittany, whether it be the crazy rocks of the Côte du Granit Rose (p. 161) or the submarine ride at St. Malo's Grand Aquarium (p. 72), it's a good idea to stock up, either before you go or while in Brittany, on some of the many wonderful story, history and colouring books featuring the region, in French or English. Good places to buy books on history and legends, including druids, Breton fairies and King Arthur, are museum/attraction gift shops such as La Maison des Mégalithes at Carnac (p. 108). Don't miss the widely available and excellent *Je colorie* colouring books on a wealth of topics, including lighthouses, prehistory and Breton legends, or the saltdough modelling book *La Bretagne en pâte à sel* (**www.edilarge.fr**). Older kids (6 and up) who speak French might enjoy *Je joue avec la Bretagne* (**www.edilarge.fr**), a book of themed games and quizzes. For the sea-themed children's books by renowned local photographer Philip Plisson, see p. 132. Other good French-language marine-themed books are the *Vivre La Mer* series (Gulf Stream), *Vacances à la Mer* (Graine de Voyageurs) and the *Au Bord de la Mer* series (Cop Breizh), all available locally or through **www.amazon.fr**.

Though most of the well-loved Madeline books by Ludwig Bemelmans, about the escapades of a French schoolgirl, are set in Paris, *Madeline Says Merci: The Always Be Polite Book* (available from **www.amazon.co.uk**) is a good way of getting youngsters aged about 4–10 interested in France and in learning some French phrases. Another classic character is Astérix; the location for his fictional settlement is thought to have been inspired by part of the Breton coast (p. 172). Astérix's countless adventures are available in French, Breton, English and lots of other languages. Bécassine, a cartoon character from the early 20th century, is a Breton farmer's daughter who becomes a servant in Paris: among her tales, available in French only from **www.amazon.fr**, are *L'enfance de Bécassine*, about her peasant childhood in Brittany.

Lastly, familiarise your family with the culinary delights of Brittany by getting a copy of *Mangez Breizh* (**www.amazon.fr** or bookshops in the region), a French-language book of traditional Breton recipes that its author Natalie Beauvais, enjoys creating with her own children. Also recommended is the English-language *Cuisine Grandmére* by Jenny Baker (**www.amazon.co.uk**), featuring authentic Breton and northern French recipes including flambéed sugared apples.

By Bus This is your least satisfactory means of getting around Brittany. For more rural areas, in particular, it's not worth the hassle, especially with children. You're most likely to use French buses within large towns or cities, such as Rennes; in this case, the basic system is that you get a ticket (about 1.20€, under-5s free) that allows you any number of trips by bus and any other urban transport system (Rennes has a tram-style metro) within the following hour. That said, most Breton cities have fairly compact and walkable centres containing most of the sights, hotels and restaurants.

By Bike If you don't bring your own bikes, tourist offices can give you lists of hire outlets, or most hotels, B&Bs, gîtes and campsites offer loan or hire. All hire shops have helmets, and most can also provide child seats and perhaps child trailers. My comment on French drivers (p. 26) should discourage you from cycling with your family on all but the quietest country lanes. A better bet are Voies Vertes (*www.voiesvertes.com*)— walking, cycling, rollerblading and wheelchair-accessible tracks on former railtracks or canal towpaths. I've detailed the best in the relevant chapters.

The site *http://troisv.amis-nature.org/sommaire.php3.* has advice on taking your bike on trains (a complex issue; you basically need to talk to the SNCF in each individual case); see also *www.randobreizh.com* for

walking, cycling and other 'nature sports'. Tourist office websites also list routes in their area.

ACCOMMODATION & DINING

Accommodation

There are few expensive hotels in Brittany; on the whole, accommodation here is seriously good value to anyone used to hotel prices in the UK, even taking into account the exchange rate. That means that even if you're on a budget you might allow yourselves the occasional splurge.

I've based the price categories used within the Accommodation sections of the sightseeing chapters on the following ranges, based on lodgings per night for two adults and two children, without breakfast, except in the case of B&Bs and the occasional hotel (as noted in individual reviews):

Very expensive: More than 290€

Expensive: 220€–290€

Moderate: 110€–220€

Inexpensive: Less than 110€

Very expensive options tend to be **châteaux-hotels** or grand old **seaside hotels** with gastronomic restaurants, swimming pools, babysitting services and more—fabulous places for the odd night or two, with a truly French feel and a welcoming attitude to children. In the expensive and moderate categories you'll find many very good seaside hotels, often with pools, though beware that some will insist on **half board** (breakfast and lunch or dinner in the hotel-restaurant) in high season, which can be limiting for those with children.

B&Bs (*chambres d'hôte*) are split between the moderate and inexpensive categories; the more rural they are, the cheaper they tend to be. Most are cosy and welcoming; often they're on farms where youngsters can pet the animals and sometimes join in with farming tasks. The inexpensive category also includes campsites, youth hostels and **gîtes** (see p. 34). The latter have long been the most popular option among families holidaying in France, since even relatively luxurious examples with pools, when broken down per head per night, represent very good value compared with hotels, and the self-catering facilities mean you save money on eating out too.

Campsites run the gamut from rowdy but fun four- and five-star affairs with huge aqua-parks, sports facilities galore and children's entertainment, to quiet sites within the grounds of historic châteaux, or green sites where the onus is on leaving a minimal environmental footprint.

I've not included many **youth hostels,** but if you're prepared for your lodging to be a bit rough and ready (generally in rooms with two bunk beds, with a sink and perhaps an ensuite shower room), they can be good places to stay, with readymade playmates for the children, communal kitchens, laundrettes and games rooms, and sometimes activities laid on. Single-parent families (p. 16) often get special rates. The French hostelling association website, *www.fuaj. org,* has links to individual hostel websites where they exist but doesn't list private hostels or those run by other organisations, such as La Mine d'Or. Expect to pay about 15€ per person in a four person room, including breakfast, plus 23€ for annual family membership of FUAJ.

Just about every hotel and B&B reviewed in this guide offers **family rooms** for up to four people; if not, then interconnecting rooms or suites with comfy sofa-beds are available. Note that 'appartement', when used in the context of hotels, usually means a suite rather than a flat with self-catering facilities. **Cots** are usually provided, either free or for a small extra fee. **Breakfasts,** though generally of decent quality whatever the price range (almost invariably Continental or occasionally in the form of a buffet, they usually feature fresh, sometimes organic, farm produce), can get a bit monotonous—you may not think it now, but there will come a day when you can barely countenance a croissant, no matter how buttery and delicious. Hotel breakfasts, in Brittany as elsewhere, can be very expensive.

Breaking Journeys without Breaking the Bank

For wallet-friendly overnight stops en route, the mighty Accor empire has several budget hotel chains with family rooms throughout France, including **All Seasons** (p. 95), **Etap**, **Formule 1** and **Ibis**. On standard rates, most offer cancellation right up to the evening of arrival, so if you get delayed en route (or conversely, make better time than you anticipated), you can just call or go online and recoup your money. Or you can just pull up at your nearest hotel when you're too tired to drive on—some even have automated check-ins where you feed in your credit card and it spits out a room code.

Hotels You're generally better off dealing directly with the accommodation providers recommended throughout this guide (or others listed on **tourist board and tourist office websites**; p. 14), rather than via a booking agency, and doing it by **email**. This allows you to explain your requirements as a family and check exactly what's provided for children, from bottle warmers and cot linen to games consoles and to have the details in writing in case of queries or discrepancies on arrival. Hotels very often offer **special offers** or **last-minute deals** on their website, but even if they don't, *always ask if a better rate is available.*

Hôtel-Résidences The family option *par excellence*, apartments in *résidences* attached to hotels give you the flexibility of self-catering together with use of hotel facilities. A very good example is the Reine Marine at St. Malo (p. 92), where you can stay in a sea-view apartment with use of a pool, sauna, bar, laundrette and breakfast delivery service, enjoy direct access to the beach, and also use the thalasso therapy (seawater cures) centre and crèche and children's club of its five-star sister hotel and restaurant. For tighter budgets, Pierre & Vacances (p. 38) offers the facilities of resort hotels in apartment-complex settings.

Gîtes & Apartments Many readers of this book will be looking for self-catering accommodation in a quaint old Breton cottage not too far from the sea, where they can relax and feel at home abroad, with the option of cooking for themselves. You get more space and lower prices than at a hotel, your children won't disturb people in neighbouring rooms, and you save money on restaurants (which children get sick of pretty quickly anyway). The downside can be a lack of things to do on a rainy day, especially if you're in a gîte without a TV/DVD player or covered pool—it's worth having a few contingency plans up your sleeve (see the Rainy Days boxes in each sightseeing chapter). Some gîtes can also be a bit grotty, filled with owners' unwanted furniture—look carefully at website photos, and check exactly what's included—if you're there for 2 weeks, you won't want to waste precious holiday hours in search of a laundrette if your gîte doesn't have a washing machine.

Luckily—at least for visitors—the gîtes market is oversaturated in many parts of France, which means you get copious choice and good deals, especially if you can hold out and wait for a last-minute deal. Good websites include *www.interhome. co.uk*, *www.frenchconnections. co.uk* and *www.cheznous.com*. With the last two you can check availability on the website but you book direct with the owner, which means they can be better value. All three offer travel discounts. The British Sunday newspapers carry ads for countless other firms arranging self-catering accommodation. Or official **French organisations** *www.clevacances.com* and *www. gites-de-france.com* have websites in English.

You can just type 'gîte' and the name of the area or nearest town into a search engine and see what it throws up—most owners now have their own websites. Make it easier for yourself by adding extra search-words such as 'child-friendly' or 'toddler' or 'swimming pool', though this may exclude suitable places that haven't set up their website properly (their problem, not yours). Or lastly, there are now family gîte specialists, chief among them *www.babyfriendly boltholes.co.uk* and *www.totsto france.co.uk*.

Children's Gîtes (*Gîtes d'Enfants*)

This school-holiday programme allows kids aged 4 to 16 to enjoy country life and outdoor activities with other children (often including the host's own family) at an establishment—usually a farm—inspected by the French department of health and social services. Activities might include butter making, rambling, making herb gardens, handicrafts, canoeing, riding and sailing. If your children are independent and enjoy discovering nature and wildlife, they may enjoy doing this for a weekend while you stay in a hotel nearby. It's generally a good idea—at least the first time—to send a child with a sibling, cousin or friend of a similar age. Expect to pay around 160€ for a weekend; some places also offer activities by the day. For children's gîtes by *département*, see *www. gites-de-france.fr*. Some owners speak English, where indicated, but this is obviously a great way for children who speak some French to improve their language skills. For **farm stays** in the Ille-et-Vilaine, see p. 73.

Prices vary by location, facilities (pools, play areas, the availability of babysitting and so on), luxuriousness and season; as a guideline, expect to pay 200€–450€ per week for a gîte for four without a pool in the Côtes d'Armor.

Finally, it's a long shot, but you may strike lucky at a **home-swap** site such as *www.home exchange.com*, where you try to match up with someone who will swap houses with you. You can sift through, say, the Brittany listings looking for someone who has listed your home country (or city) as somewhere they'd like to stay. If they like the look of your house as much as you do theirs and you can agree on a date, you get free accommodation and someone to housesit for you while you're away. Annual membership of this website is about US 89€.

Camping France has about 11,000 campsites, all of them listed on the directory *www.campingfrance.com*, with versions in English and other languages and a clickable map for searches by region or a themed search facility (sites with direct beach access, scenic inland sites, sites with indoor pools or water parks, sites with kids' clubs, sites with fitness and spa facilities and so on). It gives detailed descriptions and fees for each, and lets you book online, though it also gives phone numbers, websites and email addresses of the sites so you can do it direct.

For reliable shortcuts to the *best* campsites by area, see the reliable website *www.camping france.com*, which, again, has both contact details and website links. I've indicated some of their recommendations in the Accommodation sections of the individual sightseeing chapters of this book, alongside my own picks of the nearly 1,000 sites in Brittany; the two sometimes overlap.

I've tried to cover both smaller 'green' sites and larger sites with indoor pool complexes, kids' clubs and lots of other activities and amenities. For companies specialising in camping and mobile home holidays in these sorts of sites, including ferry travel, see p. 37 and p. 38.

Package Deals & Activity Holidays

Package deals let you buy your plane, ferry or train ticket, accommodation and other elements of your trip (such as car hire or airport transfers) at the same time, often at a discount. Alternatively, they may include hidden charges that you would avoid by booking direct with a hotel or carrier. The appeal for parents is that they *save you time* researching and booking.

Activity holidays are roughly the same with the addition of some kind of sporting, creative or cultural activity, though sometimes you make your own travel arrangements. **Escorted tours**, where you're taken around the various sites, don't generally sit well with family holidays, where you need to remain flexible in case the children get bored/tired/ill. Such holidays also take away the exhilaration of getting out there and discovering a destination for yourself—one of the best lessons you can give your children.

The following are a few of the best organisers; you'll find many more on the Internet and advertised in **Sunday papers**. Again, check that your travel insurance (p. 20) covers you if an operator goes bust.

Breton Bikes ★★★

📞 02 96 24 86 72, *www.bretonbikes. com*

In 2009, 30% of bookings with this small and very friendly Brit-run cycle-tours firm were by families with young children, so you can be sure it's well equipped for your needs. Several routes (1 or 2 weeks) are suitable for those with children, on quiet roads or cycle paths; accommodation is on campsites with play areas and lakes to swim in (or in hotels or the firm's own gîte if you prefer). Every conceivable piece of kit is available, including baby seats, baby trailers (one and two-seat), trailer-bikes, small touring bikes, tandems small enough at the back for a 6-year-old, and sleeping bags for all ages. In Whitsun Family Week the six 'fixed centre' tents at the firm's base at Gourec (near the Lac de Guerlédan; p. 172) are reserved for families.

Prices for a week in high season start from 229€ per adult, 223€ per 10–17-year-old, 112€ per 4–9-year-old and 70€ for children up to 3, including bikes, maps, tents/camping equipment, and backup (repairs, advice, etc); campsite fees (1€–6€ per adult per night) aren't included. Some travel can be arranged, and advice on your options is given.

INSIDER TIP ≫

For other family-friendly cycling holidays in Brittany, plus walks and short breaks on the coast, see *www.headwater.com*.

Brittany Ferries ★★★

📞 0871 244 1444, *www.brittany ferries.com*

This ferry company (p. 23) is also an award-winning tour operator that can make parents' lives easier by booking hotels, apartments, gîtes, camping chalets, theme parks, cycling and boating holidays and so on in conjunction with travel on its ferries, in Brittany or elsewhere in France. All properties are inspected, and—handily for those anxious about the language—there's a 24-hour telephone hotline with English-speaking staff to deal with any problems. The excellent website allows you to refine your search by requirements such as distance from a beach, availability of baby equipment and so on, and plenty of detail is provided about each property. You can also mix-and-match holidays—for instance, you might fancy treating yourselves to a posh hotel after a week in a chalet.

Firms offering similar experiences to Eurocamp are Siblu (📞0871 911 2288, *www.siblu.com*) with its own site, Domaine de Kerlann, in southern Finistère; Canvas Holidays (📞0845 268 0853, *www.canvasholidays.com*), who deal with 9 sites in Brittany, including Camping Le Ty-Nadan in Finistère (p. 240); and Thomson Al Fresco (📞0871 231 3293, *www.thomsonalfresco. co.uk*), with 3, including the Domaine des Ormes (p. 92). All can book your travel (ferry/ Eurotunnel/flydrive).

Eurocamp/Keycamp ★

📞0844 406 0402, *www.eurocamp. co.uk*

Part of the same parent company, these camping specialists offer accommodation at the same sites (a couple less with Keycamp) with small differences (for instance, at the time of writing, Keycamp was the only firm offering treehouses at the Domaine des Ormes; p. 92). The 19 sites in Brittany include campsites and holiday villages with apartments; see p. 33). Accommodation varies by site but usually includes mobile homes of various size and categories, classic tents and pitches; in some spots you'll also find more luxurious 'safari tents'. The attractions of this kind of a holiday for those with young children are lots of readymade playmates and a range of things to do (from aquaparks to organised activities) when the weather isn't so great. Travel can be arranged for you, including ferries at the best available rates.

Eurocamp Independent (📞 0844 406 0100, *www.euro campindependent.co.uk*) caters to those who prefer to travel with their own tent, caravan or motorhome, booking your ferry crossings, campsite pitches, overnight stops and insurance.

Le Boat ★

📞0844 463 3577, *www.leboat.co.uk*

This firm offers 3–14-day holidays aboard self-driven river and canal cruisers, with several routes in Brittany. The vessels are easy to steer and require no experience, and you can hire bikes to help you stop off and explore. To cover the distance requires no more than 4–5 hours cruising a day, but you need to factor in 20 minutes to get through each lock. Prices start at 1216€ per week for a four-person cruiser. The website gives travel advice and the firm can organise transport from airports and stations. Your car can be transferred whilst you're en-route during one way journeys.

Pierre & Vacances ★★

📞0870 0267 145, *www.pv-holidays. com*

Long popular with French and other Continentals but now also making massive headway in the UK market, Pierre et Vacances leads the field in self-catering holiday apartments in France, with almost 100 sites at the time of writing. Those who know Center Parcs (Europe) and Sun-parks will know what to expect from the Pierre & Vacances' resort villages, since it owns both firms—fairly basic apartments combined with a great range of family amenities, including kids' clubs. For a review of the seaside resort of Pierre & Vacances Port du Crouesty, see p. 144. There are a further 11 Pierre & Vacances *résidences* around Brittany; they do have fewer facilities and amenities than Le Crouesty resort but all are family-oriented.

Eating Out

Some people come to France for the food alone, and indeed, one of the joys of exploring this country is that you can generally walk into the most modest-looking café in any small town and be assured of getting a good meal of fresh, well-prepared food, even it's just an omelette, a *croque-monsieur* or a salad *composée* (main-course salad). With all this on offer, it's amazing that companies such as McDonald's have been able to get a foothold in France.

Most French restaurants and cafés are welcoming to children, and many have kid's menus (generally about 7.50€), though often these feature little more than *steak haché* (a hamburger patty) or ham and chips, then

ice cream, and can get very repetitive. Vegetarians are poorly catered for in this largely carnivorous country; omelettes, some main-course salads (above) and margharita pizzas are helpful standbys, but it's always wise to double check with your waiter that, for instance, pieces of ham won't sneak their way into these dishes. Naturally, in Brittany with its wonderful fresh sea-food, those who eat fish but not meat should be content.

Brittany's famous crêperies, specialising in buckwheat pan-cakes (*galettes de blé noir*) and lighter, sweeter crêpes, are another godsend for veggies. I've given my recommendations in the relevant chapters; some of them are holders of the official Crêperies Gourmandes label of quality (for others, ask for a directory at your nearest tourist office or consult www.tourisme bretagne.org). But again, you'll reach a point where you can't face another crêpe…

Restaurants and cafés gener-ally have at least one highchair, but if you're travelling by car bring a portable one (p. 22) just in case it's needed. Your only real problem as a parent in France is that mealtimes are very rigid, and you're unlikely—at least outside cities or resorts in high season—to find somewhere serving food outside standard lunch and dinner hours (gener-ally noon to 2.30pm and 7 to 10pm). For those spoilt rotten by cities with all-day eating options, this can be very frustrating. If you want to have dinner out, your only solution may be to encourage your children to have an early-afternoon nap. **Brasseries** and **crêperies** often have all-day service (*service continu*), but again, only at the seaside in season or in larger towns. I'd steer clear of the roadside **Buffalo Grill,** despite the child-friendly trappings such as all-day service and sometimes even bouncy castles.

I've tried to cover the range of options in my 'Eating Out' sections in the sightseeing chapters, recognising that if you're not staying in accommodation with self-catering facilities, the cost of eating out everyday is going to mount up. But alongside crêperies, you'll find reviews of some stunning gastronomic restaurants that welcome children—perfect for occasional treats, especially if you take advantage of **fixed-price lunch** or set menus. I've based my **price categories** on the following ranges, based on two adults and two children consuming two courses plus drinks:

Expensive: More than 75€

Moderate: 45€–75€

Inexpensive: less than 45€

The 21st-Century Traveller

Mobile Phones

It's indispensable to have your mobile phone with you if you're driving with children. Luckily,

these days it's usually hassle-free to use a British mobile phone in France: it'll simply switch over to a **French network** when you reach France, and you can call British numbers and French numbers directly, or sometimes using the international dialling code. It's wise to **check in advance with your service provider** that your phone is set up for 'international roaming', and have them explain the procedure for accessing voicemails while abroad (again, this is usually trouble-free, but do double check).

Call charges from your mobile to UK or French numbers will be higher than within the UK, and you'll also pay for incoming calls from your home country. If you expect to make or receive a lot of calls, or go abroad often, it may be worth buying an **international SIM card** to temporarily replace your UK one; see, for instance, *www.0044.co.uk*. This will give you a local number and lower calling rates. Check first that your phone is not locked to its UK network. Alternatively, if you're staying more than a few weeks or come to France repeatedly, you could buy a pay-as-you-go mobile phone from a communications shop such as France Télécom/Orange, found in all largish town centres, or even from a large supermarket.

For those from further afield, such as the **USA,** the situation is basically the same provided you have a world-capable multiband phone on a **GSM** (Global System for Mobiles) system, with 'international roaming' activated. Again, installing an international SIM card can save you money if you use the phone frequently.

Recharge your phone whenever you get the chance (many come with travel adapters you can plug into your car's cigarette lighter).

Other Phones

For information about area and international dialling codes and public phones, see p. 47.

The Internet

Most hotels now have Wi-Fi that guests can use with their own laptops and many hotels have a computer terminal for guest Internet access. Wi-Fi access is also available in many airports and cafés.

Otherwise, unless you have a smartphone, large cities and most towns of any size have a choice of Internet access points, whether in cyber cafés, public libraries or the tourist office; tourist offices will provide you with a list, or sites such as *www.cybercafe.com* and *www.cyber captive.com* can be helpful. A good French site is *www.cyber cafe.fr*. Note that if you're a touch typist and need to do a lot of emailing, French keyboards have letters in different places.

To retrieve your emails, ask your Internet Service Provider (ISP) if it has a web-based interface tied to your existing account. If it doesn't, set up a free web-based email account, with, for instance, *www.yahoo. com* or *www.hotmail.com*. You might want to start one up anyway, as backup in case of hiccups with your existing account.

FAST FACTS

Baby Equipment Most hotels, B&Bs and gîtes will provide a travel cot, often for a charge (an average of 8€); some also offer other equipment such as bottle warmers and changing mats. Note that some places don't provide linen for cots because of allergy risks. Supermarkets, especially large ones, are good for baby equipment (*matériel de puériculture*), from nappies and bottled food to baths and car seats, but if you want to go to a specialist retailer, many out-of-town *centre commerciales* (shopping parks) have baby-and-toddler supermarkets such as Bébe 9 (*www.bebe-9. com*).

Babysitters Most expensive and some moderate hotels arrange sitters for guests, usually a tried-and-tested local (or someone from an agency) rather than one of their staff. Most need at least 24 hours notice. You usually pay the sitter directly; rates average 8€–10€ per hour. Some gîte-owners also offer babysitting, either themselves or by a family member such as a daughter.

Banks Always closed on public holidays; the rest of the time they're generally open from

9.30am to 4.30pm, with a lunch break in smaller towns. In the latter they may be closed Monday afternoons but open Saturday mornings. Most have 24-hour ATMs (p. 17).

Breastfeeding You'll find this is much less common in France than the UK, and you may get stared at, especially if you're feeding an older infant. You may want to brazen it out, since breastfeeding is a right, or you might prefer to find an out-of-the-way spot.

Business Hours Shops outside large towns generally open at 9 or 10am (7 or 8am for bakeries) and close at 6 or 7pm, with a 2-hour break at lunchtime (usually 12.30 to 2.30pm). Many also open on Sunday morning (in conjunction with a market) but close Monday mornings or all of Monday. Very large supermarkets often stay open until late (9 to10pm), and larger towns have convenience stores open until late in the evening. Supermarkets increasingly open in the morning on public holidays too, except Christmas Day.

Restaurants generally open at noon until 2.30pm and then 7 to 10pm; larger towns and resorts usually have some with *service continu* (p. 40). Public museums usually close on Monday or Tuesday and on public holidays, but most tourist sites open on public and school holidays.

Brittany is a seasonal region and many attractions and hotels close for part or all of the winter;

many businesses, though not hotels and rarely restaurants, close for the whole of August, when the French take their holidays *en masse*.

Car Hire See p. 27.

Climate See 'Weather & When to Go', p. 18.

Currency See 'Money', p. 17.

Customs For the latest information on what you can and cannot bring out of France, see the English-language pages of the French customs website, **http://www.douane.gouv.fr/data/file/5461.pdf**.

Dentists & Doctors For emergency dental treatment, go to your nearest hospital or health centre.

Some upmarket hotels have doctors on call, (*médécins de service*) though they can be expensive private ones. Alternatively, local newspapers list doctors on call and chemists (p. 44) open outside normal hours, or there may be information posted outside the local *mairie*. You can also just pitch up at your local surgery and wait for an appointment; you'll have to pay for this upfront and reclaim on your EHIC (p. 20).

If you're staying in one place for a while, make a list of emergency contact details and pin them up by the front door (or your host may have provided one in their welcoming pack).

Drinking Laws Since 2009 it has been illegal to sell alcohol to under-18s (it used to be under-16s), as is supplying under-18s with alcohol that results in intoxication. France has stricter drink-driving laws than the UK (blood alcohol levels of 0.5 mg/ml rather than 0.8). Unlike in some countries, it's legal to drink in public places in France.

Driving Rules See p. 27.

Electricity In France electricity runs on 220-volt, 50-cycle AC. Visitors from the UK and Ireland need a two-pin European adapter (easily available at French supermarkets) to use their own appliance; those from North America need a voltage transformer (unless the appliance has a dual voltage switch) and plug adapter. Many hotels will loan guests adapters.

Embassies & High Commissions The Paris embassies or consulates for the UK, Ireland, USA, Canada, Australia and New Zealand are your point of contact for passport and legal problems. For contact details, see *www.expatries.diplomatie. gouv.fr/annuaires/annuaires.htm*.

Emergencies Staff in most hotels are trained to deal with emergencies, so call the front desk before you do anything else. Otherwise, for an **ambulance**, call ☏*15*, for the **police** ☏*17*, for the **fire service** ☏*18*. You'll have to pay upfront for an ambulance and try to claim back your money on your insurance. In rural areas it'll probably be quicker to drive to the nearest

hospital yourself, unless it's dangerous to move the injured person. Note that **hospitals** are sometimes signposted *hôtel de dieu* rather than *hôpital* or *centre hospitalier*.

Internet Access See p. 41.

Lost Property For lost items head to the nearest police station; for important documents such as passports, contact your embassy or consulate (p. 43); for lost credit cards, see p. 44. If you think your car may have been towed away for being illegally parked, ask at the local police station.

Mail Post offices, recognisable by their yellow signs with blue birds, are generally open Monday to Friday 8am to 7pm and Saturday 8am to noon; in towns and villages they tend to open Monday to Friday 9am to 12.30pm and 2 to 5pm and Saturday 9am to noon but close some afternoons. Postcards or letters to the UK weighing less than 20g cost 0.58€ and take 1–5 days. Stamps are sold at tobacconists (*tabacs*) as well as at post offices. If you need to receive mail while travelling, ask the sender to address it to your name c/o Poste Restante, Poste Centrale, in the relevant town. You'll need to show proof of identity and pay a small fee.

Maps For online sources to plot your route, see p. 15. On the road, arm yourself with a good French road atlas: the Michelin Tourist & Motoring atlases (available from *www.amazon.*

co.uk and at petrol stations and port shops) have the best level of detail.

Money & Credit Cards See also 'Money', p. 17. For lost/stolen cards, call the relevant company immediately: for Amex call ☏*01 47 77 72 00*, for Visa ☏*08 00 90 11 79*, for MasterCard ☏*01 45 67 84 84*, for Diners ☏*08 10 31 41 59*. For emergency cash out of banking hours, you can have money wired to you online, by phone or from an agent's office via Western Union (☏*08 00 83 38 33*; *www.westernunion.com*).

Newspapers & Magazines National dailies include *Le Monde*, *Libération* and *Le Figaro*, and all have online versions; regional newspapers are *Ouest-France* (*www.ouest-france.fr*) covering Brittany and part of Normandy, and *Le Télégramme* (*www.letelegramme.com*), with local editions for 14 cities and towns in Brittany. These newspapers are good sources for local listings of markets, cinema showings and so on. Newsagents also stock a choice of glossy magazines covering the region in French. Otherwise, English-language newspapers from the UK and USA are widely available at newsstands and newsagents, usually a day old, without the supplements and at a premium price.

Pets With many gîtes, hotels and other forms of accommodation accepting pets (sometimes with an extra fee), it's easier than ever to take a furry friend to France. The commercial website *www.visitfrance.co.uk* is a good source of pet-friendly self-catering options.

Under the Pet Travel Scheme (PETS), UK-resident dogs and cats (and even ferrets) can travel to many other EU countries and return to the UK without being quarantined. Dogs and cats are issued with a passport (by a vet) after being fitted with a microchip and vaccinated against rabies at least 21 days prior to travel. On re-entry to the UK, you need to get your pet treated against ticks and tapeworm (by any EU vet 24 to 48 hours before being checked in with a transport company approved by the scheme). For full details, check *www.defra.gov.uk/wildlife-pets/pets/travel/pets/*.

Pharmacies Staff at chemists (*pharmacies*), recognisable by a green cross, can provide first aid in minor emergencies. Rotas of pharmacies operating out of normal hours (9am to1.20pm and 2.30 to 8pm, Mon–Sat) are posted in every chemist's window and in local papers. It's a good idea to take a first-aid course yourself; there's a CD-Rom version (£15) developed in collaboration with St. John's Ambulance: see *www.firstaid forkids.com*.

Police In emergencies, call ☏*112* or ☏*17*. For theft, you have to file a report at a local police station.

Post Offices See 'Mail', above.

Safety See also p. 21, 'Travelling Safely'. The usual common

Public & School Holidays

French national holidays are called jours feriés; banks and small shops close but larger supermarkets increasingly open in the morning or even all day. Most museums close but many other visitor sites stay open, as do the majority of restaurants.

France's main public holidays are New Year's Day (1 Jan), Easter Monday (Mar or Apr), Labour Day (Fête du Travail; 1 May), VE Day (8 May), Whit Monday (late May), Ascension Thursday (late May/40 days after Easter), Bastille Day (14 July), Assumption of the Blessed Virgin (15 Aug), All Saint's Day (1 Nov), Armistice Day (11 Nov) and Christmas Day (25 Dec).

There are five school holidays a year in France: 2 weeks in February, 2 weeks at Easter, all of July and August, 1 week at the end of October, and 2 weeks at Christmas. As in the UK, holidays are staggered round the country: Brittany is in Zone A.

The following are sample dates for general guidance for Brittany, with each year varying slightly:

18 Feb–6 Mar
22 Apr–9 May
4 July–2 Sept
22 Oct–3 Nov
17 Dec–3 Jan

Though tourist sites and roads are naturally busier during these periods, especially July and August, and hotels usually more expensive, do remember that many museums, galleries and other venues host extra children's activities in the holidays, and resorts have children's beach clubs (p. 19) and special events and entertainment, such as Festival Place aux Mômes events (p. 57).

For my pick of family-friendly happenings throughout the year, from puppet festivals to son-et-lumière extravaganzas, see the 'Child-Friendly Events and Entertainment' section of each sightseeing chapter.

sense tips apply—don't leave money or valuables on display on your person or in your car, and be wary of **pickpockets** in confined public spaces; don't allow yourself to be distracted by anyone while withdrawing money at a **cashpoint**; and don't walk alone in unlit open spaces such as parks (most of which are locked out of hours anyway) or even on seemingly innocuous residential streets after dark.

Smoking France banned smoking in workplaces and other public buildings in 2007 and extended the law to cafés, restaurants and bars in 2008.

Comfort & Safety on the Beach

The cardinal rules of making the best of Brittany's beaches are as follows:

- Keep out of the sun completely between 11am and 3pm. At other times, wear a T-shirt (or better still a UV sunsuit or swimsuit), slap on a hat, and slop on the sunblock, even if it doesn't feel that hot or if you're sitting in the shade.
- Full-body UV swimsuits also have the advantage of blocking the stings of jellyfish, which have been increasingly prevalent in France in recent years. If a member of the family is stung, rinse the affected part with cool seawater and then apply a medicated cream available from any pharmacy.
- Kit your children out with 'jellies'—very practical rubber shoes that they can wear both on the beach and in the sea, to protect them from shells, glass and stings from seabed creatures.
- Invest in a pop-up beach tent to which kids can retreat to cool down or nap.
- Never swim alone; it's safest to swim where there is lifeguard cover, especially with young children—Brittany's 'Stations Familles' (p. 15) have surveillance on the most popular beaches.
- Never dive off piers or rocks: it's impossible to see what's beneath the surface.
- Save inflatables for pools; on the beach, only use them in the safe bathing area attached to a line, held firm by an adult on the beach.
- Don't let children drink or splash water from rock pools in their mouths—they can carry unpleasant bacteria. Wash hands in clean water before eating.
- Always fill holes your children have dug afterwards to prevent someone tipping in headfirst. And never let a small child crawl into a deep hole—the sides could collapse.
- If you want to doze or read on the beach, take it in turns with your partner—children need to be constantly watched on beaches.

Taxes A 19.6% national **value-added tax** (VAT; *taxe valeur ajoutée* or **TVA** in French) is included in the price of most goods and hotel and restaurant services in France. Non-EU residents can reclaim most of this if they spend 175€ or more at a participating retailer—ask for *détaxe* papers and present them at the airport; the refund can go to your credit card.

Taxis In major towns and cities and at airports, taxis can be caught from ranks (look for square signs with 'Taxi' in white on a blue background); they can also be hailed in the street if the 'Taxi' sign on the roof is lit and the small lights under it are switched off—unless you're less than 50m from a rank or 100m from a railway station. Away from main centres or airports, ask at your hotel or restaurant desk, or call a local firm—see *www.pagesjaunes.fr* (French *Yellow Pages* online) or ask at the tourist office. Check all taxis have a meter, and for airport taxis and out-of-town trips, ask the driver for an estimate before setting out.

Telephone Within France, all telephone numbers are 10 digits, including a two-digit **area code** (📞02 in Brittany) that you must dial even if you're calling from within that area. Numbers starting with 06 are **mobile numbers,** which will cost you more to call; numbers starting with 0800 and 0805 are free to dial but are only available within France (other numbers beginning 08, such as 0892 and 0820, have differing rates).

To **call a French number from abroad,** drop the initial 0 of the area code after dialling the international code (📞00 33 from the UK, 📞011 33 from the USA). To **dial the UK from France,** call the international code (📞00 44) then the British number minus the first 0 of the area code; to call the USA dial 00 1 then the number. If you don't bring your mobile (p. 40), avoid using hotel phones as charges can be high; buy a **phonecard** (*télécarte*) from a post office, tobacconist or newsagents, starting at 8€ for 50

units. Incoming calls can be received at **phone boxes** where the blue bell sign is shown.

Time Zone France is one hour ahead of **British time,** with clocks going forward by an hour for summertime or 'daylight saving', as in the UK, on the last Sunday in March and reverting on the last Sunday in October. France is six hours ahead of North American **Eastern Standard Time** (EST).

Tipping *Service compris* means a service charge has been included on your bill, but you may wish to leave an extra tip (about 15% of the total).

Toilets & Baby Changing
There are public *toilettes* on the streets of most larger towns and cities, and in some smaller places; if you can't find one, bars and cafés are normally happy for you to use theirs but for politeness' sake make a small purchase while you're there. Alternatively, try a large shop/department store or a public museum. Few places except big family-oriented tourist sites such as zoos, aquaria and museums have baby-changing facilities, so be equipped with a portable folding mat.

Water French water is safe to drink. Many restaurants automatically serve you a carafe of chilled tap water (*eau du robinet*). Bottled water is *eau minérale plat/sans gaz* (still) or *gazeuse/pétillante* (sparkling).

Weather See p. 18.

Speaking in Tongues: The Breton Language

About 300,000 inhabitants of Brittany (and some people in the Loire Atlantique) still speak Breton, which is descended from a branch of Celtic languages brought to the region by Roman–British settlers. Cornish and Welsh are the modern-day languages to which it's most closely related, and it's comprised of four dialects, though there are no set areas in which these are spoken—the language as a whole varies slightly between one village and its neighbours. It's never been an official language of France, despite efforts by supporters for state recognition, and this is one factor in its decline (1.3 million people spoke it in 1930, and around half of the population of southern Brittany spoke no other language, not even French). On the other hand, there have been some positive developments—in the 1970s Diwan schools (unfunded by the state) were set up to teach children Breton, and in 2004 the Astérix books (p. 31) were translated into Breton and Gallo (another language of Brittany, based on Latin)—an important symbolic step given that Astérix is said to be based in Brittany. And, as you venture deep into Brittany, you'll see street signs and place names in Breton as well as French.

It's not an easy language to pronounce, and you don't need to speak any to get by in Brittany, but your kids may have fun looking out for, recognising and trying out the following phrases on their travels:

Breizh—Brittany

brezhoneg—the Breton language

demat/devezh mat/salud dit—hello

kenavo—goodbye

ken emberr—see you soon

trugarez—thank you

mar plij—please

deuet mat oc'h—you're welcome

degemer mat—welcome

kreiz-kêr—town centre

da bep tu—all directions

porzh-houarn—train station

skol—school

ti/ty—house

ti-polis—police station

ti an douristred—tourist office

ti-kêr—town hall

krampouezh—crêpes

chistr—cider

3 Ille-et-Vilaine

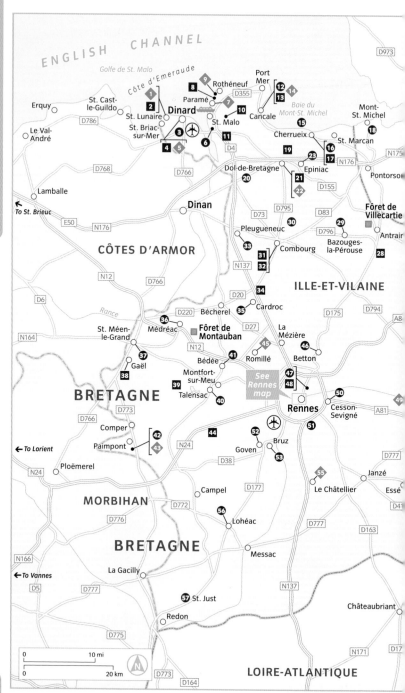

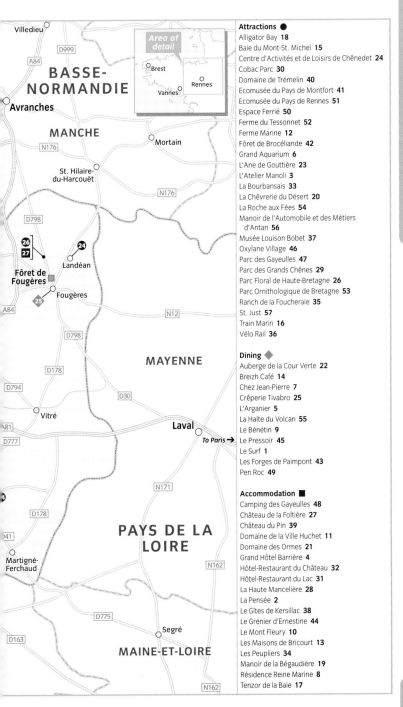

Villedieu

D999

A84

BASSE-NORMANDIE

Avranches

MANCHE

N176

Mortain

St. Hilaire-du-Harcouët

N176

D798

26
27

24

Landéan

Fôret de Fougères

Fougères

A84

25

N12

D798

D178

MAYENNE

D794

D30

D777

Vitré

A81

Laval

To Paris →

N171

D178

PAYS DE LA LOIRE

41

Martigné-Ferchaud

N162

D775

Segré

D163

MAINE-ET-LOIRE

N162

Area of detail

Brest

Rennes

Vannes

Attractions ●
Alligator Bay **18**
Baie du Mont-St. Michel **15**
Centre d'Activités et de Loisirs de Chênedet **24**
Cobac Parc **30**
Domaine de Trémelin **40**
Ecomusée du Pays de Montfort **41**
Ecomusée du Pays de Rennes **51**
Espace Ferrié **50**
Ferme du Tessonnet **52**
Ferme Marine **12**
Fôret de Brocéliande **42**
Grand Aquarium **6**
L'Ane de Gouttière **23**
L'Atelier Manoli **3**
La Bourbansais **33**
La Chèvrerie du Désert **20**
La Roche aux Fées **54**
Manoir de l'Automobile et des Métiers
  d'Antan **56**
Musée Louison Bobet **37**
Oxylane Village **46**
Parc des Gayeulles **47**
Parc des Grands Chênes **29**
Parc Floral de Haute-Bretagne **26**
Parc Ornithologique de Bretagne **53**
Ranch de la Foucheraie **35**
St. Just **57**
Train Marin **16**
Vélo Rail **36**

Dining ◆
Auberge de la Cour Verte **22**
Breizh Café **14**
Chez Jean-Pierre **7**
Crêperie Tivabro **25**
L'Arganier **5**
La Halte du Volcan **55**
Le Bénétin **9**
Le Pressoir **45**
Le Surf **1**
Les Forges de Paimpont **43**
Pen Roc **49**

Accommodation ■
Camping des Gayeulles **48**
Château de la Foltière **27**
Château du Pin **39**
Domaine de la Ville Huchet **11**
Domaine des Ormes **21**
Grand Hôtel Barrière **4**
Hôtel-Restaurant du Château **32**
Hôtel-Restaurant du Lac **31**
La Haute Mancelière **28**
La Pensée **2**
Le Gîtes de Kersillac **38**
Le Grénier d'Ernestine **44**
Le Mont Fleury **10**
Les Maisons de Bricourt **13**
Les Peupliers **34**
Manoir de la Bégaudière **19**
Résidence Reine Marine **8**
Tenzor de la Baie **17**

In many ways, the Ille-et-Vilaine doesn't feel truly Breton—its coastline, on a fairly sheltered stretch of the Channel, isn't as wild, rocky and windswept as that further west, while inland its wooded countryside may put you in mind of Normandy over the border. Yet this is still a fabulous place for a beach holiday: the oyster-farming town of Cancale and its resort Port-Mer are just the start of the stunning Côte d'Emeraude, with some wonderful stretches of sand and awesome views over the Baie du Mont-St. Michel, the bay shared by Brittany and Normandy. A short drive away, stunning St. Malo combines a walled pirates' city with an attractive seaside resort, as well as offering good shopping and an impressive aquarium. Dinard is classic family holiday territory among the well-to-do, while lesser-known St. Lunaire is more down to earth.

Brittany's capital, Rennes, is a superb place for culture, family events and boho-chic shopping. Other towns worth checking out are pretty Dol-de-Bretagne with its mysterious, legend-shrouded rocks, Fougères with its medieval remnants, and the charming Vitré.

Between the coast and Rennes you'll find the picturesque Château de la Bourbansais with its zoo and the appealing secondhand book town of Bécherel. Further south, lovers of stories and myths can get a further fix in the forest of Brocéliande (Paimpont), a wonderland of Arthurian myths and atmospheric ancient monuments. You'll also find great animal parks and rural activity centres with something to offer all ages, interesting accommodation options and many restaurants serving up the local produce. You'll come away from the Ille-et-Vilaine with more than a breath of fresh air in your lungs, and the feeling of really having escaped.

The *département* is also a good base for those visiting the world-famous Mont-St. Michel, one of the world's biggest tourist attractions, just over the border with Normandy (p. 65).

VISITOR INFORMATION

Information Centres

The French-only website of the CDT (main tourist office for the *département*), *www.loisirsac cueil35.com*, has a Liens Utiles (useful links) option listing the main tourist offices, *syndicats d'initiative and mairies*. If you're heading into the region from the direction of Paris, you might want to stop off at the **Maison Accueil Bretagne** at Erbrée just outside Vitré (summer and main hols, ☎ 02 99 49 49 45), where the kids can play in the nursery corner while you seek advice from the friendly staff about your stay.

Bécherel: 9 Place Alexandre Jehanin, ☎ 02 99 66 75 23, *www. becherel.com*.

Brocéliande/Paimpont: (*syndicat d'initiative*), 5 Esplanade de

Brocéliande, ☎02 99 07 84 23, *www.tourisme-broceliande.com*.

Cancale: 44 Rue du Port, ☎02 99 89 63 72, *www.ville-cancale.fr*, plus in high season an info point at La Criée.

Dinard: 2 Bd Féart, ☎02 99 46 94 12, *www.ot-dinard.com*.

Dol de Bretagne: 5 Place de la Cathédrale, ☎02 99 48 15 37, *www.pays-de-dol.com*.

Fougères: 2 Rue Nationale, ☎02 99 94 12 20, *http://ot-fougeres.fr*.

Rennes: 11 rue St. Yves, ☎02 99 67 11 11, *www.tourisme-rennes. com*.

St. Briac-sur-Mer: 49 Grande Rue, ☎02 99 88 32 47, *www. tourisme-saint-briac.fr*.

St. Coulomb: (*syndicat d'initiative*), Rue de la Mairie, ☎02 99 89 09 00, *www.saint. coulomb.com*.

St. Lunaire: 72 Bd du Général de Gaulle, ☎02 99 46 31 09, *www. saint-lunaire.com*.

St. Malo: Esplanade St. Vincent, ☎08 25 135 200, *www.saint-malo-tourisme.com*.

Vitré: Place Général de Gaulle, ☎02 99 75 04 46, *www.ot-vitre.fr*.

Orientation

The Breton capital Rennes is in the middle of the *département*, with the main roads radiating out from it: the N137 takes you to St. Malo (about 1hr/70km/43 miles north), the N12 goes west to St. Brieuc in the Côtes d'Armor (100km/62 miles) and on to Brest in Finistère (240km/149 miles), and the N24 travels west to Lorient in the Morbihan (153km/95 miles).

To the east, the A84, Brittany's only stretch of motorway, leads up to the Mont-St. Michel (92km/57 miles) and on into the heart of its region, Normandy.

Heading east, the N157 turns into the A81 to Le Mans in the Sarthe, your fastest route to cover the 357km (222 miles) to Paris from Rennes.

Arriving

By Boat Brittany Ferries (p. 23) sails once a day (except Sat Nov–Mar) between Portsmouth and St. Malo, leaving St. Malo late morning and Portsmouth early evening and taking between 8hrs 30mins and 11hrs. Most journeys are aboard the *Bretagne*, which, like all Brittany Ferries, offers kids' entertainment and a games room. You're also within about a 60–90min drive of Caen-Ouistreham and Cherbourg in Normandy, to which Brittany Ferries also sails.

Condor Ferries (p. 24) runs fast ferries between St. Malo and Poole or Weymouth daily in August, less frequently the rest of the year, taking around 5hrs. Some crossings require a change of vessel in Jersey or Guernsey in the Channel Islands. Boats have a children's TV room.

By Train Rennes is about 2hrs 15mins from **Paris** on the **TGV**. There's a direct TGV from Paris to **St. Malo**, taking around 3hrs (some trains also stop at **Dol-de-Bretagne**), or TGVs to St. Malo requiring a change in Rennes. For SNCF details, see p. 30.

By Air Ryanair (p. 25) runs budget flights between **Dinard** on the north coast and **London Stansted** (1 hour 5 minutes) and the **East Midlands** (1 hour 25 minutes).

There are also budget flights between Rennes airport just west of the city and Southampton, Exeter, Birmingham, Manchester and Edinburgh (most of them seasonal) with Flybe (p. 25). Rennes is also linked with Dublin by Aer Lingus (p. 25) twice-weekly in summer, and daily with Paris (CDG) with Air France (p. 25).

Getting Around

A car (or motorhome) is the only real way of getting around Brittany unless you plan to be based in one place. That said, even in the cities of St. Malo and Rennes, some of the best attractions are a little way out of the centre and a hassle to reach by public transport, especially with kids in tow.

For car hire at Dinard or Rennes airports see their websites (*www.saint-malo.cci.fr* and *www.rennes.aeroport.fr*) or organise with your airline when booking a ticket. Among the many options for car-hire at the TGV train terminals of Rennes and St. Malo is Easycar.com. Rennes is now also the region's centre for motorhome collection (p. 29).

Local tourist offices will provide details of taxi and bike-hire firms.

WHAT TO SEE & DO

Children's Top 10 Attractions

❶ **Heading** across the sands of the **Baie du Mont-St. Michel**, by tractor-drawn **Train Marin** to see mussels growing on *bouchots*, or

---

Getting Around Brittany the Green Way

Voie Vertes (*www.voiesvertes.com*), which appear through much of France and Europe as a whole, are 'greenways' designated for cyclists, walkers and horse-riders, many on old railway lines and towpaths. See each geographical chapter for details of Brittany's inherently family-friendly Voies Vertes. Another good source for walking and biking families, with 10 routes for each *département* in Brittany, is '*50 Balades Dimanches*', published by Ouest France and available in bookstores or from their website (*http://boutique.ouestfrance.fr*).

Breton Colours

on a guided walk for families. See p. 73.

❷ **Discovering** the historical sights, beaches and **Grand Aquarium** of **St. Malo**. See p. 72.

❸ **Getting to know** the low-key family resort of **St. Lunaire**. See p. 74.

❹ **Living** like a local family in hip **Rennes** with its great shopping, dining, parks and museums. See p. 60.

❺ **Exploring** the **forest of Brocéliande** with its ancient stones and Arthurian legends. See p. 67.

❻ **Swinging** from tree to tree then riding miniature boats at the **Parc des Grands Chênes**. See p. 81.

❼ **Cycling** along an old railway track on a family **Vélo Rail** at Médréac. See p. 81.

❽ **Encountering** the prehistoric sites of **St. Just** and **La Roche aux Fées**. See p. 67 and p. 70.

❾ **Spotting** the carved sea monsters at the **Rochers Sculptés de Rothéneuf**. See p. 63.

❿ **Sleeping in** a family treehouse at the **Domaine des Ormes**. See p. 92.

Child-Friendly Events & Entertainment

For the **Fête du Nautisme**, see p. 196; the best place in the department to enjoy it is St. Malo, with free sailing demonstrations and tuition on several beaches.

Bastille Day ★★

For Rennes tourist office, see p. 53.

Most towns of any size have fireworks and parties on **13th** or **14th July**, celebrating the storming of the Parisian fortress-prison representing royal authority. Rennes has perhaps the best in the region— fireworks, a parade and a ball on the large Plaine de Baud. Alternatively, the coast is a good place to enjoy a display.

Etincelles Aquatiques ★★

Etang de la Forge, Martigné-Ferchaud; ☎02 99 47 83 83; *www.etincelles-aquatiques.org. 53km (33 miles) southeast of Rennes on D41.*

This open-air extravaganza combining music, dance and fireworks involves around 250 amateur performers (of a total team of 950 volunteers, plus an audience of 5,000+) in a stunning lakeside setting. The 'story' blends local mythical and historical figures from fairies of the nearby Roche aux Fées (p. 70), 'rush-pullers' (who used to call locals to feasts by vibrating rushes), to imps. It is great fun for all ages, though the 10.15pm starting is not so suitable for smaller children. You can arrive earlier and have a dinner of sandwiches or Breton pancakes.

Date *Aug.* **Tickets** *adults 14€ adults, 6€ child (5–15).*

INSIDER TIP »

Bring a cushion and warm clothing to the Etincelles Aquatiques, and book well ahead (you can do so online, at a discount)—the four performances are very popular.

Quai des Bulles

Espace Duguay-Trouin, Esplanade St. Vincent, St. Malo; ☎*02 99 20 63 27;* ***www.quaidesbulles.com.***

St. Malo's long-standing festival of *bande dessinée* (comic strip) and cartoons attracts exhibitions by a huge variety of authors alongside around 80 stands by publishers, bookshops and fanzines. Each year there's a new film theme, with showings for all ages, plus book launches, auctions and debates.

Date *Nov. Check website to confirm dates.* **Admission** *free.*

Quartiers d'Eté ★★

Parc des Gayeulles, Avenue des Gayeulles, Rennes; ☎*02 99 36 81 08;* ***http://crij-bretagne.com/Quartiers-d-ete.html.***

This free, two-day, open-air festival in the east Rennes park Gayeulles (p. 78) is organised by young volunteers for a youthful audience—music has an ethnic slant, with hip hop, ragga and slam—and the fun and games includes quirky performance, open-air cinema, *vélo polo* (polo on mountain bikes), a graffiti wall, pony-rides, ecology lessons, temporary tattooing, jewellery-making, juggling and much more. In short, it's a bit of a mish-mash and a slightly eccentric day out. The park also has play areas.

Date *July.* **Admission** *free.*

INSIDER TIP »

For a real festival experience, stay at the Parc des Gayeulles campsite (p. 95), but be sure to reserve ahead. Otherwise, there are free shuttles to and from the centre.

Rennes sur Roulettes ★

Central Rennes; ☎*02 99 27 74 00;* ***www.rennessurroulettes.com.***

This weekend festival brings together some of the world's best rollerblading teams and individuals, competing in the women's and men's International Marathons over 50km through central Rennes. But non-pros can take part too: there's free *randonnée populaire* on the Sunday (kids need parental permission, and everyone must wear a helmet), as well as free lessons for beginners. The event also sees demos and a late-night roller-party.

Date *Apr or May.* **Admission** *free.*

The French school holidays (p. 45) see free events designed for kids aged 4 to 5 and their families in all 17 'Stations Famille', including Dinard and Cancale, as part of the **Festival Place aux Mômes** street festival. Each 'station' has a set day a week for events, which includes theatre, circus and acrobatics shows. See the Sensations Bretagne website (p. 15) for details.

Tombées de la Nuit

Rennes; ☎ 02 99 32 56 56 (tourist office); www.lestombeesdelanuit. com.

This large open-air festival has taken over the centre of Rennes for a week in July for more than 20 years. As the name says, it only gets going at sunset, but older kids love the mix of music, dance, lights, poetry, storytelling, theatre, and other street performance, much of an avant-garde nature. Most events are free, but some concerts require tickets, sold at the Fnac bookshop (p. 60) or at the tourist office (p. 53). Keep a look out in restaurants for the special dishes invented by local chefs to mark the occasion.

Date July. **Admission** mainly free, some events 2€–10€.

Towns & Cities

Bécherel, Cité du Livre ☆

For tourist office, see p. 52.

This 'book town' has the makings of a lovely family day out if you share a love of books, or a half-day combined with a visit to the **Zoo de la Bourbansais** (p. 69). The **tourist office** offers a beautifully

illustrated free French-language booklet for kids 7 and up, setting them on the trail of the town's compelling Plantagenet and linen-manufacturing history— and the local dragon too.

This sleepy little place full of ambling cats comes alive for the monthly book fair (first Sunday), Easter book festival and August 'book night'. Otherwise, there are a dozen or so bookshops with somewhat arbitrary opening times/days, so call the tourist office if you're making a special trip. The most child-friendly is the **Librairie Gwrizienn** (Rue de la Chanvrerie, ☎ 02 99 66 87 09), with second-hand French books for adults and children, including Tin Tin, old annuals, and illustrated Dickens' tales. In the adjoining *salon de thé* you can relax to classical music while the kids doodle with the paper and pencils provided or play in the town's quaint central square.

Also on the square, the **Librairie Neiges d'Antan** (rue de la Beurrerie, no phone) has English-language and other non-French books, books on Brittany, old crime novels and travel books, and kids' books.

Cancale

For tourist office, see p. 53.

Come at low tide to watch the tractors out in the oyster beds just offshore of Cancale's **Port de la Houle** and to enjoy distant views of the Mont-St. Michel (p. 65). You can buy a plastic tray of oysters from one of the stalls (at a fraction of the cost of the restaurants steps away) and enjoy them as natives do, on the beach, tossing the shells back to the ocean. Your kids might not yet have a taste for seafood (the fancy groceries along the front have biscuits and other beach munchies), but they should enjoy visiting the **Ferme Marine** (p. 71) or a half/one-day 'discovery trip' of the Bay of Mont-St. Michel (p. 65) in a *bisquine*, a sailing boat used by local fishermen c. 1810–1940 (☎ 02 99 89 77 87, *www.lacancalaise.org*). For places to stay, see p. 90.

To the north (still part of Cancale), the picturesque bay of **Port-Mer** has a sailing school (☎ 02 99 89 90 22) for ages 6 and up, and a summer Club Mickey on the beach. Further north still, the **Pointe du Grouin** is a jagged headland with impressive views, including the Ile des Landes, a reserve for great cormorants and other birds, with a lighthouse. In summer you might also spot dolphins. Sadly, tourists tend to overrun the spot.

Dinard ★

For tourist office, see p. 53.

The listed clifftop villas built by wealthy British visitors in the late 19th century are the most recognisable image of the 'Cannes of the North'. The curious mixture of British and French ambiances is reflected in the two famous people it is best associated with—Alfred Hitchcock, after whom a prize in the

Oysters for sale in Cancale

Petits Pirates

Croisières Chateaubriand (Gare Maritime du Barrage de la Rance, ☎02 99 46 44 40, *www.chateaubriand.com*) run *bateau-promenades* on the lovely Rance estuary that divides Dinard from St. Malo (p. 61), taking you past islands, coves, old watermills and *malouinières* (merchants' country dwellings), and lots of marine wildlife, including herons, cormorants and—if you're lucky—seals. Trips last 1 to 3hrs and include lunch or dinner cruises with seafood-based menus (29€–70€pp, including crossing) and an under 12s 'Pirate's Menu' (20€) including a cheese crêpe, *steak haché* and potato gratin, chocolate cake, and unlimited drinks.

town's British film festival (October) is named, and Pablo Picasso, who came here on several family holidays.

These days, it's a focal point of the thalassothereapy industry and has several large, clean, sandy beaches, foremost among them the Plage de l'Ecluse and Plage de St. Enogat. Along with the Plage du Prieuré, they have kids' clubs in high season. Watersport tuition is on offer here, from sea-kayaking and sailing to kite-surfing or diving, and there's a seawater swimming pool at the Digue de l'Ecluse.

Another draw for families is its **Parc de Port Breton,** with play areas offering sea views, a 'pets corner' with llamas, wallabies and more, and a walkway in the shape of the tree-based Celtic zodiac (from which Druids believed you could deduce your main personality traits). For a touch of culture, ask at the tourist office about their French-language heritage booklets with games. Dinard is also very handy for the many attractions of St. Malo (p. 61). For places to stay, see p. 90.

INSIDER TIP
Dinard's **Nouvelles Impressions** (42 rue Levavasseur, ☎02 99 46 15 95) is one of the rare bookshops outside Rennes to stock English-language titles, as well as travel guides, books on Brittany and the sea, and a kids' selection.

Dol-de-Bretagne ★
For tourist office, see p. 53.

This town just inland of the Bay of the Mont-St. Michel is best known for its stones, specially the **Mont-Dol,** a now-landlocked former island rising from the flat landscape north of the town. The spot where Europe's largest mammoth skeleton was found, the Mont was once home to rhinos, cave lions and wolves, and is said to be the place where St. Michael battled Satan before leaping in victory over to the Mont-St. Michel (some people claim you can see his footprint, and marks made by the devil's claws).

The second stone is the 125–150 tonne **Menhir de Champ-Dolent** south of town. One of the most impressive standing stones of the region, it's said to have fallen from the skies to separate two brothers locked in a feud. Dol, which is featured on the Bayeux Tapestry, is a 1.5hr drive away in Normandy, has an impressive cathedral and Romanesque townhouses with original carvings.

Fougères

For tourist office, see p. 53.

A few hops from the border with Normandy, this attractive town is dominated by its brooding medieval fort and a ruined castle with intact water-wheels and ramparts. Older kids might also like the **Atelier–Musée de l'Horlogerie Ancienne** (↡02 99 99 40 98), a 16th-century building devoted to timepieces old and modern, with demonstrations by a watchmaker. As well as clocks and watches dating back as far as 1600, there are music boxes and animated tableaux with automated figures. You might also hop aboard the petit train for a guided tour of Fougères, including the medieval quarter and upper town.

Rennes ★★★

For tourist office, see p. 53.

The capital of Brittany, Rennes is the liveliest spot in terms of **festivals and events** (p. 55) and the place to combine culture and shopping. Make sure you enjoy a ride on the hyper-modern automated **metro** system, which forms a strange contrast with the colourful timberframe medieval houses and cobbled lanes. There's also the superb **Parc du Thabor** (p. 78), a **farm museum** (p. 70), the excellent **Musée de Bretagne** and **Espace des Sciences** (p. 76), an exceptional fine arts museum (p. 76) and several traditional carousels.

Possibilities for retail therapy include a **Fnac** book- and multimedia store (Centre Commercial Colombia, ↡08 25 02 00 20) and a **Fnac Eveil et Jeux** (Centre Commercial La Visitation, ↡08 92 35 06 66, *www.eveiletjeux. com*), a children and babies specialist, with many products, from toys to furniture, tested and rated by parents. For designer childrenswear, try **L'Atelier des de Courcelles** on

Keeping in Touch the Old-fashioned Way

The stone Télégraphe de Chappe amidst marshland in the Bay of Mont-St. Michel (p. 65) 10km (6 miles) northeast of Dol de Bretagne is among the last vestiges of a remarkable late-19th-century telegraph system that prefigured the modern telephone line. About 50 such posts were dotted across the country at 15–20km (9–12 miles) intervals to provide a relay link between Paris and Brest in Finistère, with messages taking just 20 minutes to cross the distance of 600km (375 miles). The restored building is now open for visits in summer, when you can watch the replica arm functioning and see displays about the system.

Half-timbered buildings in Rennes

Rue Leperdit (📞 02 99 80 56 09); for kids' furniture and **Vibel** (8 Rue Edith Cavell, 📞 02 99 78 35 75) is a hip address. For treats for weary parents, **Lostmarc'h** (17 Rue Hoche, 📞 02 23 20 39 02) sells beauty and bath products (plus scented candles) made with Breton marine ingredients.

The city also has a travel book-shop selling French and English language guides, the **Librairie du Voyage** (20 Rue Capitain Drey-fus, 📞 02 99 79 68 47), while on Saturday mornings it hosts France's third-biggest **market**. For places to stay, see p. 90.

INSIDER TIP

A novel way to appreciate Britta-ny's capital and its green sur-roundings is with **Urbavag** (📞 02 99 33 16 88, **www.urbavag.fr**). This firm has small electric boats that you can hire out without a licence and take for a spin on the Vilaine river and Ille-et-Rance canal through and around Rennes. A five-person boat costs

from 15€ for half an hour. Note that you get a 25% discount if you have a **City Pass,** a booklet of discount vouchers on various Rennes sights, hotels, restau-rants and other amenities, avail-able from the tourist office and costing 13€ for two days.

St. Malo ★★★

For tourist office, see p. 53.

Famous for its gnarled 17th- and 18th- century *corsaires* or 'pirates with a permit' (who had royal warrants to attack foreign com-mercial vessels), St. Malo sprawls out from its *ville intra-muros*, the historic hub, which has wide ramparts you can stroll on and good beaches with lots of waters-ports opportunities (ask at the tourist office or try the Centre Nautique de Rance, which oper-ates in the sheltered estuary of the Rance just south of St. Malo (📞 02 99 58 48 80, **http://perso. orange.fr/cn.rennes**).

RENNES

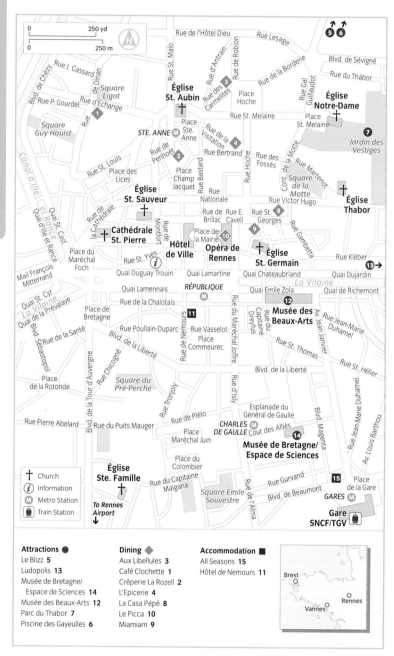

Attractions ●
Le Blizz **5**
Ludopolis **13**
Musée de Bretagne/
  Espace de Sciences **14**
Musée des Beaux-Arts **12**
Parc du Thabor **7**
Piscine des Gayeulles **6**

Dining ◆
Aux Libellules **3**
Café Clochette **1**
Crêperie La Rozell **2**
L'Epicerie **4**
La Casa Pépé **8**
Le Picca **10**
Miamiam **9**

Accommodation ■
All Seasons **15**
Hôtel de Nemours **11**

Market Days in the Ille-et-Vilaine

The department's major markets are as follows (all are morning-only):

Cancale	Sun
Dinard	Tues and Thurs, then a big one on Sat
Dol-de-Bretagne	Sat
Fougères	Sat
Rennes	Tues, Thurs and Fri mornings, then vast ones on Wed and Sat
St. Lunaire	Sun (Apr–Sept)
St. Malo	daily except Mon
Vitré	Mon and Sat

The beaches include the **Plage du Bon Secours,** from which you can sometimes walk out (study the tide warnings first) to **Grand Bé island,** where the writer Chateaubriand is entombed (as a child he played on the rocky Plage de l'Eventail nearby). In summer you can also walk out to the **Fort National,** a one-time execution site with a drawbridge, jail and powder magazine (there are English-speaking guides). There's a **petit train touristique** and a appealing, if pricey, carousel by the Grand Porte. The highlight, though, is the **Grand Aquarium** on the fringes of town (p. 72).

Accommodation (p. 90) is better outside the walled centre—notably in the city's seaside resort of **Paramé** stretching northeast as far as **Rothéneuf** with its amazing **Rochers Sculptés.** Created by a deaf-dumb priest as a way of expressing himself, these gargoyle-like figures represent a local

Beach leading away from St. Malo

Pop Pops & other Seaside Shopping

St. Malo is more than just a ferry stop or a site of historical interest that happens to have a handful of good beaches, it also offers some superb shops. However short your time here, find time for **La Droguerie de Marine** (66 rue Georges Clemenceau, St. Servan-sur-Mer, ☎ *02 99 81 60 39*) ★★, an ancient marine hardware store that still sells classic products for sailors such as Marseille soap, brushes, paints, varnishes and waxes, knives and storm matches. Look deeper inside, though, and you'll find an eclectic treasure trove and a brilliant place for gifts. Kids' eyes are inevitably drawn to the Pop Pop boats—little tin craft that move when you place a little candle into them—but there's an array of other toys and games, plus ship's models, compasses, barometers, tin whistles and decorative objects from linen to mirrors. The grocery section stocks local delicacies such as fish ravioli from Le Guilvinec, lobster soup, salted-butter caramels and beer. Appropriately, it's like being on an exotic ship. If it inspires you to sail forth, there's a book section with three main themes—the Sea, Brittany and Travel—including English-language books.

Sportmer (5 place aux Herbes, ☎ *02 99 40 23 32*) is a classic, unpretentious toyshop in the centre of St. Malo, crammed full of toys and games from ships' models to up-to-date TV-related merchandise. It's a useful stop off on the way to the nearby Plage du Bon Secours (p. 63), with plenty of buckets and spades, balls, nets for dabbling in rockpools, kites and more. For Breton stripes (p. 8) and other stylish clothes for adults and kids, head for the **Boutique Coudémail** (51 Rue Ville Pépin, ☎ *02 99 19 81 29*), which stocks the kidswear line Elle Est Où La Mer? (p. 132).

A **Galerie Plisson** (p. 132) has also opened in the old town (9 rue des Cordiers, ☎ *02 23 18 44 80*), selling the photographer's famous seascapes in various formats, from postcards to large canvases, plus his children's books, and there are three branches of Comptoir de la Mer (p. 176), one on Place Chateaubriand and two on Avenue Franklin Roosevelt (plus two more in the *département*, in Cancale and Le Vivier-sur-Mer).

For **markets** in the Ille-et-Vilaine as a whole, see p. 63.

family of *corsaires* devoured by sea monsters after a battle with other pirates. It's astonishing to imagine the priest clambering down the vertiginous rock face every day for 25 years, chiselling away. Those with toddlers or babes-in-arms might find the rough-hewn steps a challenge, and sensible shoes should be worn.

In summer, St. Malo is home to the **Labyrinthe du Corsaire** (Route de Quelmer La Passagère, ☎ *02 99 81 17 23*, *www.labyrinthe ducorsaire.com*), a huge corn maze by the sea, with bouncy castles at the centre, giant wooden games and other entertainments.

INSIDER TIP ⟩⟩

As well as a Channel ferry port (p. 22), St. Malo is the starting point for trips by small ferries (*vedettes*) to Dinard (p. 58), the uninhabited island of Cézembre with its fine sand beach, and—in the Côtes d'Armor—Cap Fréhel (p. 163) and the town of Dinan (p. 158). Contact Vedettes de St Malo, 📞 *02 23 18 02 04*, *www.vedettes-saint-malo.com*.

Vitré

For tourist office, see p. 53.

A delight of medieval streets, squares and buildings, this designated Ville d'art et d'histoire can provide a charming introduction to Brittany for those heading into the region from the east. Most impressive is the town's

Rochers Sculptés de Rothéneuf (see p. 63)

very handsome castle, begun in the 11th century and housing a small museum. Ask at the castle reception desk to hire a 'Jouer en famille à Vitré' pack (10€ plus presentation of ID required), containing adult tickets to that and Vitré's second castle—that of Madame de Sévigné, with an exhibition on the famous 17th-century letter writer and lovely formal gardens—together with games, crayons, an MP3 player and a mini telescope.

In summer only, visitors to the town can see the **Musée de l'Abeille** (📞*02 99 75 09 01*), an off-beat little 'museum of the living bee', with five active hive colonies (safely behind glass) and, in August (3pm daily), the chance to see honey being extracted.

Fun Days Out

Baie du Mont-St. Michel
★ ★ ★ **ALL AGES**

www.baie-mont-saint-michel.fr

This bay of glittering sand flats stretching out between Brittany and Normandy is one of France's most awesome sights—and one of its deadliest, with quicksand and Europe's fastest-moving tides still claiming lives today as they did those of medieval pilgrims attempting to reach the **Mont-St. Michel** (p. 68). The best time to visit it is in June, for the annual grand **Rando-Baie** programme (📞*02 33 89 64 00*, *www.rando-baie-mont-saint-michel.fr*) of fantastic family-based events in the bay, run from the Maison de la Baie at Genêts in Normandy but with some activities taking place in Cherrueix (home to the Maison du Terroir). A warning: Victor Hugo described the tides in the bay being as 'swift as a galloping horse' (they come in at 1m/3ft a second, with roughly 14m/46ft between high and low water marks). **Never walk in the bay without a guide.**

Midway between St. Malo and the Mont-St. Michel, the **Maison de la Baie du Vivier sur Mer** (℡*02 99 48 84 38, www.maison-baie.com*) is a nature centre that brings the bay, especially its main trade of mussel farming, alive for all ages—partly through imaginative and interactive displays and a film on marine life in the bay. A visit is best combined with an hour tour of the bay in the 'Mytili-Mobile' tractor-drawn cart (a longer 2hr tour takes you to see mussels growing on bouchots amidst the sands), or, better still, with one of the guided walks lasting 3 to 7hrs (over a distance of 8 to 25km). One walk, the Balade Découverte (3–4hrs over 8km), was conceived specially for families and includes shell-hunting.

> **INSIDER TIP** »
>
> Only 5 minutes from the Mount, at Beauvoir, you'll find **Alligator Bay** (℡*02 33 68 11 18, www.alligator-bay.com*), where you can see about 200 alligators, crocodiles and caimans and pet around 300 tortoises, some of them giant specimens from the Seychelles. Other residents include snakes and chameleons, and there are child-friendly observation points and feeding sessions.

The Mont-St-Michel

Cobac Parc AGE 1 & UP

Le Parc de Haute Bretagne, Lanhélin; ℡02 99 73 80 16; www.cobac-parc. com. 13km (8 miles) southwest of Dol-de-Bretagne on D78.

One of those amusement parks with a rather 'home-made' feel the French seem to specialise in, this is still a good standby for a family day out when everyone's had their fill of beaches. Of the many attractions, the big draws are the new pirate ship, the traditional carousel, the rope bridge over the boating lake and the 'monkey bridge' between trees. Most are aimed at kids roughly 5 and over, but there are possibilities for tots, from petting goats to splashing in the toddlers' pool (the waterpark is open June–Aug). Eating options include a self-service café with waffles, ice creams and the like (plus a kids' menu), and there are picnic spaces.

Time half a day. Open daily 11am–6pm; check website for seasonal variations *(closed Oct–Mar)*. **Admission** 16€ adult, 13.50€ child (3–11). **Amenities** 🏠 🅿 🎪 ⛱ 🍴 🍷 🛒 ♿

Fôret de Brocéliande

⭐ ⭐ **AGE 7 & UP**

For tourist office, see p. 52.

Also known as the Fôret de Paimpont, these woods and moorland west of Rennes are the centre of Breton Arthurian legends—possibly because an 11th-century lord of the forest brought back tales of King Arthur and the Knights of the Round Table after fighting in England during the Norman Conquest. Today tourist trails take in atmospheric sites where events involving characters from the legends are said to have taken place, and Neolithic remains such as menhirs and dolmens dot the landscape.

The Château de Comper (just within the Morbihan) houses the **Centre de l'Imaginaire Arthurien** (📞 02 97 22 79 96, *www.centre-arthurien-broceliande.com*), with exhibitions about the area and legends (texts and videos are in French only). It also hosts storytelling events and guided walks through the forest. Beside the château, the **Lac de Comper** (or 'Grand Etang')—or at least the bottom of it—is where magician Merlin is reputed to have created a castle of crystal for the fairy Viviane.

Another Arthurian site is the **Fontaine de Barenton,** a spring where Merlin and Viviane are said to have met, reputed to have powers for bringing rain and curing madness (hence the name

of the nearby village of Folle Pensée—'Mad Thought'). Books and crafts on Arthurian and other Celtic and medieval themes, plus local produce, can be found at **Au Pays de Merlin** (Rue du Général de Gaulle, Paimpont, 📞 02 99 07 80 23).

For places to stay in the area, see p. 90.

Time: *half a day to a day.* **Amenities** *(centre)* 🅿 ♿

> **INSIDER TIP »**
>
> The Brocéliande forest is also a scenic area for walking and riding (tourist offices sell 'Topo-Guides' detailing 3–20km/2–12-mile circuits) together with mountain biking (hire is available at Au Pays de Merlin; see above).

St. Just ⭐ **AGE 7 & UP**

48km (30 miles) southwest of Rennes off D177.

This exceptional Neolithic site, famous for the diversity of its dolmens and megalithic buildings and set on a beautiful area of heath, is comparable in many ways with Carnac (p. 107) but is utterly untouristy. Sites of interest are dotted over several kilometres, a highlight being the **Demoiselles de Cojoux** or **Roches Piquées**—quartz standing stones that may have been part of a larger alignment, and that according to legend are young girls turned to stone for dancing at prayer time.

A 7km 'discovery circuit' gives an insight into human activity here, starting from 7,000 years ago, and also lets you

A Mystical Mount in a Bay of Wonders?

A rocky islet 2km (just over a mile) off the coast of Normandy, topped by a dramatic Benedictine abbey and Romanesque church, the Mont-St. Michel (☎ *02 33 60 14 30*, *www.ot-montsaintmichel.com*) is a UNESCO World Heritage Site and also France's most-visited attraction outside Paris. It's often thought to be in Brittany—in fact, many Bretons still challenge Norman ownership of it, claiming that it's only there now as a result of the river Couesnon, the historic border between Brittany and Normandy, having changed course.

Only about 50km (30 miles) east of St. Malo, the Mount is easily visited by those holidaying in Brittany. A Roman stronghold, it first became home to a monastery in the 8th century, after, according to legend, the archangel Michael told the Bishop of Avranches to build a church here (reinforcing his message by burning a hole in the bishop's skull with his finger; you can see the skull in the church at nearby Avranches). A site of pilgrimage for many years, its influence waned with the Reformation, and after the Revolution it served as a prison until a campaign led to it being declared a historic monument in 1874. Your children may recognise it from a scene in *Mickey, Donald, Goofy: The Three Musketeers* (2004), and it also inspired the design of Mina Tirith in *The Lord of the Rings: The Return of the King* (2003).

That said, it's not the most child-friendly of sights, with its steep cobbled lanes, tacky souvenir shops and restaurants, and tourist hordes (don't bring a buggy). But if you come outside high season or in the evening you can still catch inklings of a mysterious aura. The best bit for kids—apart from the incredible views over the glistening sandflats of the Baie (p. 65), dotted with ant-like walkers—is the Archéoscope, a multimedia space with a son-et-lumière show about the mount's history, construction and legends (in French, but with great footage from a helicopter). You can also visit the abbey itself, including the spooky crypts, a Musée Maritime with model boats and displays on local tides and ecology, and the Musée Historique, with waxwork prisoners, reconstructed *oubliettes* (prison cells set in dungeon floors), torture instruments, weapons, and a 19th-century periscope that lets you look at the bay.

A pass to all of the Mount's sights costs 18€ for adults and 9€ for children aged 10 to 18. There's nowhere good to eat, so bring a picnic or head for nearby Pontorson, where the charmingly named Tartines Bavardes ('Garrulous Sandwiches'; 32 Rue St. Michel, ☎ *02 33 60 67 04*) serves great paninis, quiches, tarts and desserts.

appreciate the natural surrounds; there are green arrows to follow, plus info points along the way,

but you can also pick up free leaflets at **La Maison Nature et Mégalithes** at St. Just itself (Allée des Cerisiers, 02 99 72 69 25, *http://landes-de-cojoux.com/*). In summer La Maison organises events such as a prehistoric festival and *fest noz,* astronomy nights and woodland games; year-round there's a permanent exhibition on Neolithic peoples and their relationship with nature.

Time half a day to a full day. **Open** *main site is open access. La Maison: May, June, Sept and Oct Wed–Sun 2–6pm; July and Aug daily 9.30am–12.30pm and 2.30–7pm; Nov–Apr Sun 2–6pm.* **Admission** *main site free; exhibition at La Maison 5€ adult, 3€ child (8–16), 12€ family.* **Amenities** *(La Maison)* 🅿 ♿

Animal Attractions

L'Ane de Gouttière FIND
AGE 5 & UP

Raingo; 02 99 80 04 82; *www. anedegouttiere.com. 10km (6 miles) southeast of Dol de Bretagne on D85.*

Kids with a hectic pace of life will learn to chill out as they discover the northern Ille-et-Vilaine from the back of a donkey—one of them named Scoubidou—with this French-speaking firm. The donkeys will also carry picnics and gear, but parents must lead the creatures on foot. Trips range from half-day tours of the area around Epiniac itself to 2 days or more, venturing as far as the Mont-St. Michel (p. 68)—staff will help you to devise your itinerary and organise your accommodation (campsites, B&Bs on working farms and the like). For those taking longer treks (but also those simply keen

to learn), there are also Initiation sessions including donkey care (hoof-cleaning, brushing, saddling and so on). The young family who run this organic farm also sell their own produce, including merguez sausages.

Time from half a day to several days. **Open** *all year by reservation.* **Admission** *Initiation 25€ per donkey, half-day ride 25€, 1-day ride 40€, 2-days or more 35€ per day.* **Amenities** 🅿 🏕

La Bourbansais ★ ALL AGES

Pleugueneuc; 02 99 69 40 07; *www.labourbansais.com. 33km (20.5 miles) south of St. Malo off N137.*

This charming zoo with an almost tropical atmosphere is part of a castle and park, so you can take in some history and culture in the same outing. Bounded by a rich, shady forest (the deer and wolf enclosures merge into the trees), La Bourbansais is lush with palms, colourful flowers and other plants, to the point where it's often difficult to see the animals through the foliage, but they seem to have a decent amount of space, and there are daily feedings to watch.

If you join a 50-minute guided tour of the beautiful castle's period interiors (there are combined or separate tickets for the zoo and castle), reward the kids with a turn on the bouncy castles and other play equipment (and a maze July–Sept), though you may be surprised how much fun they have just running around the formal gardens with

Fairies with Biceps?

Delighting lovers of the prehistoric and fairytales alike, **La Roche aux Fées** or 'Fairies' Rock' near Essé (40km/16 miles southeast of Rennes) is one of the most impressive dolmens (Neolithic gallery tombs) in all France, at 20m in length, 6m in width and 4m in height (65 × 20 × 13ft). According to one legend, fairies flew the 40-or-so huge red-schist slabs, weighing up to 40 tonnes, here about 5,000 years ago. Other legends have it that this was a dragon's lair, the tomb of a Roman emperor, and a site of human sacrifice.

Some locals claim that it's impossible to walk round the Rock and count the same number of stones twice; unless you're about to wed and do the counting by full moon, in which case, if the numbers do tally, your marriage will last. The rock's entrance is aligned with the rising sun at the winter solstice, which means the interior is illuminated on December 21.

Make sure you wear sensible shoes to visit as this is an uphill walk (you're rewarded with great views over the countryside).

their pyramid hedges and weathered statuary. The grounds also host daily displays (Apr–Sept) involving falconry and hunting hounds.

There's a snack restaurant serving *steak frites*, Italian ices, *barbe à papa* (candyfloss) and more, plus a shady picnic area.

Time half a day to a full day. **Open** Apr–Sept daily 10am–7pm; Oct–Mar daily 2–6pm. **Admission** 16.50€ adults, 12.50€ child (3--12). **Amenities** ♈ ☕ 🅿 🪧 ⛰ 🏠 ♿

La Chêvrerie du Désert ALL AGES

Plerguer; ☎02 99 58 92 14. 8km (5 miles) west of Dol-de-Bretagne off D676.

You're never far from a friendly (often overfriendly) goat in Brittany, but this small 'discovery farm' is worth an early evening visit if you're in the area, to watch the goats being milked (5.30pm). Otherwise, the entry fee is on the high side to see dwarf goats in their enclosure (which kids can enter), Vietnamese pigs, Poitou donkeys, Ouessant sheep (p. 204), Jersey cows and a variety of birdlife. There's also a shop selling the farm's goats' cheese, jam and honey, cider, apple juice and other produce.

Time: 1–2hrs. **Open** Apr–June Wed–Sun 2.30–6.30pm; July–Aug daily 11am–6.30pm. **Admission** 6.50€ adults, 5.50€ children. **Amenities** 🅿 🏠 ♿

Ecomusée du Pays de Rennes ★ ★ ★ ALL AGES

Ferme de la Bintinais, route de Châtillon-sur-Seiche, Rennes; ☎02 99 51 38 15; www.ecomusee-rennes-metropole.fr. From city centre, take Ave Henri-Fréville, then follow signposts in direction of Noyal-Chatillon-sur-Seiche.

La Bintinais on the outskirts of Rennes was once one of the city's largest farms, and this three-storey museum retraces the history, through artefacts, machinery and furniture, enlivened by audiovisual displays, interactive games and films. There are also two new spaces for free, drop-in, interactive workshops, aimed at both kids and adults—Chlorophyll, with a plant theme, and Kératine, on the subject of animals, including skeletons and models. They're open on alternating days in the school holidays (2–6pm Tues–Sat, 3–7pm Sun). Within the 19 hectare grounds you can see about 20 threatened local breeds, including some rather fetching spotted pigs.

Time half a day. ***Open*** Apr–Sept Tues–Fri 9am–noon, 2–6pm; Sat 2–6pm, Sun 2–7pm; Oct–Mar Tues–Fri 9am–noon and 2–6pm, Sat 2–6pm, Sun 2–7pm. Closed public hols. ***Admission*** 4.60€ adults, 2.30€ child (6–14). ***Amenities*** 🅿 🛍 ♿

Ferme Marine AGE 3 & UP

L'Aurore, Cancale; 📞 *02 99 89 69 9; www.ferme-marine.com. 16km (10 miles) east of St. Malo on D355.*

There can be few better places to tour a working oyster farm than scenic Cancale (p. 58). Visitors to this family enterprise get to see farming techniques, including the hauling in of the mesh bags, and oyster sorting by hand (an arduous task), plus a display of seashells from around the world that appeals more to youngsters—toddlers love the giant shells, some as big as themselves.

Time 1hr. ***Open*** mid-Feb–June and mid-Sept–Oct Mon–Fri 3pm (in French); July–mid-Sept daily 2pm (in English). ***Admission*** 6.80€ adults, 3.60€ children, 18.70€ family ticket (2 adults and 2 or more kids). ***Amenities*** 🅿 🛍 ♿

Ferme du Tessonnet ALL AGES

Goven; 📞 *02 99 42 02 55; http:// foireanimalieredegoven.e-monsite. com/. 19km (12 miles) southwest of Rennes on D21.*

Château de la Bourbansais

This 6 hectare farm is a breeding centre for 50 plus threatened species, including Girgentana goats from Sicily, recognisable by their spiralling horns up to 70cm, Mangalitza pigs, with dense curly black hair on their back, and miniature pigs from the USA. Activities include pony rides for young kids (2.30€), and you can feed some of the animals.

Time 2hrs. *Open* July and Aug Mon–Fri and Sun 2–7pm; Sun and public hols mid-Apr–June and Sept 2–7pm. *Admission* 4€ adults, 3€ children. *Amenities* 👤 ♿

Grand Aquarium

★ ★ ★ **ALL AGES**

Ave du Général Patton (towards Dinard), St. Malo; ☎02 99 21 19 00; www.aquarium-st-Malo.com.

The highlights of this excellent aquarium outside St. Malo's walled centre are the amazing Nautibus mini submarines, which make 6-minute tours of an underwater pool full of marine flora, fauna and mock wrecks—the turbulence is designed to be part of the fun. Aimed at younger children, the brilliant Bassin Ludique has a touchpool with rays, turbots and more, and interactive installations such as the Sirène Anémone, which calls out to its siblings if you get too close. The Anneau des Requins or 'Shark Ring', is a massive circular aquarium where you recline on soft mats as lemon sharks, nurse sharks, sandbar sharks, sand tiger sharks, turtles and a giant grouper swim around you, to soft music and subtly pulsating

lighting (call ☎02 99 21 19 07 for details of overnight stays in the Ring). Other rooms are cleverly themed (oil rig, lab with bubbling test tubes, wreck and so on), with stories told by a fictional explorer (in French only) but an emphasis on serious ecology. The aquarium has a restaurant but also space to picnic.

Time 2–3hrs. *Open* daily 10am–6pm. Call to check seasonal opening hours and late-night openings. *Admission* 15.50€ adults, 9.50€ child (4–14). *Amenities* 👤 ♨ 🏕 🍽 ♿

Parc Ornithologique de Bretagne **ALL AGES**

53 Bd Pasteur, Bruz; ☎02 99 52 68 57; www.parc-ornithologique.com. Approx 14km (8–9 miles) south of Rennes off D177.

This wooded park brings together birdlife from all over the world, from Siberian geese to Australian black swans, so there's quite a racket going on most of the day. Some creatures—such as parrots—are familiar from zoo visits; others, including golden pheasants from China and Lady Amherst pheasants from Tibet and Burma, are more novel. The beady-eyed birds of prey also exert a fascination. Strolling around the duck and geese filled lake is pleasant on a sunny day; there are tables and benches where you can sit and have a snack, plus a cute bar with a terrace and a gift shop.

Time 90 mins. *Open* Apr–June, Sept daily 2–7pm; July and Aug daily 10am–noon and 2–7pm; Oct–mid-Nov and mid-Feb–Apr Sun 2–6pm. *Admission* 6.50€ adults, 3.90€ child (3–12). *Amenities* 🍷 🍴 👤 🏕 🔋 ♿

If your children love animals, are independently minded and speak good French, they may enjoy a stay on a French farm. At Talensac west of Rennes, for instance, **La Ferme de Trénube** (*www.trenube.com*) offers activities based on farm life and crafts for 6 to 12-year-olds, costing 370€ for a week but with shorter stays and day visits available. East of Rennes, **La Haute Hairie** (St-M'Hervé, ☎ *02 99 76 72 88*, *www.ferme-pedago.fr*) offers 'holiday colonies' for ages 4 to 9 and 10 to 13, with pony or horse-riding and related games, bread-making, nature discovery, treasure hunts, campfire and all sorts of other fun. Accommodation is in a gîte for the younger kids and tents for the older ones.

For nearby hotels with spas where you might treat yourself while the kids are on the farm, see Accommodation from p. 90.

Train Marin ★ ★ AGE 3 & UP

Cherrueix; ☎ 02 99 48 84 88; www. train-marin.com. 38km (23.5 miles) east of St. Malo on D85.

These yellow tractors and trailers take you out into the other-worldly landscape of the vast bay of Mont-St. Michel—up to 5km (3 miles) at low tide—to see mussels clustered on *bouchots*—the wooden posts on which they're cultivated, which vanish beneath the water at high tide. It's incredible to see how tiny the creatures start out. You also watch a demonstration of dredging for shrimps (children can join in if they like) and see huge wooden traps dating from around AD 1000, still used to catch fish. The whole trip takes two hours; the live commentary in French takes in the history of the bay and its legends as well as mussel farming. Advance booking is essential, but you also need to arrive 30 mins ahead of your slot otherwise your place might be sold to someone else.

Remember your wellies—it's a muddy outing!

The Maison de la Baie at nearby Le Vivier-sur-Mer (p. 66) runs similar tractor-drawn trips out to see mussel farming.

Time *2hrs.* **Open** *times vary hugely due to tides; call for details.* **Admission** *12€ adults, 8€ child (4–11).* **Amenities** 🅿

INSIDER TIP »

Cherrueix's exposed 7km (4 mile) beach is an amazing place to learn to kite-surf, against a background of picturesque old windmills (the last of 11 that once stood here). Contact **Noroit Club** (☎ *02 99 48 83 01*, *www. noroit-club.fr.fm*) for details.

Best Beaches

See also especially **Port-Mer** (Cancale; p. 58) and **Dinard** (p. 58). **St. Malo** (p. 61) has excellent sands for children in its seaside resort of Paramé, though there are few amenities or organised activities.

Anse Du Guesclin and Plage de la Touesse ★

For tourist office (St. Coulomb), see p. 53.

A gloriously wild croissant-shaped beach on the quiet coastal road between St. Malo and Cancale, the Anse du Guesclin, has nothing but sand to play on and sparkling rockpools to delve in. The dramatic Fort Du Guesclin overlooking it, set on a little island that's cut off at high tide, was home in the 1950s and '60s to singer Leo Ferré and his famous pet chimp Pépée. Meanwhile, just east of the Anse, the **Plage de la Touesse** will particularly please teen fans of Colette—the novelist found inspiration for *Le Blé en Herbe*, about a family holiday in Brittany, while living in a villa here from 1911 to 1926.

St. Lunaire ★ ★ ★ FIND

For tourist offices, see p. 53.

Named after an evangelising monk said to have lived to 115—his Gallo-Roman sarcophagus is in the 11th-century church and his sandal marks are supposedly visible on the Pointe du Décollé, where he's claimed to have stepped offshore after chopping through fog with his sword. The village of St. Lunaire was transformed from a fishing community into a chic resort in the 1860s, with wide boulevards, grand villas, hotels and a casino. Things calmed down after the 'Années Folles' of the 1920s, and now this is a placid family resort retaining the stunning sea vistas

that—some contend—inspired Debussy to write parts of *La Mer*.

St. Lunaire's four lovely beaches include **La Grande Plage,** with a kids' club in July and August and swimming lessons for ages 3 and up in a heated pool. Right nearby you'll find mini-golf and the town's Yacht Club (☏02 99 46 30 04, **www.ycsl.net**), offering a sailing tuition on all sorts of vessels, with a starting age of 7, plus a 'Jardin des Mers' activity programme for 5- to 8-year-olds in July and August. The same firm has an outpost, **Point Passion Plage,** on the **Plage de Long-champ** stretching out of town to the east, where you can hire sea canoes, bodyboards, surfboards and sand yachts. Don't miss the surprising wonderful 'snack bar', **Le Surf** (p. 85), towards the western end of this beach.

St. Lunaire's **Tennis-Club** (☏02 96 46 31 11) offers lessons and courses for kids, and, in summer, junior and family tournaments, while **Les Ecuries** (☏02 99 46 06 20, **www.equitation-saint-lunaire.fr**) has a '*pony club*' for ages 5 plus and rides in the area.

For places to stay, see p. 90.

INSIDER TIP

Nestling up against St. Lunaire, the pretty estuary town of **St. Briac-sur-Mer** has more great beaches and a centre full of *brocantes* (junk shops) and the largish **Tant Qu'il y Aura la Mer** (☏02 99 88 32 72), stocking kidswear. Take kids to spot the green stone mackerels that adorn the church (the fish were seen here as a herald of spring).

Museums

L'Atelier Manoli ⭐ AGE 3 & UP

9 Rue du Suet, La Richardais; 📞*02 99 88 55 53. 2km southeast of Dinard on D114.*

This museum and sculpture garden on the site where the artist Manoli lived has more than 300 outsize works and models based around three main themes: the human figure, 'assemblages' and animals (the 'Bestiaire'). It's fun to look at the 'assemblages' and try to work out what discarded objects they were created from (including saws and nails), but kids have the best fun exploring the pathways and green lawns, where sculpted animals, gravity-defying human figures and strange creatures lurk amidst the vegetation.

*Time 1–2hrs. **Open** Apr–June, Sept and Oct Sat, Sun and school and public hols 3–7pm; July and Aug daily 10.30–12.30pm and 3–7pm. **Admission** 4.50 € adults, children under 10 free. **Amenities** 🅿️ ♿*

Ecomusée du Pays de Montfort AGE 5 & UP

2 Rue du Château, Montfort-sur-Meu; 📞 *02 99 09 31 81,* ***http://ecomusee paysmontfort.free.fr**. 27km (17 miles) west of Rennes on D125.*

Within a tower that is all that remains of the town's 14th-century castle, this museum provides a lesson in life's simpler pleasures, with its displays on toys from pre-Industrial times. In place of Playstations and plastic contraptions, kids can see toys made from wood and other natural country materials both for and by children, and be inspired to see what can be created from leaves, flowers and even fruit and vegetables. In addition, the museum has displays on medieval Montfort, regional costumes from 1840 to 1940, local legends, architecture and photography.

*Time 1hr 30mins. **Open** Apr–Sept Mon–Fri 8.30am–noon and 2–6pm, Sat 10am–noon and 2–6pm, Sun*

Oyster beds at Cancale (see p. 71)

2–6pm; Oct–Mar Tues–Fri 9am–noon and 2–6pm. **Admission** 4€ adults, 2€ child (6–16).

INSIDER TIP

A 20-minute drive west of Mont-fort, in St. Méen-le-Grand, is the offbeat little **Musée Louison Bobet** (5 rue de Gaël, 02 99 09 67 86), dedicated to a local hero who won three consecutive Tours de France (1953–55). Bobet is said to have got so fast by delivering bread for his dad, the local baker. He also brought thalassotherapy (seawater cures) to Brittany.

Manoir de l'Automobile et des Métiers d'Antan AGE 4 & UP

La Cour Neuve, Lohéac; 02 99 34 02 32; www.manoir-automobile.fr. 35km (22 miles) southwest of Rennes on D177.

This vast museum in the grounds of a 17th-century manor houses a collection of 400 or so cars, from chunky 1930s Talbots to sleek Ferraris and modern Formula 1 cars, plus a few thousand scale models. Around 230 waxwork tableaux with utterly unlifelike manne-quins in period costume add a touch of humour to proceedings, livening things up for family members who might not be as car-crazy as others. As well as old forms of transport such as horse-drawn carts, they evoke a variety of bygone trades.

Time 1hr 30mins. **Open** Tues–Sun and public hols 10am–1pm and 2–7pm, also Mon in July and Aug. **Admission** 8.50€ adults, 7€ child [10–16]. **Amenities** 🍸 ☕ 🖼 🛍

INSIDER TIP

A good way to spend the rest of the day after visiting the Manoir de l'Automobile is boating and canoeing on the **Vilaine river** in nearby Messac (02 99 34 78 18). The latter town is also one of the bases for Crown Blue Line cruising holidays.

Musée des Beaux-Arts
AGE 2 & UP

20 Quai Emile Zola, Rennes; 02 23 62 17 45; www.mbar.org.

Rennes's fine arts museum, crammed with artworks and arte-facts from Ancient Egypt to the present is a doozy, with highlights including pieces by contemporary Breton artists and Pablo Picasso's *Baigneuse*, one of several works he painted at Dinard (p. 58). Your kids might enjoy joining in one of the free, 1hr drop-in work-shops (in French) for kids 4 to 11 (school holidays only), or for kids 5 to 14, Croqu'musée ('Bite-sized Museum') workshops one Wednesday a month (2.50€; booking required). For younger kids (aged 2–2½) there are free 'discovery' sessions every Friday, on topics such as Animals or Mothers. Or you can just pick up one of the themed family booklets or colouring booklets at reception.

Time 1–2hrs. **Open** Tues 10am–6pm, Wed–Sun 10am–noon and 2–6pm. **Admission** 4.58€ adults, 2.88€ child. **Amenities** 🛍 ♿

Musée de Bretagne/Espace de Sciences ★★★ AGE 4 & UP

10 Cour des Alliés, Rennes; 02 23 40 66 70 (Musée); 02 23 40 66 40

(Espace des Sciences); www.les champslibres.fr.

Rennes's must-visit **Champs Libres** building is home to the city library, the vastly expanded Musée de Bretagne and the Espace des Sciences (Science Centre). The **Musée de Bretagne,** Brittany's regional museum, should be on any visitor's list, particularly the exhibition 'Bretagne est Univers', which, designed to resemble a city, with 'streets' and 'squares' between the main displays, traces the region's history and identity through objects, costumes, videos and more, from paleolithic tools to a Minitel computer. **Mille et Une Images,** another permanent exhibition, evokes the region from a more poetic point-of-view, with sound and light effects creating a 3D universe in which paintings, posters, photos and old engravings are experienced as a 'flow' of sensations, rather than in any chronological or thematic order. Children are most interested by the many Breton toys and games on display, including a wooden Poule Picorante ('Pecking Hen') from 1935. New since 2009 are free Explorer backpacks with binoculars, a map and a compass, for those with kids 7 and up, taking you on a route lasting 1hr to 1hr 30mins (the accompanying text is in French). There are also regular, free, 1hr 30min workshops—again in French— on such themes as mosaic design or Neolithic pottery, aimed at kids aged 6–12.

The **Espace des Sciences** comprises a state-of-the-art planetarium, hosting three of six 1hr shows each afternoon, plus exhibition spaces. The first, the **Salle Euréka,** hosts 6-monthly exhibitions on topics such as dinosaurs. The **Salle de la Terre** ('Earth Room') looks at the geology of northern France's Armorican peninsula through big-screen films, 3D models, multimedia displays, a mini earthquake simulator and an amphitheatre with daily shows and discussions. Lastly, **Laboratoire de Merlin** forms the discovery zone with 30 hands-on scientific installations that allow you to, for instance, make a ball hang in the air, or learn about water pressure. Again, it has a little amphitheatre with daily science displays. Visits to the 'Labo' are restricted to 1 hr— put your names down for a slot at reception as soon as you arrive at the museum.

The building's free-to-enter **city library** has two whole floors of kids' books and magazines, plus heaps of children's events, including storytelling, film screenings and music sessions. Les Champs Libres also has a **café** with a lovely terrace and a great **shop** selling items relating to the exhibitions, including books, DVDs and postcards.

Time half a day to a full day. **Open** *Tues noon–9pm, Wed–Fri noon–7pm, Sat and Sun 2–9pm.* **Admission** *Musée de Bretagne or Espace des Sciences: 4€ adults, 3€ child (8–16). Joint tickets available.* **Amenities** BF

The Musée de Bretagne/Espace des Sciences will keep you and your crew out of mischief for a good day. But those in the city for longer should check out the **Espace Ferrié** (Avenue de la Boulais, Cesson-Sévigné, ☎02 99 84 32 43, *www.espaceferrie.fr*). This 'transmissions museum' has themed zones documenting human communication from pre-historic smoke signals, with lots of hands-on displays. You might combine a visit with a play at Ludopolis (p. 80).

Parks & Gardens

Parc Floral de Haute-Bretagne ☆ FIND ALL AGES

Le Châtellier; ☎02 99 95 48 32; *www. parcfloralbretagne.com. 12km (7 miles) north of Fougères on D19.*

These themed gardens inspired by all five continents have many child-pleasing touches that make this park a true adventure for younger visitors: a *T. rex* lurks in the 'Prehistoric Garden', for instance, and a minotaur in the 'Knossos' City'. There are also three mazes, carnivorous plants and a hanging bridge over the Valley of the Poets. Bring a picnic to eat in the shady designated areas (one covered) or enjoy the tea room in the castle, spreading out onto its terrace. You can also stay in the castle (p. 97).

Time *2hrs.* **Open** *Sun, public hols Apr–mid-Sept and July and Aug daily 10.30am–6.30pm; Apr–June and Sept daily 10am–noon and 2–6pm; March and Oct–mid-Nov daily 2–5.30pm.* **Admission** *9.20€–9.80€*

adult, 8.20€ teenagers (13–18), 7.20€ child (5–12), 30€ family ticket (2 parents and any number of kids). **Amenities** 🍴 P ⛱ 🏕 ♿

Parc des Gayeulles
☆ ☆ FIND ALL AGES

Avenue des Gayeulles, Rennes; ☎02 99 28 56 62.

Rennes's biggest park, on its northeast fringes, blends woods and lakes with copious leisure opportunities, including a tree-top adventure course (p. 81), an ice rink (p. 80), all-weather pool (p. 80), pedal-boats, bike paths, tennis courts, mini-golf, skate-board/Rollerblade ramps, and large lawns and picnic areas. Look out for the city farm, welcoming families with kids aged 8 to 16 for free educational visits on Tuesdays, Thursdays and Fridays late afternoon. And if you like the park so much you want to linger, there's also a lo-fi campsite here (p. 95). In July a brilliant youth festival (p. 56) is held in the park.

Time *1 day.* **Open** *summer daily 8am–8.30pm; winter daily 8am–5.45pm.* **Admission** *free.* **Amenities** 🍷 🍴 P 🖼 ⛱ 🏕 ♿

Parc du Thabor ALL AGES

Place St. Melaine, Rennes; ☎ 02 99 28 56 62.

One of the loveliest public gardens in all France, on a site abandoned by Benedictine monks after it become a favourite spot for duels (in the sloping area known as Enfer, or 'Hell'), Rennes's central Parc du Thabor is a great picnic and walking spot, with diverting topiary animals and statues, a carousel and outdoor *babyfoot* (table football), as well as a botanical garden and an orangery hosting changing exhibitions. Don't miss the enchanting Jardin des Catherinettes with its fountains, grottoes and mysterious island. Come on a Sunday and blend in with the Rennes families walking off their lunch. Or if you're here in summer, especially during the Tombées de la Nuit festival (p. 57), catch a concert or a Breton music and dancing show (Wed in July).

Time half a day. **Open** summer daily 7.15am–9.30pm; winter daily 7.30am–6pm. **Admission** free. **Amenities** 🍷 ☕ ♿ 🪑 ⛺ ♿

For Active Families

For watersports in the area, see also **Best Beaches** (p. 73).

Centre d'Activités et de Loisirs de Chênedet
⭐ **AGE 4 & UP**

Route Forestière de la Villeboeuf, Landéan; 📞 *02 99 97 35 46; www. chenedet-loisirs.com. 8km (5 miles) north of Fougères on D177.*

This activity centre deep in the forest of Fougères (p. 60), with its megaliths and other Druid remains, welcomes families as well as school groups, though you need to speak reasonable French. As well as horse-riding in the surrounds, it offers themed equestrian stays, one of them learning horse-related circus skills. Young riders can also stay

in a tepee camp, with storytelling around a campfire. Alternatively, there are now several Mongolian yurts (wood-framed tents) on site, in addition to the lakeside campsite and communal gîtes. You can cook for yourself in the shared facilities or there's a restaurant for half or full-board stays.

Time depends on activity and length of stay. **Open** check website for details. **Admission** prices vary according to accommodation and activity. **Amenities** ♿ 🍴

Domaine de Trémelin ⭐
ALL AGES

Lac de Trémelin, just south of Iffendic; 📞 *02 99 09 73 79; www. domaine-de-tremelin.fr. 38km (24 miles) west of Rennes off D72.*

This leisure base on a wooded lake-shore site caters for everyone, from toddlers to thrill-seeking teens and adults. Young kids like the clean, supervised beach, pedaloes and electric boats, karts, bouncy castles, play areas and mini-golf; older ones can swing through the trees on special circuits (starting at age 3), ride a giant zipwire, canoe on the lake, hire mountain-bikes and more. If you want to stay, there are 20 basic gîtes for six to eight people or a campsite, and a bar-restaurant with a sunny terrace. In high season, there's a holiday feel to the place, with *bals musette* (traditional dance hall entertainment) and *fest-noz* (p. 16).

If you wonder about the cheesy fake sword sticking out of one of the rocks, remember that

In addition to the museums listed on p. 75–77, the following can be useful options when the weather isn't your friend.

Le Blizz: 8 Avenue des Gayeulles, Rennes, *02 99 36 28 10*, *www.leblizz.com*. Brittany's only two-rink ice-skating venue (one is Olympic, the other is a 'fun' rink), situated in the Parc des Gayeulles (p. 78), with special luges that under-5s can be pushed around on (or push each other around on).

Centre Culturel Jean Rochefort: Bd des Cap-Horniers, St. Lunaire, *02 99 46 08*, *www.saint-lunaire.fr*. A very active cultural venue by the sea, with a lively programme including children's shows and family film screenings (the latter sometimes in *version originale*—subtitled rather than dubbed).

Dolibulle: Rue de l'abbaye, Dol-de-Bretagne, *02 99 80 71 75*, *www.prestalis.com*. An indoor pool complex including a 'fun pool', a paddling pool, and a 40m slide.

Enigmaparc: Zone d'Activités du Bois de Teillay, Quartier du Haut Bois, Janzé, *02 99 47 07 65*, *www.enigmaparc.com*. An offbeat indoor leisure park for kids about 6 and up, offering a journey through scenes from ancient Egypt, the Middle Ages, the Celtic world and Asia, with mazes, puzzles and games requiring either physical and mental dexterity.

Ludopolis: ZA La Rigoudière, Cesson-Sévigné, Rennes, *02 23 45 62 72*, *www.ludopolis.eu*. An indoor soft-play centre for ages up to 12, with a café serving mainly fair trade and organic products. It's handy for the **Espace Ferrié** (p. 78).

Piscine des Gayeulles: Avenue des Gayeulles, Rennes, *02 23 21 11 50*, *www.rennes.fr*. Another attraction in the Parc des Gayeulles (p. 78), this pool complex was scheduled to reopen in a new state-of-the-art building as this guide went to press. The retracting roof makes it an all-weather option, and there's a kids' pool, wave pool and 'diving ditch' unique in the region, but no slides.

Les P'tits Pirates: 22 Rue de la Croix Desilles, St. Malo, *02 99 81 13 67*, *http://lesptitspirates.wifeo.com/*. An indoor softplay venue for kids aged 2–12, with a ball pool, ball cannons, mini-karting and more.

Royal Kart: Zone d'Activités La Montgervalaise, La Mézière, *02 99 66 42 59*, *www.royalkart.com*. An indoor karting track for adults and children 7 and over, plus a snack bar.

this is King Arthur country (see Brocéliande; p. 67).

Time half a day or more. **Open** 24hrs daily. **Admission** free to site;

individual rates for each activity and type of accommodation. **Amenities**

Parc des Grands Chênes

★★★ **ALL AGES**

Forêt domaniale de Villecartier, Bazouges La Pérouse; ☎06 88 72 73 40; www.parcdesgrandschenes.fr. 35km (22 miles) northwest of Fougères on D796.

Paradise for little nature lovers, 'Big Oak Park' in the Villecartier forest offers adult and acrobatic routes through the trees, with a minimum age of 5, plus a Port Miniature with an electrically powered replica ferry, tug, steamboat or fishing boat to steer between scale models of Breton lighthouses and other landmarks. You can also go orienteering or walking along the signposted paths, ride ponies or go out in a pedalo. Note that you're far from any facilities, so bring a picnic to eat by the lake and lots to drink.

Time half a day. Open July and Aug daily 9.30am–7pm; Apr–June and Sept–Nov Sat 2–7pm, Sun and public and school hols 9.30am–7pm (last entry 4pm). Admission 25€ adults, 15€ child (10–13), 10€ child under 10. Amenities P ⛱

INSIDER TIP »

Sporty families should head for the **Oxylane Village** health and leisure complex (ZAC de Pluvignon, ☎0810 507507) just north of Rennes at Betton. For younger kids, Premiers Pas Sportifs is a specially designed space where they can get to grips with bikes and scooters, as well as Rollerblades (alongside adults), under the watchful eye of a tutor. There's also the Activeway 2.5km (1.5 miles) track for anyone who wants to walk, run, mountain-bike or horse-ride, several play areas, a sports club offering a variety of activities, huge sports fields, a restaurant, a café and picnic areas, a branch of the Decathlon sports shop and a plant nursery. Lastly, Oxylane is home to a **Fôret Adrenaline** treetop adventure course (p. 131), for ages 2 and up. There's another one in Rennes, at the Parc des Gayeulles (p. 78), for ages 5 and up.

Ranch de la Foucheraie

AGE 3 & UP

Cardroc; ☎02 99 45 82 55; www. ranch-de-la-foucheraie.com. 31km (19 miles) northwest of Rennes off D27.

This French-speaking riding centre on the edge of the forest surrounding the Château de Montmuran is a great place for older kids to ride amidst bucolic scenery and picturesque chateaux, by the hour, day, weekend or (for those 11 and up) week— the latter go as far the Mont-St. Michel (p. 68) or the Forêt de Brocéliande (p. 67), or further afield in France, with nights spent in communal gîtes along the way. Highly qualified and friendly guides accompany all rides. Younger kids can come for pony rides from the age of three.

Time from 1hr to a full wk. Admission 1wk ride for ages 11–17: 530€ per person. Check website for further details.

Vélo Rail ★★★ **ALL AGES**

Train station, Médréac; ☎02 99 07 30 48; http://lagaredemedreac.free. fr/. 38km (24 miles) northwest of Rennes on D220.

The Port Miniature, Parc des Grands Chênes (see p. 81)

These wacky two-person contraptions (two bikes joined together) run on old rail tracks on a choice of two circuits, one covering 6km (nearly 4 miles) and taking about an hour to complete, the other covering 14km (nearly 9 miles) and taking two hours, or more if you break for a picnic. Under 8s don't ride but sit in a sort of hammock swung between the bikes, while people of reduced mobility can enjoy the same scenery (the Néal valley, forest of Montauban and megalithic remains) from a motorised wagon for up to 20 (advance booking and at least eight people required). There's also a road train with commentary, the renovated station to visit, with new displays and waxworks relating to the railway, mountainbike hire and a café.

Time from 1hr to half a day. **Open** June–Sept daily 10am–6pm; Apr, May and Oct, Sun and public hols 2–6pm (departures on hour); rest of year by arrangement. **Admission** Vélo Rail 6€ per rider, 3€ per child in 'hammock'; wagon or train 7€, 5€ child (under 8); station free with activities or 2€. **Amenities** 🍵 P ⛱ 🚲

Voie Verte Dinard–Dinan ★
ALL AGES

23km (14 miles) from Dinard to Dinan; www.voiesvertes.com.

This 'Green Route' takes you 23km (14 miles) from Dinard on the coast inland to the Côtes d'Armor town of Dinan (p. 158). The route takes you along an old railway track and then along the Rance towpath, by bike, on foot or on horseback. See the website (above) for bike hire and repair outlets for this route, along with places to stop en route, whether hotels or sights of interest.

Alternatively, you could take the **Véloroute du Marais de Dol,** which is in fact two interconnected circuits, each of 25km (15.5 miles), to explore the area around the Bay of Mont-St. Michel (p. 65), using quiet roads. See the Rando Breizh website (p. 224) for more details.

FAMILY-FRIENDLY DINING

The Ille-et-Vilaine is a gourmet's delight—fresh local produce includes flat oysters from Cancale (p. 71), mussels grown on wooden stakes in the Baie du Mont-St. Michel (p. 73), and the tender *pré-salé* lamb that has grazed on the herby salt-marshes around the bay. Seaside dining is predictably good, but inland you'll find some treasures too, especially in Rennes with its hundreds of restaurants and cafés.

The Coast & Dol de Bretagne

You're never far from a child-friendly eatery at the region's coast with its family resorts.

EXPENSIVE

The *bateau-promenades* run by **Croisières Chateaubriand** (p. 59) include lunch and dinner trips with kids' menus. The **Grand Hôtel Barrière** (p. 90) also offers kids' menus at all meals.

Le Bénétin

Rochers Sculptés, Rothéneuf, St. Malo; 02 99 56 97 64.

Far from the tourist hordes, at the tip of the bay by the Rochers Sculptés (p. 63), this stylish restaurant—which burnt down but has been rebuilt since the first edition of this guide—has a splendid decked terrace and succession of small gardens with unobstructed views out into the wide blue bay. If the weather's not up to it, the dining room has huge bay windows with the same vista, plus wood-burning stoves that make it cosy out of season. Though the standard of cuisine is high and the decor fashionable, the atmosphere is relaxed, and there's a lounge with plump sofas where you can sit if the kids get twitchy at the table. The sophisticated menu depends on the market but might include Cancale oysters, veal tagine with preserved lemons and artichokes, and apple crumble with vanilla ice cream. Kids pay a good-value 11€ for smaller versions of any of the main dishes plus a dessert. Note that at weekends—or daily in high season (June–Aug)—Le Bénétin stays opens in the afternoon as a *salon de thé.*

Open July and Aug Thurs–Tues noon–2.30pm and 7.30–10pm; Sept–June Thurs–Mon noon–2.30pm and 7.30–10pm. **Main courses** 18€–24€. **Amenities** 🎫 🍴 ⚲

MODERATE

For the **Grain de Vanille** tea-room in Cancale, see p. 90.

L'Arganier ★

3 Rue Winston Churchill, Dinard; 02 99 16 90 39.

This attractive Moroccan behind Dinard's seafront is a good place to know about when you've over-done it on the seafood platters and crêpes, serving well-prepared tagines and couscous—inherently child-friendly fare. There's a kids' menu (8€) offering a small main course and ice cream, but normal portions are generous so if you have tots you may be able to share your dish. The English-speaking staff couldn't be more obliging, often offering free mint tea at the end of meals. Try to come when there's a special event in town, as the restaurant puts on North African dance displays.

Open *Tues 7.30–9.30pm, Wed–Sun noon–2pm and 7.30–9.30pm. Closed mid-Oct–mid-Mar.* **Main course** *9€–16.50€.* **Amenities** ⬚ ℃

Auberge de la Cour Verte ★★

Route de Rennes, Dol-de-Bretagne; ☏02 99 48 41 41.

A little inland, this old stone farmhouse houses a restaurant offering a versatile choice of country fare, grills and crêpes. You can enjoy a house cocktail outdoors on the flower-filled terrace while the kids work up an appetite on the play equipment in the courtyard. Inside, it's cosy and intimate, with beams, old photos, a log fire over which local meats are expertly grilled, and views of the chef at work. There's a small, fairly standard children's menu (9€), but the dishes are wide-ranging—including soups, salads, omelettes, mussels, galettes and crêpes, and ice cream—so only the fussiest eater will go hungry. You can also order smaller portions according to how hungry you are. Leave room for the home-made rice pudding or *crème brûlée*. The young English-speaking staff are delightful with

kids and adults alike, and if you don't finish your wine they'll pack it up for you to take away. Book well ahead for the justifiably popular Sunday lunches, especially in summer (the restaurant is recommended by the nearby Domaine des Ormes—p. 92—so is no insider secret, alas).

Open *Wed–Sun noon–2.30pm and 7–10pm.* **Set menus** *8–29€.* **Amenities** ⬚ 🎵 🎵 ℃

Breizh Café ★★ FIND

7 Quai Thomas, Cancale; ☏02 99 89 61 76.

With sister crêperies in Paris's chic Marais district and in Tokyo, this relative newcomer to Cancale's quayside was always going to stand out from the crowd. The décor is a playful modern take on traditional Breton motifs, while in the kitchen the emphasis is on top-quality ingredients—which make the excellent galettes and crêpes, whether classic or more adventurous, a tad more expensive than in the tourist traps nearby. Kids love the little *amuse-galettes* and *amuse-crêpes*, rolled like sushi and dipped in salted-butter caramel with orange or ginger, while parents should take note that this is one of the few places where you can try Cancale's rare Tsarsaya oysters. If you have to wait for a table, there are big squashy leather sofas around a cosy hearth.

For the more adventurous, **La Table Breizh Café** upstairs

serves gastronomic Japanese cuisine based on Breton seafood.

There are five guest rooms available too, one of them a family suite for up to six (78€ for 2 people, then 20€pp); breakfast is served in the Appartement, inspired by Japanese *ryokan* (inns).

Open Sat–Wed noon–9.30pm, daily in school hols. **Main courses** 5€–13.50€. **Amenities** ⌣

Chez Jean-Pierre VALUE

60 Chaussée du Sillon, St. Malo; ☎ 02 99 40 40 48.

A warm welcome, sea views and well-priced if unexceptional Italian food await you at this bright place on the coast road away from St. Malo *intra-muros*, decorated with old posters. Children are made welcome with chair-stilts or highchairs and an under 12s menu (8.50€) with a wide choice, including steak or turkey escalope with pasta or chips, or five varieties of pizza (including a spicy Vesuvio), then plain or fruit yogurt, ice cream or seasonal fruit. The main menu runs from open sandwiches via good pizzas and pasta dishes to grilled meats with pasta, chips or green beans. Save your sweet tooth for the speciality apple pizza with rum and raisin ice cream. It's next to an Ibis hotel, so JP's can get inundated with tourists, with the inevitable impact on service, but there is a take-out/delivery service.

Open daily noon–2pm and 7pm–midnight. **Main courses** 9€–14.50€. **Amenities** ⌷ 🎧 ⌣

Le Surf ★ ★ ★ FIND VALUE

Plage de Longchamp, St. Lunaire; ☎ 06 80 26 08 58.

Little more than a covered terrace and a line of blue plastic tables and chairs along the sea wall, this blink-and-you'll miss it *snack de plage* overlooking St. Lunaire's longest, wildest beach (p. 74) has a tiny kitchen that produces a decent range of enjoyable food: paninis (from smoked salmon to Nutella with banana), *croques* or crêpes, or steak, *moules de bouchot*, whole lobsters (order a day in advance), or salads simple or elaborate (the Indonesian—king prawns with seaweed butter, basmati rice, rocket and shallots cooked in lemon juice—*rocks*). There's so much on the menu, plus an ice cream cabinet, that everyone comes away happy, if you can bring yourself to leave—it's all too easy to linger over a kir, cider, herbal tea or hot chocolate as the kids explore the rockpools below.

Open Apr–mid-Nov Tues–Sun and school hols 12.30–2pm and 7.30–9.30pm; mid-Nov–Mar Tues–Sun 12.30–2pm ; Fri, Sat only 7.30–9.30pm (can vary according to weather and custom). **Main courses** 3€–19.50€. **Amenities** ⌣

Rennes

It's hard *not* to find somewhere great to eat in this hip, buzzing city, especially in summer when the crowds take over almost every square as restaurant and café terraces battle it out for space. The below are just a few reliably good suggestions. Others worth singling out are: **Miamiam** (📞*02 99 38 90 04*), just down the road from La Casa Pépé, serving eclectic food (think tomato and mozzarella *brik*, or honey and ginger roast pork with mash) amidst funky, colourful décor; **L'Epicerie** (2 Rue des Fossés, 📞*02 99 38 76 70*), a cool, laidback bistro with great open sand-wiches, daily-changing soups, home-made cakes and desserts; and **Le Picca** (Galeries Théâtre, 📞*02 99 78 17 17*), a brasserie with a plum location beside the opera house and a terrace looking onto the carousel on the Place de la Mairie, plus a wide-ranging menu.

MODERATE

La Casa Pépé ★ ★

29 Rue St. Georges, Rennes; 📞*02 99 38 99 55.*

The best pizzas in Rennes, and perhaps the Ille-et-Vilaine as a whole, keep locals flocking to this sunny pizzeria, so come early for dinner, and if you can, book for both dinner and lunch. Be prepared for a bit of a squash, too, though the summertime ter-race eases the strain. Whether you want something classic or a bit more outré (honey pizza, anyone?), or other Italian dishes including pasta and meat escalo-pes, count on huge portions and fair prices. The spinach and gor-gonzola gratin is to die for, as is the chocolate fondant.

Open Mon and Tues noon–2pm, Wed–Fri noon–2pm and 7–10.30pm, Sat and Sun noon–10.30pm. **Main course 7€–15.50€. Amenities** 🍴 ☕

INEXPENSIVE

There's a family-friendly café in the Musée de Bretagne (p. 76) building.

Aux Libellules ★ ★ FIND

17 Passage des Carmélites, Rennes; 📞*02 99 12 19 51.*

With sturdy but funky furniture, bright creatures painted on its walls and an array of toys, games and children's books at custom-ers' disposal, this 'intergenera-tional café'—open since 2008—is a great place to chill out as a family over a lunch of savoury tarts and crumbles, *croques*, soups and scrumptious desserts, including kid-friendly servings. Outside lunch hours, there's a tempting menu of home-made cakes, all in child's size portions, plus a huge choice of teas, hot chocolate, smoothies and juices. Most ingredients are organic, and you can stock up on ethical baby products while here. If you're in town for a while, take note of the work-shops, creative evenings (every-thing from baby massage to knitting or mosaic-making) and 'animations' (storytelling, sing-ing, board games and so on).

Open Tues 2–6pm, Wed–Fri 10am–6pm, Sat 10am–6.30pm. **Main course 4€–9€. Amenities** 🖼 🍴 ✳

INSIDER TIP ▶▶

There's another family restaurant and tea-room, **Café Clochette** (📞*02 99 35 80 89*), just outside the centre at 37 Rue de Dinan, with a kids' corner with wooden toys and secondhand books, and even a quiet corner where your baby can nap. Food is veggie, with gluten-free options, and there's free Wi-Fi. Call before coming, though, as opening times are quite restricted—and changeable.

Crêperie La Rozell ★★★ FIND

14 Rue Penhoët, Rennes; ☎*02 99 78 20 01.*

A holder of the Crêperie Gourmand label—a sure sign of quality (p. 39)—this delightful central spot looks tiny from its pretty façade but unfolds into a large rear garden filled with plants and is extremely popular with local families (booking is advised). The under-12s' menu (8.50€) comprises a drink and a galette followed by an animal-themed ice cream served in a moulded pot that doubles up as a toy to take away. Of course, there are wonderful à la carte galettes and crêpes on offer too—among them house specialities with black pudding (*boudin noir*) and butter-cooked apples, or with marinated strawberries and violet ice cream. For those looking for variety, you can get 'snacks' such as omelettes, *steak haché* or black pudding with chips. The apple juice and cider selection includes some very good organic bottles.

Open *daily 11.45am–2pm and 7–10pm; all day on summer weekends.* **Main course** *2.20€–10.50€.* **Amenities** 🏧 ♿ ☕

West of Rennes

Good places to eat in this rural neck of the woods are naturally harder to find than in the capital or by the sea, especially if you're with children.

MODERATE–EXPENSIVE

Les Forges de Paimpont ★★ FIND

Les Forges, Plélan-le-Grand; ☎*02 99 06 81 07.*

La Casa Pépé, Rennes

This utterly charming restaurant run by four generations of the same family lives up to its surrounds—the legendary forest of Brocéliande—with its stunning exterior (complete with vintage car), quirky yet stylish décor, and lake views. The food, too, takes its inspiration from local produce, including lots of game and meats grilled over an open fire. It's the perfect setting for a Sunday lunch *en famille*, though the slightly formal setting may be off-putting for those with noisy younger kids. However, all children are made welcome, with the 7.50€ *menu enfant* featuring simple dishes such as *steak haché* with sauté potatoes, followed by ice cream. There's an *à la carte* menu, although the set menus may tempt you into being more adventurous and trying new things. Whatever you do, don't miss the famous Délices des Forges dessert—apple crisp with cider caramel—and on your way out, stock up on home-made terrine, salmon rillettes, onion jam, smoked salmon and duck breast.

Open summer Tues–Sun noon–2pm and 7–9pm, winter Tues and Sun noon–2pm, Wed–Sat noon–2pm and 7–9pm. **Main course** 8.50€–20€. **Amenities** ⬚ 🛈 ☏

The **Domaine de Tremelin** (p. 79) at Iffendic has a child-friendly restaurant.

Le Pressoir ★

16 Place de l'Eglise, Romillé; ☏02 99 23 28 59. 26km (16 miles) northwest of Rennes on D21.

This bright and congenial crêperie handy for Bécherel offers almost 50 kinds of *blé noir* galettes, many quite unusual—parents might like to try La Lucette with home-made *steak tartare* (raw mince), egg and Emmenthal cheese; children might prefer the house speciality, the prawn-cocktail-like Le Pressoir with avocado, crab and prawns. Be sure to leave room for the dessert crêpes—especially, La Rousse, with vanilla ice cream and home-made caramel with salted butter. For non-pancake fans, there are also main-course salads and grilled meats, including a good-value daily special. A new farm-produced cider is on offer each month, or choose from a good range of inexpensive wines.

Open Tues–Sun noon–2.30pm and 7–10pm. **Main courses** 5.50€–12€. **Amenities** 🛈 ☏

South & East of Rennes

Like the area west of Rennes, this largely rural environment is not the best-endowed with family-friendly eateries.

Pen Roc ★ ★ FIND

La Peinière, St. Didier, Châteaubourg; ☏02 99 00 33 02, www.penroc.fr. 29 km (29 miles) east of Rennes on D857.

This unexpected outpost of high gastronomy sits within a tranquil three star hotel with a pretty outdoor pool and a spa in a rural setting halfway between Rennes and Vitré, making it a great alternative to staying in the

Breton capital. Though its offerings are experimental—the likes of Breton oysters on a Swiss chard and marrow 'spaghetti', and local hare on pumpkin and liquorice purée—the extremely solicitous staff might tempt your kids to try dishes and combinations they may otherwise have turned their noses up at. The kids' menu itself (under-10s, 13.90€) is ambitious but not off-puttingly so, featuring crab and salmon buckwheat wrap or local rillettes with croutons for starters, followed by local fish fillet or roast Jonzé chicken with fried potatoes and seasonal vegetables, then home-made ice cream with meringue or a plate of crêpes.

Most ingredients are grown in the hotel's own large garden. Overall, prices might seem high but various set menus make eating here easier on the wallet. There's also a superb sommelier to guide you through an outstanding wine list of mainly local bottles.

The hotel's modern, functional exterior hides lodgings of considerable appeal. Some rooms and suites (98–198€; one under 12 stays free in a parent's room) have whirlpool baths; others are blessed with private terraces overlooking the garden or pool.

Open daily 12.30–2pm and 7.30–9pm (exc Sun eve Oct–May). **Main course** 23€–29€ (exc lobster dishes). Amenities ☐ 耳 ✆

La Halte du Volcan FIND

Le Châtellier, Plechâtel; ✆02 99 43 75 65. *34km (21 miles) south of Rennes on D77.*

Handy for those visiting La Roche aux Fées (p. 70), this informal restaurant derives its name from the fact that the hill it stands on to the south of Rennes was once thought to be a very old volcano, after thick black smoke was seen coming out of it (later found to be due to the spontaneous combustion of organic materials mined there). Serving lunches made up of traditional dishes such as salt-marsh lamb (p. 83) and seafood platters, La Halte du Volcan is so family-friendly it has not only a play area within its large grounds but also a riverside animal park (separate entry fee) with llamas, Vietnamese potbellied pigs, kangaroos and more. You can also play quoits or *boules*, and fish nearby.

Open daily 10am–5pm. **Main course** 5€–12.50€. **Amenities** 耳 ∧ ✆

Crêperie Tivabro FIND

3 Place du Marchix, Fougères; ✆02 99 17 20 90.

This characterful crêperie—sister to the Breizh Café in Cancale (p. 84)—is set in a stunning half-timbered house in the heart of medieval Fougères, not far from the castle (p. 97), and has a small garden. The choice of galettes, crêpes and ciders, often featuring organic ingredients, is unusually wide, with a number of surprises, and the serving staff are a delight.

Open Tues–Sat noon–2pm and 7–10pm, Sun noon–3pm. **Main course** 4€–11.50 €. **Amenities** 耳 ✆

FAMILY-FRIENDLY ACCOMMODATION

The truly plum accommodation in the Ille-et-Vilaine is, unsurprisingly, to be found by the coast, although there are a few gems inland.

The Coast & Dol de Bretagne

The Ille-et-Vilaine has great seaside options to suit all kinds of families, travelling on every kind of budget.

VERY EXPENSIVE

Grand Hôtel Barrière ★

46 Avenue George V, Dinard; ☎*02 99 88 26 26, www.lucienbarriere.com.*

Well-to-do French parents come to the Grand—hotel of choice for French and foreign stars during Dinard's British film festival—to splurge and relax while their kids make friends at its Club Diwi and Co (open mornings in the school holidays and public holiday weekends; age range 4–12; €15 per session), offering activities such as sandcastle contests, cookery classes and circus skills, plus seasonal treats such as Easter egg hunts. The elegant hotel, which looks over the ramparts of St. Malo (accessible by sea taxi), has a largish indoor pool, a new Phytomer spa, a sauna and a hammam. Families tend to stay in interconnecting rooms, with sea or garden views; they're light and airy, with pastel nautical stripes and small balconies. Regular Family Getaway offers include a double Classic room and connecting or close-by kids' room from 175€ and 88€ per night. Children's menus are offered at all the dining venues, but you may well find that the food doesn't live up to the high prices.

90 rooms. **Rates** *140€–220€; suites 230€–440€; extra bed 40€ per day; cot free of charge.* **Amenities** 🏊 🍸 ☕ 🚲 📷 💼 🍴 ⚙ **In room** 💻 📺 🗄 📺

Les Maisons de Bricourt ★★★

Cancale; ☎*02 99 89 64 76; www.maisons-de-bricourt.com. 16km (10 miles) east of St. Malo on D355.*

Celebrity chef Olivier Roellinger has colonised much of his native town with this chic empire, which comprises **the Gîtes Marins,** five seaside cottages for two to eight people; **Cottage Les Rimains,** a tiny clifftop house with four double rooms; **Château Richeux,** a small hotel with a restaurant; **Grain de Vanille** tearoom; and **L'Entrepôt Epices Roellinger,** selling his spices, chutneys, seaweed creations and so on. The latest additions is **La Maison de Gwenn,** a foot massage studio, and **La Cuisine Corsaire** cookery school, where you can book 2hr family lessons for a minimum of four people at 200€ per adult and child, (plus extra if you need an interpreter).

The **stunning Gîtes Marins** with their New England décor have superb kitchens, spacious living areas with all mod cons plus kids' story and colouring books, and terraces with BBQs.

Best Picnic Spots

Aside from beaches, the following are great picnicking venues in the Ille-et-Vilaine:

Deep in the **forest of Brocéliande,** p. 67
Domaine de Trémelin, p. 79
Parc Floral de Haute-Bretagne, p. 78
Parc des Grands Chênes, p. 81
Along the Vélorail Circuit at Médreac, p. 81
Parc Thabor, Rennes, p. 78

A few steps away is a veg and herb garden where you can pick ingredients, then the clifftop, where an old customs officers' track leads down to Cancale port or to the Pointe du Grouin (p. 58). Cottages have shrimp nets if you want to garner further items for dinner. Breton breakfast (cake, crêpes, soft rolls and bread) is left in a basket outside your door early each morning, and logs are provided so that, if the sea wind bites, you can snuggle up next to a roaring fire.

22 units. **Rates** *Château Richeux 160€–290€, apartment from 290€, extra bed 28€; Gîte Marin for 4 or more from 380€, extra bed free. Cot free.* **Amenities** 🦐 🍴 ☕ 🗲 ⛶ 🛎 ⛿ *In* **room** *(gîtes)* ☒ ⬚

INSIDER TIP ››

Even if you stay elsewhere at Les Maisons de Bricourt, go visit the **Château Richeux** to explore its gardens and orchards with their beehives, donkeys and Ouessant sheep.

MODERATE

For bed & breakfast at Cancale's **Breizh Café,** see p. 84.

Le Mont Fleury

2 rue du Mont Fleury. St. Malo; 📞*02 23 52 28 85; www.lemontfleury.com.*

For those seeking something a little out of the ordinary, this restored 18th-century *mal-ouinière* (merchant's dwelling) in a quiet suburb of St. Malo is decorated with artefacts and artworks amassed by the ex-pilot owner during his travels. The bed and breakfast rooms are similarly eclectic, ranging in theme from Africa to nautical. The Oriental room can fit an extra bed to accommodate three, the Chinese room sleeps up to five over two levels, and the American room sleeps up to six over two levels, so this is a good address for larger families, though the mezzanines are accessed via steep spiral stairs so think twice about coming with toddlers. The pleasant grounds have a hammock and sun-loungers.

5 units. **Rates** *room for 3 people 108€– 133€, room for 4 people 141€–151€, room for 5 people 164€–174€. Cot free.* **Amenities** ⬚ *In room* 📶

Résidence Reine Marine

★ ★ ★ **VALUE**

*65–67 Avenue JF Kennedy, Paramé,
St. Malo;* 📞*02 33 18 48 58; www.
reinemarine.com.*

St. Malo's famous Thermes
Marins (*www.thalassotherapie.
com*) includes a seawater therapy
centre, a spa for those more into
pampering, and the seaside
Grand Hôtel, offering connecting
rooms for families (some newly
modernised) and a very good
children's club (in July–Aug
there's also a beach club for 3–10
year-olds in front of the hotel).
However, this little empire also
extends to two smaller, cheaper
hotels and a golf hotel, and—best
for families—two self-catering
residences where guests can
equally enjoy access to the wellness facilities and kids' club. The
Neptunia beside the Grand Hôtel
offers studios (double bed and
sofabed); the Reine Marine a
20-minute walk along the beach
at low tide has secure parking and
pristine modern one and two
bedroom apartments for up to six
(living rooms have sofabeds).
Prices vary widely according to
whether you have a sea view and
the time of year but even in high
season they're a steal given that
the *résidence* has an indoor pool,
sauna, bar, games room with
widescreen TV and board games,
laundry, and order-in breakfast
service (or buffet breakfast in the
bar by advance booking). Highchairs, cots and changing mats
can be reserved and babysitting
arranged. There's a minimum
three-night stay.

67 units. **Rates** *1-bedroom apartment for up to 4 people 72€–248€,
2-bedroom apartment for up to six
people 90€–356€; weekly rates also
available, with 15% discount on 2nd
wk at certain periods, ask about thalassotherapy packages.* **Amenities**

In
room

Domaine des Ormes ★ ★

Epiniac; 📞*02 99 73 53 00, www.
lesormes.com. 10km (6 miles) southeast of Dol-de-Bretagne on D4.*

This vast holiday park offers a
quite extraordinary choice of
accommodation, activities and
facilities in its parkland based
around a 16th-century château.
The most exciting accommodation is the **treehouses** (some are
accessible by miniature treetop
adventure courses so reserved for
those with older kids, others are
designed to be safe for kids as
young as 2), with breakfast left at
the foot of your tree each morning to winch up. But there are
also some new 'cabane-huttes' or
nature lodges, built from natural
materials and tucked away in
wooded areas for a Hansel and
Gretel/Three Little Pigs feel,
plus wooden chalets and datchas
(Russian log cabins). Then,
more conventionally, there's a
three-star hotel with its own
pool, some plush rooms in the
golf **clubhouse**, a *résidence-hôtel*
with **studios and apartments,**
four stone **gîtes** with gardens,
well-appointed **mobile homes**
and a **four-star campsite.** The
hotel and golf clubhouse boast
relatively upmarket restaurants,

but there's also a campsite restaurant for pancakes and grills, and a pizzeria with a take-out option.

Leisure facilities include a waterpark (five pools, one with a wave machine new in 2010), riding, a treetop adventure course and zipwire, tennis and table-tennis, bike hire, golf and crazy golf, archery, pedaloes, kayaks and surf bikes, cricket, football tournaments, basketball and fishing. Summer sees a raft of additional 'animations'. Some activities are free, others bear an extra charge, but overall this is a good-value option.

Rates Tree house107€–114€ per night for 2 adults then 32€ per child (2–16); double hotel room 78€–110€ then 17€ extra person; studio or apartment 398€–898€ per week; gîte 495€–1150€ per week; wooden cottages (nature lodges, chalets and datchas 465€–998€ per week; mobile homes 364€–1350€ per week; camping pitch 15€–25€ per night for one person, additional person 4.20€–7.50€, child (2–12) 2.60€–4.60€. Weekend rates available for some accommodation. *Amenities* [WIFI] [image] [image] [image] [image]

INSIDER TIP »

The Domaine des Ormes is bookable directly or with tour operators including **Eurocamp** (p. 38). Not all the accommodation options are offered by all UK operators, but you may find a better deal with them, especially when booking in sterling and via their websites.

Manoir de la Bégaudière [FIND]

6 la Bégaudière, Le Mont-Dol; ℡02 99 48 23 46, *www.manoirdela begaudiere.com. 3.5km (2 miles) north of Dol de Bretagne on D155.*

Ivy-clad and boasting turreted towers, this stunning property, offering four gîtes for up to six people and two bed and breakfast rooms for up to four, is about as stylish as they come, with creamy walls, chic modern furniture and unobtrusive nautical theme. Though not the kind of place you'd choose to bring energetic toddlers for a week of mayhem—the gîtes are more like swanky urban flats—it's a great place to stop over with slightly older children on your way deeper into Brittany or on your way back to the Channel (gîtes can be rented for 2-night breaks). Of the gîtes, try to nab Côté Mer, a three to six person duplex with a terrace; the best of the *chambres d'hôte*, Côte Champs, has its own garden plus a separate bedroom.

6 units. Rates Gîte for 2–4 people 300€–550€ per week, for 4–6 people 325€–320€ per week; B&B 80€ night for 2 people, then 15€. *Amenities* [image]

INEXPENSIVE

Campsites recommended by the reliable **Camping de Qualité** (*www.campingqualite.com*) include the small, family-oriented **Tenzor de la Baie** (*www.le-tenzor-de-la-baie.com/*) at Cherrueix (offering yurts in addition to mobile homes and tent pitches) and the larger, more commercial **Domaine de la Ville Huchet** (*www.lavillehuchet.com*) on the way into St. Malo, where 'extras' are 'fisherman's hut' style mobile homes and three apartments in stone buildings.

La Pensée ★ ★ FIND

5 Rue de la Grève, St. Lunaire; ☎ *02 99 46 03 82, www.la-pensee.fr/.*

This exceptional little place in charming St. Lunaire (p. 74) offers double bed and breakfast rooms with kitchenettes, plus self-catering apartments and houses for two to five people, most of it year-round. Styles vary, but all have lovely wooden furniture and decor, mosaic-tiled bathrooms and kitchens, and pretty colour combinations—Ariane, a house for four to five, will delight little princesses with its pale and hot pinks and its sweet wrought-metal furniture Some rooms have views of the former Grand Hôtel (now apartments); most have a little garden or veranda. You're just moments from the lovely Grande Plage, too. A delicious breakfast featuring home-made jams and scones can be provided even in the self-catering apartments. The bed and breakfast is closed during July and August.

15 units. **Rates** *apartment for 4 people 95€–120€ per night, apartment for five people 125€-135€, double B&B room 55€–65€. Reductions in rate apply from the 2nd or 3rd night according to season.* **In room** ☒ ☐

INSIDER TIP ❯❯

Of note mainly for its impressive lakeside castle (open for visits) that was the boyhood home of the writer Chateaubriand, **Combourg** makes for a pleasant, low-key place to stop-over for those travelling to or from the ferry at St. Malo. Its **Hôtel-Restaurant du Lac** (☎ *02 99 73 05 65, www.hoteldulaccombourg. com*) has a lakeside garden with children's play equipment, while the **Hôtel-Restaurant du Château** (☎ *02 99 73 00 38, www.hotelduchateau.com*) has triples and family rooms. Both are moderately priced.

Domaine des Ormes treehouse (see p. 92)

Rennes

Surprisingly, the Breton capital has no upper-end hotels that are worthy of recommendation. However, the good budget options more than make up for this.

INEXPENSIVE

All Seasons FIND

15 Place de la Gare, Rennes; 02 99 67 31 12. www.all-seasons-hotels. com.

Part of the mighty Accor empire, this chain offers functional, clean, modern accommodation at unbeatable prices—family suites with two connecting rooms or two single beds in the lounge area can be had from as little as 80€ for no-cancellation advance bookings. However, be sure to play about with the rates on the website, as some deals include breakfast. Rooms, cleverly designed to maximise the very restricted space, are perfectly adequate for those passing through or sightseeing for a couple of days (note that there are showers not baths). Children are warmly welcomed with crayons, games and other treats at check-in, children's magazines, board games, an activity corner with computer games near reception, and baby equipment. This Rennes outpost is opposite the train station, so expect some noise—but then that's true of all of lively Rennes! Note that you can cancel up to 6pm on your day of arrival if you have a flexible booking. Note also that the Accor website (*www.accor.com*)

has more detailed information on room options than the main website.

*99 units. **Rates** doubles from 57€, family suites vary but average about 100€. Cot free. **Amenities** 📶 🖥 🐾 In room A/C 📶 📺*

Camping des Gayeulles
★ ★ ★ FIND

Rue Maurice Audin, Rennes; 02 99 36 91 22; www.camping-rennes. com.

This bring-your-own-tent and caravan and camper-van campsite in a forest park on the northeast outskirts of Rennes (10 minutes by car) is a family paradise, situated within the wonderful Parc des Gayeulles (p. 78). The campsite itself is blissfully simple, with a play area and a small grocery. There are 30 year-round Premium pitches with water and electric outlets, and an additional 98 three-star pitches from April to October, with electrical hook-up points, and 50 no-star Seasonal Tourism pitches in July and August, spreading out onto the neighbouring rugby pitch. Central Rennes is a short bus and Métro hop away.

*178 pitches (high season). **Rates** tent pitch 3€–5.70€, then 3.50€ per person, 1.50€ per child (under13) and 1.50€–1.70€ per car. **Amenities** 📶 🧺 ⛺ 🍼*

Hôtel de Nemours FIND

5 Rue de Nemours, Rennes; 02 99 78 26 26; www.hotelnemours.com.

Rennes has a surprising scarcity of good lodgings, but this tarted-up two-star in the centre is all you need given that you're unlikely to be spending much time indoors, with all that the Breton capital has to offer (p. 60). The décor is stylish for this price range, with neutral colours, good bed linens, old photos of Rennes on the walls, and flatscreen TVs; the bathrooms feel a touch shabby by comparison. Extra beds can be added to certain doubles, or you can get a 'suite' for three or four people, with a sofa-bed, two TVs and a shower. Breakfast is generous and of good quality, although the dining room is a bit cramped. Periodic Internet offers can make this option even better value.

29 units. **Rates** *74€–87€, suite for 3 or 4 people 97€. Extra bed 10€. Cot free* **In room amenities** 📶 ▢

West of Rennes

As with eateries, this largely rural area has quite a limited choice when it comes to family accommodation.

MODERATE

Château du Pin

Iffendic; 📞 *02 99 09 34 05; www. chateaudupin-bretagne.com. 38km (24 miles) west of Rennes on D30.*

This sober 19th-century country house surrounded by tall oaks and meadows isn't the place for those with rowdy toddlers, but older, bookish children may love the literary-themed rooms resembling something from a bygone, more elegant era, as well as the setting a few kilometres

from 'Merlin's Tomb' and other Arthurian sites (p. 67). Of the five rooms, three are doubles, while Victor Hugo and George Sand are both family suites, each with a double and a twin room sharing a bathroom. Both are scattered with books and have quirky touches such as straw teddy bears. Breakfast is a copious Continental affair that you can run it off in the large grounds. You can also get evening meals by prior arrangement (27€, 10€ under10s), with a highchair provided. Alternatively, there's a pretty gîte for five people including a baby, available Oct–Mar.

6 units. **Rates** *double room 85€– 270€; family suite 125€–184€; gîte 380€–520€ per week. Cot free.* **Amenities** 📶 **In room** ✏ ▢ ✖

INEXPENSIVE

The only camping in this area recommended by **Camping de Qualité** (p. 93) is the small-scale family-friendly **Les Peupliers** (*www.les-peupliers-camping.com*) in the grounds of a 16th-century manor house at Tinteniac.

Le Gîtes de Kersillac

Gaël; 📞 *02 99 07 76 78; http:// broceliande.gîteskersillac.com. 49km (30 miles) west of Rennes on D30.*

These sweet stone cottages in the grounds of a tranquil dairy farm are not only named 'Arthur' and 'Judicäel' in reference to local folklore—their walls are adorned with murals of fairies, forest scenes and more. Though whimsical, they're practical and comfy, with solid rustic furniture, good beds, and dishwashers and washing machines. Both have a double and a twin room plus a sofabed so sleep up to six, plus two bathrooms and a terrace. They share table tennis and table football facilities. Guests are free to look round the farm and watch the cows being milked.

2 units. **Rates** *243€–438€ per week (nightly rates also available).* **Amenities** 🖥 *In room* 🖊 ✖ 🧳 🛏

Le Grénier d'Ernestine ★ ★

Les Basses Barres, Bréal-sous-Montfort; 📞 *02 99 60 34 03; www.grenier-ernestine.com. 18km (11 miles) southwest of Rennes off N24.*

In keeping with the surrounding area with its elves, fairies and mythical knights, this guesthouse is a childhood paradise for kids and adults alike, with five homely rooms dotted with old dolls, teddies and toy cars, and a little farmyard with donkeys, ponies, dwarf and Alpine goats, and more. The welcoming owner often regales young visitors with stories about the animals. There are five spacious, antique filled rooms—a ground-floor one for those with reduced mobility, two doubles with room for an extra bed, and two rooms with a double bed, a single bed and a small double on a mezzanine level. Alphonsine has direct views onto the farmyard. Breakfast includes home-made cake and jams created to old recipes. The cosy breakfast room and

salon extends out onto a terrace when the weather permits, where you can enjoy evening meals (28.50€) or cold platters (18€) by request. The hosts have five kids so won't be bothered by yours running around.

5 rooms. **Rates** *room for 4 people 75€ (weekly rates available). Cot free.* **Amenities** 🚲 *In room* 🛏

South & East of Rennes

Again, this countryside around Rennes is not the most fertile hunting ground for family-friendly lodgings.

MODERATE

For the **Pen Roc** at Châteaubourg 30km (18.5 miles) east of Rennes, see p. 88.

Château de la Foltière ★ FIND

Le Châtellier; 📞 *02 99 95 48 32; www.parcfloralbretagne.com. 12km (7.5 miles) north of Fougères on D19.*

Set in the idyllic Parc Floral de Haute Bretagne (p. 78) to which guests have free access, this stunning manor house offers four double rooms to which you can add a spare bed for a child, and one suite that can accommodate up to five in two adjoining bedrooms. The interiors are classically French without being stuffy so those with younger kids won't feel uncomfortable. The couple who run it couldn't be friendlier or more helpful.

5 units. **Rates** *140€–150€, extra bed 30€ (free to under-3s); suite for 4 people 208€.* **Amenities** ☕ 🏃 🖼 *In-room* 🛏

INEXPENSIVE

There's a small **municipal campsite** (☎ *02 99 43 75 65*) beside the Halte du Volcan restaurant.

La Haute Mancelière ☆

Tremblay; ☎ 02 99 97 74 20; www.brittany-cottages.co.uk. 25km (15.5 miles) northwest of Fougères on D155.

The high quality and child-friendliness of these three stone cottages in a 17th-century *longère* or longhouse within large lawned gardens means you have to snap them up early in the high season. Set in a peaceful hamlet yet well-placed for the coast, these buildings have been tastefully converted, retaining their exposed beams and stone walls. Facilities include a pool with a retractable roof, play equipment, a boules court, free bicycle loan, and DVD, books and games loan. There's also plenty of baby equipment to borrow, including stairgates. Les Hirondelles sleeps four plus a baby, Les Alouettes sleep six plus babies, and Les Chouettes sleeps 12 plus babies. All have open-plan living-dining areas and private terraces. Guests get a 20% reduction on crossings with Brittany Ferries (p. 23).

3 units. **Rates** *gîte for 4 people 335€–715€ per week, gîte for 6–8 people 460€–1150€ per week, 2-night rates available Oct–May. Cot free.* **Amenities** *In room*

4 Morbihan

MORBIHAN

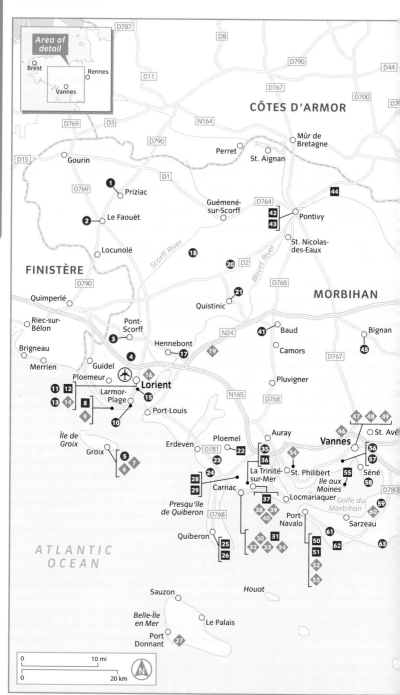

Attractions ●

Alignements de Carnac/ Musee de Prehistorie J. Miln—Z. le Rouzic **35**
Alignements de Kerzehro **23**
Aquarium du Golfe **56**
Barrage d'Arzal **66**
Centre Nautique de Kerguelen **10**
Château de Suscinio **61**
Cité de la Voile Eric Tabarly **13**
Domaine de Kerguéhennec **45**
Ferme du Monde **79**
Golfe du Morbihan **57**

Haras National de Hennebont **17**
Insectarium de Lizio **73**
Kéroman Submarine Base **11**
L'Abeille Vivante et La Cité des Fourmis **2**
L'Odyssaum **3**
L'Univers du Poète Ferrailleur **74**
La Maison de la Chauve-Souris **18**
La Thalassa **15**
Le Cartopole **41**
Le Clos du Tay **80**
Les Passagers du Vent **24**
Moulin à Papier de Pen-Mur **67**
Musée de la Poupée **72**
Musée de la Résistance Bretonne **77**
Musée des Châteaux en Allumettes **69**
Oh Bonheur des Gosses **59**

Parc Aquanature de Stérou **1**
Parc Celt'Aventures **63**
Parc de Branféré/Fondation Nicolas Hulot pour la Nature et l'Homme **68**
Parc de Préhistoire de Bretagne **83**
Parcabout Chien Noir **5**
Reserve Naturelle Marais de Séné **58**
Tropical Parc **84**
Village de l'An Mil **20**
Village de Poul-Fetan **21**
Zoo de Pont-Scorff **4**

Dining ◆

A L'Aise Breizh Café **47**
Atlanville **46**
Bar–Pizzeria de Pont Kerran **19**
Brasserie Edgar **48**
Côte et Saveurs **49**
Crêperie Bara-Breizh **60**
Crêperie Chez Renée **27**
Crêperie de la Pompe **32**
Crêperie des Forges **71**
Crêperie Saint-François **39**
Hippopotamus **16**
Hôtel Restaurant de la Marine **33**
L'Equinoxe **52**
L'Escale **53**
La Casa Varadero **14**
La Plancha **40**
Le Gavrinis **54**
Le Jardin des Saveurs **76**
Le Quai **38**
Le Safran **7**
Le Vivier **9**
Les Enfants Gat'thes **81**
Maison Chevillard **30**
Memes Tra **34**
O Thon Bleu **6**
Végétarium **82**

Accommodation ■

Auberge des VoyaJoueurs **78**
Camping Le Clos du Blavet **42**
Camping Pen Palad **8**
Carnac Thalasso & Spa Resort **31**
Château de Trédion **70**
CLAJ La Mine d'Or **64**
Dihan **22**
Ferme de Lann Hoëdic **62**
Hotel Bellevue **25**
Hôtel de l'Europe **43**
Hôtel L'Ancre d'Or **65**
Hôtel Le Roi Arthur **75**
Hôtel Mercure **12**
La Grande Metairie **36**
Le Lodge Kerisper **37**
Le San Francisco **55**
Miramar Crouesty **50**
Pierre & Vacances Port du Crouesty **51**
Plouharnel Youth Hostel **29**
Sofitel Thalassa **26**
Ty Louisette **44**
Villa Mine Lann **28**

Mauron
Comper
D773
D766
N24
Paimpont
72
Les Forges-de-Paimpont
D38
Josselin
N24
Ploërmel
ILLE-ET-VILAINE
75
76
73
74
Lizio
78
D776
D772
Carentoir
79
St. Marcel
D8
D73
77
N166
D5
La Gacilly
69
Rochefort-en-Terre
D777
80 81 82
St. Just
izole
Malansac
Questembert
83
84
Redon
Le Guerno
68
D775
Vilaine
165
D5
D1
Muzillac
67
66
Arzal
D164
Pénestin
64
65
D773
St. Lyphard
Pontchâteau
LOIRE-ATLANTIQUE
D774

Though home to one of the world's most famous megalithic sites, Carnac, the Morbihan is perhaps the *département* of Brittany least familiar to visitors from outside France. Its name, 'little sea', refers specifically to the inland sea of the Golfe du Morbihan with its fragmented landscape of tiny islands. But there are plenty of other attractions too—offshore islands accessible by boat-trip, great resorts and beaches, and, inland, nature parks and quirky little museums that bring Breton culture alive.

Carnac itself (the site, not the town) suffers from tourist overload in the high season, but within a stone's throw of it are some spots where you can still experience the mystery up close. Thousands of the stones aligned here date back further than Stonehenge or the Pyramids, to the Neolithic period when agriculture developed, and are thought by some to have been a lunar observatory. Experts are still scratching their heads as to their significance or how the ancients could even have placed some of them without powered machinery.

The Morbihan is a wonderful place for seaside accommodation, some traditional and others more chic and/or novel, as well as for thalassotherapy centres (p. 146) with childcare. The seafood here, unsurprisingly, is first rate.

VISITOR INFORMATION

For all of the region's tourist offices and *syndicats d'initiative*, see the French-only CDT website, *www.morbihan.com*.

Information Centres

Belle-Ile en Mer: Quai Bonnelle, Le Palais, ☎02 97 31 81 93, *www. belle-ile.fr*.

Carnac: 74 Avenue des Druides, ☎02 97 52 13 52, *www.ot-carnac.fr*.

Erdeven: 7 Rue Abbé Le Barh, ☎02 97 55 64 60, *www.ot-erdeven. fr/*.

Golfe du Morbihan: Ile aux Moines (mairie), ☎02 97 26 32 31, *www.mairie-ileauxmoines.fr*.

Ile d'Arz (mairie): ☎02 97 44 31 14, *www.iledarz.fr*. Or contact Vannes tourist office.

Gourin (syndicat d'initative): 24 rue de la Libération, ☎02 97 23 66 33.

Houat (mairie): Le Bourg, ☎02 97 30 68 04.

Ile de Groix: Port-Tudy, ☎02 97 84 78 00, *http://groix.tourisme. free.fr/wordpress/*.

Josselin: 4 Rue Beaumanoir, ☎02 97 22 36 43, *www.paysde josselin-tourisme.com*.

Lorient: Maison de la Mer, Quai de Rohan, ☎02 97 84 78 00, *www.lorient-tourisme.fr/*.

Pénestin: Allée du Grand-Pré, Pénestin, ☎02 99 90 37 74, *www. penestin.com*.

Ploërmel: 5 Rue du Val, ☏02 97 74 02 70, *www.tourisme-ploermel. com*.

Pontivy: 61 Rue du Général de Gaulle, ☏02 97 25 04 10, *www. pontivy-communaute.fr/*.

Quiberon: 14 Rue de Verdun, ☏08 25 13 56 00, *www.quiberon. com*.

Rochefort en Terre: 7 Place du Puits, ☏09 77 39 40 60, *www. rochefort-en-terre.com*.

Vannes: Quai Tabarly (port), ☏08 25 13 56 10, *www.tourisme vannes.com*. Plus information point at the Parc du Golfe in high season.

Orientation

The main N165 slices up through the region from the Loire Atlantique (see p. 148), taking you on into Finistère (p. 189–p. 240). It runs virtually parallel to the coast, whizzing you past the main Morbihan towns of Vannes and Lorient. Vannes is 122km/76 miles south of Quimper and 116km/72 miles south of Brest in Finistère.

From Vannes (49km/30 miles) and Lorient (86km/53 miles), two major roads, the N166 and the N24, take you inland as far as Ploërmel, there converging to take you on to Rennes (68km/ 42 miles) in the Ille-et-Vilaine.

Arriving

By Boat There are no international ferry points in the Morbihan; your closest is **Roscoff** in

Finistère (p. 199), about 190km (118 miles) from Lorient.

By Train Some fast **TGVs** between **Paris** and Quimper in Finistère stop at **Vannes, Auray** or **Lorient** (about 3 hours 35 minutes from Paris); see p. 30 for SNCF details.

By Air Lorient Bretagne Sud airport is linked with **Waterford** and **Kerry** by Ireland's budget airline **Aer Arann** (p. 25) during the summer months, and year-round with **Paris** (Orly) and **Lyon** on **Air France** (p. 25). For schedules, see *www.lorient. aeroport.fr*.

Alternatively, **Ryanair** (p. 25) has low-cost flights from **East Midlands, Leeds** and **Dublin** (Republic of Ireland) to the city of **Nantes** (112km/70 miles south of Vannes) in the Loire Atlantique region (see p. 148).

Getting Around

As elsewhere in Brittany Morbiban has scant public transport and your own wheels or a hire car is essential. **easyCar.com** offers **car-hire** from **Lorient** and **Nantes** airports as well as **Lorient, Auray** and **Vannes** train stations, or you can often book car-hire at the same time as you do your online flight or train tickets.

This is also a very popular spot with motorhomers, with your closest pick-up point Rennes in the Ille-et-Vilaine (p. 60). For more on hiring a **motorhome**, see p. 29.

WHAT TO SEE & DO

Children's Top 10 Attractions

❶ **Sailing** around the Golfe du Morbihan, stopping off to catch crabs on the Ile aux Moines. See p. 112.

❷ **Monkeying around** in the treetops at Celt'Aventures or Parcabout. See p. 130 or p. 131.

❸ **Learning** all about sailing, submarines and Nazi history and Cité de la Voile and former U-boat base at Lorient. See p. 134.

❹ **Admiring** the glimmering golden cliffs of the Plage de la Mine d'Or. See p. 123.

❺ **Exploring** the château, animal park and botanical garden of the Parc de Branféré. See p. 119.

❻ **Puzzling** about how ancient peoples moved the gigantic Grand Menhir Brisé. See p. 109.

❼ **Cruising** lazily along the Nantes-Brest canal, or cycling along its towpaths. See p. 223.

❽ **Finding out** about the 5,000km (3,125 mile) odyssey of the salmon as it returns from the Atlantic, at the Odyssaum. See p. 119.

❾ **Creating** giant sand sculptures during the Breizh Sable Tour. See below.

❿ **Let your** offspring have fun in the kid's club whilst you enjoy a peaceful thalassotherapy session. See p. 146.

Children-Friendly Events & Entertainment

For the Brittany-wide, school-holiday Festival Place aux Mômes, see p. 57. For Stations Sensation Bretagne in the region, see p. 201.

Also see p. 196 for the Fête du Nautisme sailing event and p. 55 for the Couleurs de Bretagne painting competition.

Bastille Day

France's greatest annual celebration sees events across the region, usually including fireworks. Two great places in the Morbihan to join in the festivities are Josselin (p. 105), which hosts a medieval festival including activities in the castle grounds, and Vannes, when locals don traditional costume and horse-drawn carriages ply the streets.

Date 14 July. For tourist offices, see p. 102 and p. 103.

Breizh Sable Tour ★★ FIND

www.sensation-bretagne.com

This mini sandcastle festival tours a handful of Breton resorts each year: in 2010 the hosts were the Morbihan—Port du Crouesty (p. 144), Pénestin (p. 123) and Carnac (p. 121)—and Finistère (p. 189). Sand sculptor Laurent Dagron exhibits his own large-scale works but also leads free workshops so that others can learn to create their own giant sand-sculpture. There are also best-sandcastle competitions and night-time illuminations.

Date 3wks in July. **Admission** free.

Festival des Artisans d'Art et Modèle Réduit

Lizio, 19km southwest of Ploërmel on D174, www.lizio.fr/f_artisans.php.

Home to the Insectarium (p. 119) and the Univers du Poète Ferrailleur (p. 127), Lizio is also a centre for artists and craftspeople, and each August this 'Petite Cité de Caractère' hosts a festival in which more than 150 artisans and model-makers display and sell their wares to a soundtrack of traditional Breton music. Highlights include model cars, boats on a pond, free face-painting workshops, an old-fashioned carousel, and a miniature steam train ride. There's a free *fest-noz* (p. 16) in the evening, and a food tent at lunch and dinner.

Date *early Aug.* **Admission** *free.*

Festival Interceltique ★ ★

Lorient; ☏ 02 97 21 24 29; www. festival-interceltique.com.

This huge gathering of Celts from all over the world, now more than 40 years old, takes over much of Lorient (see p. 106) for 10 days in late July/early August. As well as Celtic traditional, classical, folk, jazz and rock music and dancing, it puts a big emphasis on Breton games and sports, with demonstrations and free tuition in *boules*, skittles, tug-of-war and the like. Another highlight is the Grand Parade, with more than 3,000 Celtic musicians, pipers and dancers in national costumes.

Date *late July/early Aug.* **Admission** *mainly free; ticket prices for concerts vary.*

Fête de la Crêpe ★ ★

Gourin; 55km (35 miles) northwest of Lorient off D769.

Brittany's pancake festival is hosted by the region's biggest industrial crêpe producer, in its castle just outside town. Over two days you can taste crêpes cooked over an open fire as well as chitterling sausages (for which nearby Guémené-sur-Scorff is famous), watch cooking demos, dancing and Celtic music concerts, see displays and shows on rural traditions, peruse craft stalls, and play traditional Breton wooden games. Don't miss the annual attempt to break the local record for the biggest pancake. Contact the local tourist office for more details (p. 102).

Date *late July.* **Admission** *free.*

Towns & Cities

Josselin

For tourist office, see p. 102.

A charming medieval town with well-preserved half-timbered 16th- and 17th-century houses and host to a great Saturday-morning market. Josselin is dominated by its splendid castle, first built (in wood) around AD 1000 and boasting carved dragons and other monsters on its Gothic inner façade. Though you can tour some of the ornate rooms, full of antique furniture, family portraits and gifts from

History Brought to Life

For those whose kids are old enough to take in a dose of horrible history, or even those who want an alternative day out and a gentle introduction to serious matters with younger kids, **Lorient's former submarine base Kéroman** cannot be recommended highly enough (you can lighten the atmosphere by combining it with a visit to the Cité de la Voile; p. 125). Here, largely intact, the concrete monoliths of the Nazi base where 30 submarines could be sheltered are stark reminders of a chilling episode of history that resulted in the destruction of almost 90% of the town of Lorient itself.

Visitors are free to wander round much of the old base (or take a guided tour), but do watch out with children as the harbour-sides are unfenced. On-site you'll find **La Tour Davis/Musée Sous-Marin** (℡06 07 10 69 41, *www.musee-sous-marin.com*; admission 5€, under 16 3€), a 'museum under the sea' containing the simulator that was used to train all French submarine crews in evacuation and rescue techniques for more than 50 years after the base was taken over in 1953, including a decompression chamber. Fifty-minute guided tours are run by passionate diving and history specialists (who speak good English). You then visit three exhibition rooms, including an audiovisual space re-creating the experience of life in a submarine in all its claustro-phobia, including U-171 as it sank off Groix (p. 113) and other Atlantic wrecks; a soundtrack of a diver's breathing makes it all the more haunting.

Also on the site since May 2010 is **Le Sous-Marin Flore** (℡02 97 65 52 87, *www.la-flore.fr*; admission 8€, children 5–17 6.20€), an inter-active museum about submarines, with videos on Lorient's history, a reconstructed submarine interior, and the chance to have a look inside the actual Flore submarine itself.

Note that you can get combined tickets to all venues at the base, plus the neighbouring Cité de la Voile (p. 125).

royals, the highlight for kids (or at least girls) is the **Musée de la Poupée** (℡02 97 22 36 45, *www. chateaujosselin.com*). Housed in the old stables, this famous col-lection of around 600 antique dolls and intricate dollhouse fur-niture (now added to by a few other toys and games) belonged to the Duchess of Rohan, a dis-tinguished poet, whose ancestor,

the 14th Duke, a politician, still lives here.

Lorient

For tourist office, see p. 102.

The Morbihan's largest town by population size, Lorient, an important seaport among 17th-century merchants trading with India, was largely destroyed dur-ing World War II, when the

Allies tried to bomb Nazi U-boat bases that had been built here, and, failing, bombed the town itself. It remains a major fishing port and docks for cargo and passenger ships, but tourism has grown in recent years in the form of yachting marinas, attractions such as the Cité de Voile Eric Tabarly (p. 125) and La Thalassa (p. 126), and most of all the huge Festival Interceltique (p. 105) attracting nearly 0.75 million people. For places to stay and eat, see p. 140 and p. 134.

Vannes

For tourist office, see p. 103.

Located on the Golfe du Morbihan (p. 112), this historic market town—birthplace of François I, Duke of Brittany and the *départemental* capital—has a cathedral mentioned in *The Three Musketeers* and a medieval centre of narrow cobbled streets lined by gabled houses, still surrounded by some of the old ramparts. The Château-Gaillard is a history and archaeology museum (℡ 02 97 01

63 00) open June–Sept where you can play spot-the-animals, from seabirds to monkeys. Vannes is also a good place for shopping (p. 132), with its fair share of independent shops and boutiques.

A *petit train touristique* scuttles around between Easter and early November, and there's also a free summer shuttle between the centre and the Parc du Golfe leisure complex 10 minutes away, home to the town's aquarium and to its butterfly house (p. 117).

For places to stay and eat, see p. 140 and p. 135.

Fun Days Out

Alignements de Carnac/ Musée de Prehistorie J. Miln—Z. le Rouzic
★ ★ AGE 6 & UP

Museum: 10 Place de la Chapelle; ℡02 97 52 22 04; www.museede carnac.com. Site and Information Centre: ℡02 97 52 29 81; www. carnac.monuments-nationaux.fr.

The historic market town of Vannes

Carnac is the most famous—and busiest of the prehistoric sites—an area bristling with around 3000 megaliths, menhirs, dolmens and tumulus (see p. 107)—built between 4500 and 2000 BC. For the moment, the site has free access in winter but in summer can only be visited by 1hr guided tour (some in English, German or Spanish). Be aware that at the moment, it's not buggy or wheelchair-friendly. The information centre, the **Maison des Mégalithes** has a brilliant gift/book-shop with an impressive range of materials for kids, and marked trails, picnic tables, and occasional kids' and adults' workshops.

Now generally believed to have been a place of worship, or perhaps a lunar observatory that helped the ancients observe the movement of stars, the alignments were once thought by some Bretons to have been erected by *korrigans* (fairy or dwarf) or by giants, and some modern-day theorists even claim they were made by aliens.

There are three main fields of alignments: **Menec,** the largest, with 1,099 menhirs in 11 rows, some up to 4m (13ft) high; **Kermario,** with 1,029 menhirs in 10 rows plus the **Géant du Manio,** the area's tallest menhir at more than 6m (20ft); and **Kerlescan,** the smallest but best-preserved, with 555 menhirs in 13 rows.

Scattered between are some isolated remnants, many concealed in pine-scented woodland; the most interesting is the vast **Tumulus St. Michel,** covering a dolmen and two burial chambers, once housing 15 stone chests filled with bone remains, axes, pottery fragments and jewellery that are now in the **Musée de Prehistorie J. Miln—Z. le Rouzic,** a museum that brings the history of the site to life by emphasising that the alignments were created by real people like us. The 6,500-plus objects, found during digs, include ceramics, tools, and jewellery, and you can also view maps, models and a film. Weekend and school holidays see archaeology-based workshops for kids, family activities and walks around some of the lesser-known Neolithic sites in the area. With younger kids, the **Parc de Préhistoire de Bretagne** (p. 115) is more suitable.

For places to stay and eat, see p. 140 and p. 135.

Breton stone cross near Tumulus St. Michel church in Carnac

Ancient Tongues: a Neolithic Vocabulary

Cairn: piles of stones surrounding a tomb or tombs
Cromlech: a circle of standing stones
Dolmen: a megalithic burial monument made of large stone slabs
Enceinte: standing stones forming a circle or quadrilateral
Menhir: a tall, upright stone, isolated or in alignments
Tumulus: a large tomb built of piled-up stones or earth

Time 1–2hrs, inc shop. **Open** site & information centre: May and June daily 9am–7pm; July and Aug daily 9am–8pm; Sept–Apr daily 10am–5pm. Museum: Apr–June and Sept Wed–Mon 10am–6pm plus Mon in school hols; July and Aug daily 10am–6pm; Oct–Dec, Feb and Mar Wed–Mon 10am–12.30pm and 2–5pm plus Mon in school hols. *Admission* museum: 4.50€, under 18 free.

> **INSIDER TIP** ❯❯
> In summer a free shuttle ferries visitors between Carnac's museum, standing stones and beach resort (p. 121).

Alignements de Kerzehro
⭐⭐ AGE 6 & UP

Just south of Erdeven, 9km (5.5 miles) north of Carnac on D781.

If you want to ogle ancient stones without the crowds (or fences) of Carnac (see above), this is your place—you don't even need to get out of your car, as the D781 south from Erdeven takes you through the middle of some of the 1,000 stones, which are 10 rows wide at their thickest point. There are also four huge menhirs, the **Giants of Kerzehro,** two standing and two lying on the ground, apparently encircled by stones; one even seems to have a semi-human face, though this is probably due to the elements. As with the Carnac alignments, the true meaning of the geometric configurations remains a mystery.

Ask at the Erdeven tourist office (p. 102) for their free maps outlining a Circuit des Mégalithes et Châteaux and a Circuit du Grand Arc Mégalithique, and about mountain-bike hire. At the top of the D781, you might also want to take a small detour to Etel and its **Musée des Thoniers** (☎02 97 55 26 67, *www.museedesthoniers. fr*), a small museum about local tuna trawlers and the wildlife of the Etel estuary, sometimes hosting kids' games and workshops.

Time from 1hr driving to several hrs cycling. *Amenities* 🅿 🍽 🔒 Ⓥ ♿

> **INSIDER TIP** ❯❯
> Rock devotees should make a detour to the **Grand Menhir Brisé** ('Big Broken Menhir') on the megalith-rich Locmariaquer peninsula south of Carnac. One of the largest stones worked on by prehistoric people, it's possibly the heaviest object ever moved by humans without the

powered machinery (no one knows how). Some theorists claim it's the central point of the lunar observatory of Carnac.

Belle-Ile en Mer ★★ ALL AGES

The largest Breton island, 14km (9 miles) off the Quiberon peninsula, has a mild climate and gorgeous beaches, but it's no insider secret—Parisians setting up second homes here have made it chic and expensive. Like Parisians, stick to the calm beaches and harbours of the northeast coast; the southwest's Côte Sauvage ('Wild Coast') has vicious cliffs that inspired some of Monet's Impressionist paintings, especially the **Aiguilles** ('Needles') **de Port Coton**.

To avoid the crowds of the biggest beach, **Les Grands Sables,** in high season, hire bikes, mopeds or a car. (It's best

Aiguilles de Port Coton

to leave your own car in a car park on the mainland—places on ferries are limited and expensive.) Most of the good beaches are between Locmaria at the southern tip and the island's capital, **Le Palais,** although local youngsters flock to **Port Donnant** the west side to bodyboard.

Otherwise, you can climb the 213 steps of the **Phare Grande** lighthouse, take a bus or taxi tour of the island or go horse-riding, from age 2 and up (☎02 97 31 64 32). Older kids might be impressed to learn Alexandre Dumas set part of his adventure yarn *The Man in the Iron Mask* on the island.

If you want to stay over, **Hôtel La Désirade** (☎02 97 31 70 70, *www.hotel-la-desirade.com*) has three family suites, with charming nautical decor and an outdoor pool; **Hôtel Le Clos Fleuri** (☎02 97 31 45 45, *www. hotel-leclosfleuri.com*) also has family rooms overlooking a lovely garden and will happily organise a babysitter. For places to eat, see p. 137.

Seasonal (Apr–Sept) ferries from Quiberon to Le Palais (35 minutes) and Sauzon (50 minutes), ☎0820 056 156 or ☎02 97 35 02 00, *www.compagnie-oceane.fr* or ☎0820 056 000 or ☎0825 134 100, *www.smn-navigation.fr/www. compagniedesiles.com*. There are also seasonal crossings from Vannes and Port-Navalo (☎0825 132 100, *www.navix.fr*).

Time *1 day or more.* ***Fares*** *50€ adult, 9.50€ child 4–17, 27€/18€ day return.*

Phare Grande

Combine a castle visit with a stop at the nearby **Musée Régional des Petits Commerces et des Métiers** (✆ *02 97 41 75 36*), where 30,000-plus objects from the 17th century to the 1950s, displayed in re-created workshops and shops, bring to life around 60 old trades.

Time 2hrs or more. *Open* Feb, Mar and Oct daily 10am–noon and 2–6pm; Apr–Sept daily 10am–7pm; Nov–Jan daily 10am–noon and 2–5pm. *Admission* 7€, 2€ child 8–17, 15 € family (any number of children). *Amenities*

Château de Suscinio
⭐ FIND **AGE 6 & UP**

Sarzeau; ✆ *02 97 41 91 91; www. suscinio.info. 23km (14 miles) south of Vannes on D780.*

Strikingly situated between ocean, forest and marshland, this one-time hunting residence of the Dukes of Brittany has been restored to its former glory in recent years. The summer months (June–Sept) see daily half-day visits on various themes, including a general tour and talks; meanwhile kids can take part in an educational workshop. Otherwise, you can take a self-guided tour with a free audioguide (available in English), or just enjoy a wander. In the holidays, there are special tours and workshops (also in French only) for kids 6–12, for which advance booking is preferred.

Domaine de Kerguéhennec
⭐ **ALL AGES**

Bignan; ✆ *02 97 60 44 44; www. art-kerguehennec.com. 30km (19 miles) north of Vannes on D1.*

This uncompromising contemporary art venue and cultural meeting place in an 18th-century château is best visited for its grounds. Here—free of charge—you can roam the lawns, woods and lakeside in search of the 20-plus works by major artists such as Brit Tony Cragg, whose *Gastéropodes* is a huddle of outsize cast-iron shells in which you might make out tortoises or rifle holsters as well as snails. Kids are free to climb all over the pieces should they feel so inclined—the most fun is the *Tortue de Corentin*, a green-painted brass tortoise that was actually designed by a local schoolboy, Corentin Sénéchal, in collaboration with a resident artist. Otherwise, unless you're a fan of modern installation art, you'll probably be most impressed by the scenery—the park is home to a *sentier botanique* (botanical trail) with labelled trees and plants.

The château itself (open only in summer) hosts temporary exhibitions by modern artists. New French-language family workshops (adults 8€, children 4€) for those with kids 6 and over are linked either with these exhibitions or with the sculptures outside. The onsite Café du Parc serves snacks and light meals.

Time *3hrs.* **Open** *mid-Jan–June and Sept–mid-Dec Tues–Sun 11am–6pm; July and Aug Tues–Sun 11am–7pm.* **Admission** *free.* **Amenities** ☕ ♿

INSIDER TIP

For something a little different to standard cruisers, try **Le Passeur des Iles** (📞*06 22 01 67 72*, *www.passeurdesiles.com*), a little 1960s turquoise-painted wooden boat that does a variety of routes and tours in the gulf. Among them are trips to the world-famous Gavrinis cairn on a tiny island in the Golfe—5,500 years old and boasting elaborately decorated slabs along the sides of its passage tomb, constituting some of the world's most significant megalithic art.

Golfe du Morbihan

★ ★ **ALL AGES**

Covering 100 square kilometres (39 square miles), this inland sea busy with fishing vessels, oyster boats, yachts, canoes and jet-skis is sprinkled with lush islands and islets—one for every day of the year according to legend, and many of them home to Neolithic remains. Of the 40 or so islands, most are private but you can visit the **Ile aux Moines** where you'll discover beaches (see p. 122), fishermen's cottages, winding pathways, old fountains, chapels, ruined windmills and megalithic vestiges amidst pine and fig trees, and the **Ile d'Arz,** with more old windmills and peaceful coves dotted along the coastal path right round the island (guided nature tours are run in high season). You can hire bikes on both, and seasonal tourist infopoints by the boat jetties give out free maps.

Among several companies running cruises around the Gulf, including stop-offs on one or both islands, Izenah stands out for its family-friendly itineraries (📞*02 97 26 31 45, www.izenah-croisieres.com*, one of which ('Formule 2') is especially recommended for those with young children since you can spend as much time as you like exploring the Ile aux Moines before catching a half-hourly boat back to Port-Blanc. Navix (see p. 110) also offers trips with alternative departure points; if you're staying on the southern side of the Gulf, these may be handier. For the **Hôtel San Francisco** on the Ile aux Moines, see p. 141; for places to eat, see p. 135.

You could also discover the Gulf by kayak or motorboat with **Varec'h** (📞*02 97 57 16 16, www.bretagne-kayak.com*; from 19€ an hour for a two person kayak; kids must be able to swim

25m), or fly over it by hot-air balloon with **Montgolfière Morbihan** AGES 12 & UP, around 200€pp, ☎02 97 62 76 00; *www. montgolfiere-morbihan.com*.

Time half or full day.

INSIDER TIP ≫

If you come in summer, choose Arz over Moines—the latter tends to be the focal point for tourists and can get crowded.

Houat ALL AGES

14km (9 miles) off Quiberon Peninsula.

Stranded in the Atlantic between Belle-Ile (p. 110) and the mainland, the islands of Houat and Hoëdic derive their names from the Breton for 'duck' and 'duckling'. Houat, the largest (5km or 3 miles long and 1.5km at its widest point), has magnificent unspoilt beaches, **Treac'h er Goured** and **Treac'h er Salus**, where you can hunt for crabs, lobsters, conger eels and colonies of wild mussels and oysters. That may inspire you to visit the **L'Eclosarium** (☎02 97 52 38 38; open May–Sept) or 'hatchery', a research centre with displays on microscopic life in the sea as well as the island's history.

The population amounts to less than 350, most of whom live in the main village, also named Houat, and home to a couple of hotels, restaurants, a crêperie and a bar. Outside this village you'll see just one tree on the whole island, which you can explore on foot or by mountain bikes hired by the port. The site

communes.com has rooms and apartments let by islanders.

For ferries to Houat from Vannes, Locmariaquer and Port-Navalo, plus ports in the Loire Atlantique (Apr–Sept), ☎08 25 13 41 00, *www.compagniedesiles. com*. Tickets cost 28€ adult, 18€ child, 5€ under 4. The same company runs ferries to Hoëdic from the same ports. Or you can sail to Houat (limited cars) and Hoëdic (no cars) from Quiberon: ☎08 20 05 61 56 or ☎02 97 35 02 00, *www.compagnie-oceane.fr*.

Time 1 day.

INSIDER TIP ≫

If you sail to Houat from Vannes, the trip is much longer but lets you take in the Golfe du Morbihan (p. 112) en route, for the same price.

Ile de Groix ALL AGES

For tourist office, see p. 102.

The 'Island of the Witch'—*Enezar Grroac'h* in Breton—lies just off Lorient, but getting out of the congested Rade de Lorient makes the journey longer than you'd expect. Aside the remains of some megaliths and forts, find rabbits, honeysuckle plants and a fine coastline to explore on foot or by bike. Try the sandy beaches of Primiture on the east or the wilder shoreline and cliffs of Piwisy to the west. The former, including the popular **Plage des Grands Sables** (one of Europe's few convex beaches, shifting at a dramatic pace), are often streaked with red dust from garnets—an inexpensive gemstone abundant in local rocks.

The island's chief claims to fame are **Le Trou de l'Enfer** (Hell's Hole), and the **Pointe des Chats** ('Cats' Point'), an area of dazzling multicoloured schist rocks, but there are other distractions: **Port-Tudy**, once one of France's biggest tuna-fishing ports, has an Ecomusée (📞 *02 97 86 84 60, http://ecomusee. groix.free.fr*), with occasional workshops on the likes of nautical knots, while Kerbus has both a snail farm **L'Escargoterie** (📞 *02 97 86 58 94, www.lescargoterie.fr*) and a goat farm (📞 *02 97 86 87 52*) you can visit.

A sailing school, **Sellor** (*www. sellor-nautisme.fr*) offers kids' sailing courses combined with seashore exploration sessions, while Level 1 divers aged 14-plus can explore various wrecks off the island's coast with **Subagrec** (📞 *02 97 86 59 79, http://assoc. pagespro-orange.fr/subagrec*), including a German submarine. You can also go **horse-riding** (📞 *02 97 86 57 61*). For the weird and wonderful Parcabout treetop acrobatics course and 'nests', see p. 131. The island's website lists accommodation ranging from hotels to campsites and a youth hostel; for places to eat, see p. 135.

Passenger ferries can be boarded from Locmiquelic or Doëlan (📞 *08 20 05 60 00, www. smn-navigation.fr*), both take 50 minutes. Tickets cost 26€ adults, 18€ child 4–18, 5€ under 4. Alternatively, you have the option to take your car when

Port-Tudy, Ile de Groix

sailing from Lorient (📞 *08 20 05 61 56* or 📞 *02 97 35 02 00, www. compagnie-oceane.fr*).

Time *1 day.*

Oh Bonheur des Gosses ALL AGES

Kerperdrix la Vache Enragée, St. Armel; 📞 *02 97 43 90 38; www. ohbonheurdesgosses.com. 16km (10 miles) south of Vannes on D780.*

Though small-scale, this little outdoor *parc à loisirs* is a good half-day option for those with younger kids who need to blow away some energy, with bouncy castles (don't forget socks), giant wooden toys, water games and dwarf goats to pet. There's masses of picnic space, and a kiosk selling ice creams, drinks and cakes or the wonderful

Crêperie Bara-Breizh is in the same town (p. 137).

Time half a day. *Open* mid-Apr daily 1–6pm; May, June and Sept Wed, Sat, Sun and holidays 11am–7pm; July and Aug daily 10am–8pm. *Admission* 6.50€ adults and children over 1m tall. *Amenities* 🅿️ ☕ 🅿️ 🥘 ♿

Parc de Préhistoire de Bretagne ⭐ ALL AGES

La Croix Neuve, Malansac; ☎ 02 97 43 34 17; *www.prehistoire-bretagne.com.* 42km (26 miles) east of Vannes on D153.

This 'park to take you back in time' a little way northeast of the Parc de Branféré (p. 119) might be just the ticket for young kids for whom the ancient alignments at Carnac (p. 107) are too dry. The circuit takes you past more than 25 life-sized scenes of dinosaurs, animals and early humans, including *Homo erectus*—not at all convincing, but that's all part of the fun and the Cro-magnon dancing scene

will have you in stitches. Unusually, all the info boards are in English, Dutch, German and Spanish as well as French.

Things are more low-key elsewhere in the vast and wild wooded park, where you pass old wells and slate quarries, and walk around five pretty lakes edged by cliffs. The reception centre has a picnic space, a bar selling snacks and ice creams and a shop with fossils and minerals.

Time 3hrs. *Open* late Mar–mid-Oct daily 11am–7pm (last Admission 5pm), mid-Oct to early Nov Sun and school days 1–6.30pm. *Admission* 10.50€ adults, 6.50€ child 5–11. *Amenities* 🍸 ☕ 🅿️ 🥘 🛍️

Village de Poul-Fetan
⭐ ALL AGES

Quistinic; ☎ 02 97 39 51 74; *www. poul-fetan.com.* 39km (24 miles) northeast of Lorient on D156.

Restoration of this tiny 16th-century hamlet began in 1979, less than 10 years after the last of its handful of inhabitants left,

Crepe-making, Village de Poul-Fetan

and was so painstaking, you'd be forgiven for thinking you're on a film set—especially given the presence (every afternoon June–Sept) of costumed characters acting out scenes from the daily lives of 19th century peasants, including milking, wool-dying and butter- and crêpe-making. Kids love the protected domestic animals who populate the farmland, including Breton cows, horses, sheep and pigs, but there are also displays of old farm machinery and peasant costumes, a re-created 1850s interior, pottery and bakery workshops, a craft shop and a 'tavern' serving local produce. There are tours of the village (some in English) over summer.

Time 4hrs. **Open** Apr and May daily 2–6.30pm; June and Sept daily 11am–6.30pm; July and Aug daily 10.45am–7pm. **Admission** Apr and May: 6€ adult, 4€ child 6–16; June–Sept 7€ adult, 4€ child 6-16. **Amenities** 🍸 ☕ 🅿 🚻 ♿

Animal Attractions

L'Abeille Vivante et La Cité des Fourmis ★ AGE 3 & UP

Kercadoret, Le Faouët; 📞02 97 23 08 05; www.abeilles-et-fourmis.com. 40km (25 miles) northwest of Lorient on D769.

Set on a characterful old farm, 'The Living Bee and City of Ants' allows a close-up view of insect activity, with working hives of all shapes and sizes, displays about bee-keeping through history, live stick insects, and—best of all— 'Ant City', which includes a metre-high domed colony made from twigs and pine needles by forest ants, which kids can access by means of tunnels leading to glass viewing pods. Entry includes audio/video commentary in various languages.

The shop sells local produce, bee themed products, plus toys and books.

Time 1hr. **Open** Apr–June daily 10am–noon and 2–6pm; July and Aug daily 10am–7pm; Sept–mid-Nov daily 2–6pm. **Admission** 7€ adult, 5€ child 4–12. **Amenities** 🅿 🛏 🚻 ♿

INSIDER TIP 》

There are two smaller-scale sites within striking distance of Poul-Fétan. At Melrand, the **Village de l'An Mil** (📞02 97 39 57 89, **www.melrand-village-an-mil. info**; admission 5€ adult, 4€ child 6–16), an abandoned medieval hamlet hosting frequent activities focusing on everyday peasant life and archaeology as well as housing several breeds of rare farm animal. Then at Kernascleden, **La Maison de la Chauve-Souris** (📞02 97 28 26 31, **www. maisondelachauvesouris.com**) is a discovery centre showing infrared footage of a live bat colony in the eaves of the local church. Best of all are the Bat Nights, where you watch the creatures flying over the village pond.

Aquarium du Golfe ALL AGES

Parc du Golfe du Morbihan, Vannes; 📞02 97 40 67 40, www.aquarium-du-golfe.com. Free shuttle bus runs from Vannes in high season.

It certainly doesn't scale the heights of Océanopolis (p. 210), but Vannes's small aquarium has an original focus—it looks at the Golfe du Morbihan (p. 112), the Red Sea and the Amazon in its three separate sections. Some of the most interesting inhabitants are the hairy Golfe du Morbihan seahorses and the morgate, a cuttlefish whose eggs you might spot on local beaches in summer, resembling bunches of black grapes. From further afield there are the obligatory but no less awesome sharks, Nile crocodiles and green turtles. Much thought has gone into making visits easier for those with children: there are wheeled highchairs to push babies and toddlers round at a height at which they can see into the tanks, changing facilities, and a crêperie, brasserie, ice cream counter and bar in summer, as well as a lawn for picnics.

Since the aquarium only merits an hour or two's visit, take advantage of the money-saving joint pass available with the nearby **Jardin des Papillons** (02 97 40 67 40, *www.jardinaux papillons.com)*, a tropical space full of freeflying butterflies.

Time 1hr 30mins. *Open* Jan–Mar and Oct–Dec daily 2–6pm (plus 10am–noon school hols); Apr–June and Sept daily 10am–noon and 2–6pm; July and Aug daily 9am–7.30pm. *Admission* 10.80€ adult, 7.50€ child 4–11. *Amenities* aquarium:
🍷🖼️🍺📎🎏🎪🍴🏺♿🚷 ;
Jardin: 📎🏺🚷

INSIDER TIP

Vannes's rather unscenic Parc du Golfe du Morbihan 10 minutes from the town centre is home not only to the city's aquarium and butterfly house and to the

family-friendly Brasserie Edgar and Mercure hotel (p. 140)—it's also where you'll find the **Aquatic Club** (*02 97 40 51 51, www.aquatic-club-vannes. com*), a long-established and innovative centre dedicated to water activities and swimming tuition for babies and children. Family play sessions are available. In 2008 an adjoining wellness centre, Balnéo Form, was added.

Barrage d'Arzal ★ AGE 4 & UP

Arzal; *02 99 90 88 44. 35km (22 miles) southeast of Vannes on D139.*

This flood dam built at the entrance to the Vilaine estuary in 1970—enroute to the Plage de la Mine d'Or (p. 123)—contains a 70m (230ft) long *passe à poissons* ('fish pass') that lets migrating fish through on their way back up the river. An observation room lets you watch, from very close up, the fish on their way through, while a guide tells you (in French) about the various species you might see—mullets, sea trouts, eels, sea lampreys and occasionally salmon—and their habits. There are also display boards and a video. It's a low-key but interesting sight.

Time 1hr. *Open* May and June Sat, Sun (and holidays) 3–6.20pm; July–mid-Sept Wed–Sun 3–6.20pm. *Admission* 3€ adult, free under 18.

Le Clos du Tay ★ FIND AGE 2 & UP

Le Tay, La Gacilly; *02 99 08 04 25; www.closdutay.com. 32km (19 miles) southeast of Ploërmel on D8.*

As well as accommodation, this country manor just outside La Gacilly (p. 138) also offers donkey trekking for anything from 2 hrs to a week. Shorter outings follow footpaths around the river Tay—for longer ones, staff will load up the donkeys with tents plus your bags and a picnic before you head off into the Brocéliande forest (p. 67) or along the Nantes–Brest Canal (p. 223). Two adults are needed for longer treks—one to lead the donkey carrying the pack-saddle, one to lead the donkey saddled up for a child weighing up to 40kg/6 stone (if you have two or more kids, they'll have to take it in turn to ride).

Time 2hrs to a week. *Open* all year by advance booking. *Prices* (excluding optional accommodation and picnics): 20€ one donkey for 2hrs; 185€–205€ one donkey for 1wk; 10% discount on 2nd donkey. Deposit of 150€ for rides of more than 1 day. *Amenities* 🏕 🎋 ⛺ 🍴 🛍

Ferme du Monde ★ ★ ALL AGES

Le Bois Brassu, Carentoir; 📞02 99 93 70 70, *www.lafermedumonde.com*. 38km (24 miles) southeast of Ploërmel on D118.

The 'World Farm', home to more than 400 domestic animals in five zones representing the five continents, was conceived and created by handicapped workers, and one of its events is a festival with open-air performances by handicapped artists. Other events are a Children's Day (June) and a Breton Day with traditional food and music. Set in a wooded park, the farm features yaks, zebus (a humped cow), buffalo, camels, Texas longhorns and Cameroon sheep, all housed in large enclosures, plus a children's farm where little ones can pet dwarf goats, Ouessant sheep, ponies, a Vietnamese potbellied pig, donkeys and more, as well as get a free pony-ride. There's also scale model of a Breton village with automated figures, a *petit train* and, inside the 16th-century manor within the grounds, a fast-food restaurant, a bar and a shop with local produce, including 'milk jam' (better than it sounds).

Time half a day to a day. *Open* Apr, May and Sept daily 10am–6pm; June–Aug daily 10am–7pm; Oct–mid-Nov Wed, Sat, Sun and school hols 10am–6pm. *Admission* 8.50€ adult, 5€ child; free under 4. Petit train: 2.50€ adult; 1€–2€ child. *Amenities* 🍵 🧸 🍸 🧺 📷 🚃 ⛺ 🍴 🛍

Haras National de Hennebont ★ AGE 3 & UP

1 Rue Victor Hugo, Hennebont; 📞02 97 89 40 30; *www.haras-hennebont. fr*. 10km northeast of Lorient on D724.

This stud farm took over a former Cistercian abbey in 1857, but more than its architecture, horse-lovers flock to see events such as the grand 'Spectacle Equestre' with its stallion parade, competitions, demonstrations, riding courses and quizzes. Outside these events, you can visit the stables, saddlery, smithy, modern 'discovery space' with many hands-on displays, and small screening room.

Time 2hrs. *Open* July and Aug daily 10am–7pm; May, June and Sept Mon, Sat and Sun 2–6pm, Tues–Fri 9.30am–12.30 and 2–6pm; French Easter holidays and autumn half-term Mon–Fri 9.30–12.30 and 2–6pm, Sat and Sun 2–6pm. *Admission* 7.10€ adult, 5.50€ child 5–17, 21€ family (any number of children). *Amenities* P 🏠 ♿

Insectarium de Lizio   ALL AGES

Rue du Stade, Lizio; 📞 *02 97 74 94 31, www.insectarium-de-lizio.fr. 20km (12 miles) southeast of Ploërmel on D174.*

In a characterful town of ceramic and weaving workshops, this old cottage stands out—instead of kilns and looms it houses scorpions, praying mantises, trap-door spiders, millipedes up to 30cm (12 inches) long, stick insects and more besides. The exhibition spaces focus not only on the insects themselves (housed safely in more than 30 terrariums) but on their role in maintaining the natural status quo by, as in the example of the ladybird in Brittany, eating aphids before they destroy tomato plants. The display boards (in French) explore other ways insects help humans, and microscopes and magnifying glasses allow you close-up views. Don't miss the room where tricks of scale give you an idea of what it must feel like to be an insect. You can picnic in the quiet garden.

Time 1hr. *Open* Apr–June, Sept and Oct daily 2–6pm; July and Aug daily 10am–7pm; French Easter holidays and autumn half-term daily 10am–noon and 2–6pm. *Admission* 7€ adult, 5€ child 4–16. *Amenities* 🏕 ♿

L'Odyssaum ★★ AGE 3 & UP

Pont-Scorff; 📞 *02 97 32 42 00; www.odyssaum.fr. 14km (8.5 miles) north of Lorient on D6.*

The perfect counterpoint to the commercialised zoo nearby (p. 120), this tranquil eco-museum is based around an open-air *station de comptage* where wild salmon are captured and anaesthetised to be weighed, measured and aged during their migration back from the Atlantic to their native river to breed and die (a process designed to keep track of how many make the return journey). Next to the *station*, the **Moulin des Princes,** once home to Breton royalty, now houses an exhibition about the salmon's amazing 5,000km (3,000 mile) odyssey.

Time 2hrs. *Open* July and Aug daily 10am–7pm; May, June and Sept Mon, Sat and Sun 2–6pm, Tues–Fri 9.30am–12.30pm and 2–6pm; French Easter holidays and autumn half-term Mon–Fri 9.30am–12.30pm and 2–6pm, Sat and Sun 2–6pm. *Admission* 5.70€ adult, 4.30€ child 5–17, 16.90€ family (any number of children). *Amenities* P 🏕 ♿

Parc de Branféré/Fondation Nicolas Hulot pour la Nature et l'Homme ★★★ GREEN   ALL AGES

Le Guerno; 📞 *02 97 42 94 66; www.branfere.com. 38km (24 miles) southeast of Vannes on D139.*

Like the Bourbansais in the Ille-et-Vilaine (p. 69), Branféré combines guided visits of a stately château with a pretty animal park full of native and exotic species. It also has a botanical garden and—uniquely—a nature school teaching families how to live in harmony with the world around them. The weekend and school-holiday residential 'discovery courses' allow families to take part in activities such as nature-based sports (canoeing, tree-climbing and hiking) and study biodiversity and sustainability (how to make your house more eco-friendly, and so on). There's also a course for kids aged 7–13 and their grandparents, and another in which children and parents hang out with the park's animal-keepers.

Accommodation is youth-hostel style, with meals in the park's panoramic restaurant utilising local produce (often organic/Fair Trade) and crêpes. Prices are reasonable—around 149€ per child and 178€ per adult for two days and nights, with all meals (not drinks), unlimited access to the animal park and botanical garden, and mountain-bike use.

In 2010 the Parc became home to the second Parcabout treetop adventure course (p. 131).

Time from half a day. *Open* early Feb–early Apr and early Oct–mid-Nov daily 1.30–4pm; early Apr–early July Mon–Fri 10am–5pm, Sat and Sun 10am–5.30pm; early July–early Sept daily 10am–6pm; early Sept–early Oct daily 10am–5pm; last admission 90 minutes before closing. *Admission* 13€ adults, 8.50€ child 4–12. *Amenities* 🍷 🍴 🅿 🛖 ⋀ 🍴 🛍 ♿

Reserve Naturelle Marais de Séné FIND ALL AGES

Near Séné; 📞 *02 97 66 92 76; www.reservedesene.com. 4.5km (3miles) from Vannes on D199.*

This tranquil spot on the southern edge of the Golfe du Morbihan (p. 112), has a Nature Centre where you can learn all about the local birdlife—borrow a pair of binoculars and walk the new 3.8km (2.4 mile) circuit (buggy and wheelchair accessible) around marshland, dotted with five observatories (there are another three for those prepared to walk a bit further). Ask about special events, including nature walks in the area.

Time 2hrs. *Open* Feb and Mar daily 2–6pm; Apr–June daily 2–7pm; July and Aug daily 10am–1pm and 2–7pm. *Admission* 5€ adult, 2.50€ child 7–17, 12€ family. *Amenities* Ⓥ ♿

Zoo de Pont-Scorff ALL AGES

Pont-Scorff; 📞 *02 97 32 60 86; www.zoo-pont-scorff.com. 14km (9 miles) north of Lorient on D6.*

Out-of-the-way but expectedly huge, this zoo has hilly (if attractive and flower-filled) grounds crossed by steep, winding pathways leading around to the 120 or so species (buggy-pushers and toddlers with easily tired legs beware), including elephants, big cats, zebras and rhinos. Enclosures tend to be on the small side, though some imagination has gone into their design—there are Moorish buildings, for instance, for the friendly giraffes who stroll over to eat popcorn from your hands. Other

A giraffe at the Zoo de Pont-Scorff

highlights are an area where you have to identify the animal dung used to fertilise certain plants, and a farm enclosure set around an island of monkeys, with tame ducks and sheep. There are good daily shows plus refreshment stops, shops and baby-changing facilities.

Time about 4hrs. **Open** daily 9.30am–5pm. **Admission** 16€ adult, 10.50€ child 3–11. **Amenities** 🍷 📷 🍺 🅿️ 🎠 🧺 🍴 💼 ♿

Best Beaches

Beach resorts in the Morbihan listed as 'Stations Familles' by Sensations Bretagne (p. 57) are as follows: **Carnac, Quiberon, Arzon/Port Crouesty/Port Navalo**, and **Pénestin**. All host **Festival Place aux Mômes** (p. 57) events in the school holidays. See also the Fun Days Out section (p. 107) for family-friendly beaches on the islands of the Morbihan.

Note that the southern part of the **Lac de Guerlédan** (p. 172) is in the Morbihan.

Carnac-Plage ★

15km (9 miles) southwest of Auray on D186. For tourist office, see p. 147.

Though world-famous for its Neolithic megaliths (p. 107), Carnac also has its own sheltered beach resort backed by pine woods. Family-friendly amenities there include **kids' clubs** on the five beaches and a great **yacht club** (📞 *02 97 52 10 98*, *www.yccarnac.com*) running various introductory courses for all ages, including a 2hr family starter sailing lesson (38€ per person), sailing tours of Quiberon bay (29€ per person) and diving **AGE 8 & UP**. The **thalasso therapy centre** (*www.thalasso-carnac.com*), has accommodation in several family-oriented residences/hotel (p. 147) and, in summer (July–early Sept, Thurs from 6pm), **Nocturnes** evening markets with local produce and crafts, Breton music and a *fest noz* (p. 16).

If you can drag yourself away from the beach, Carnac's charming upper town, **Carnac-Ville**, is well worth a stroll.

> **INSIDER TIP** ›
>
> It's generally cheaper to eat up in Carnac-Ville. **Maison Chevillard** (Rue du Tumulus, ☎02 97 53 05 56) is an excellent bakery and patisserie offering sandwiches, croques, pizzas and pastries to take away or enjoy in its tea-room. **Crêperie de la Pompe** (Place de la Chapelle, ☎02 97 52 07 78) serves good crêpes but also more substantial fare. The family-friendly **Hôtel Restaurant de la Marine** (Place de la Chapelle, ☎02 97 52 07 33), which has family rooms for up to five people, also offers a superb value lunchtime menu. If you do eat down by the sea, **Memes Tra** (Boulevard de la Plage, ☎02 97 52 26 87) is a buzzy brasserie that attracts lots of families; if you can't stay away from the beach, takeaway pizza and ice creams are available. Alternatively, there's a second (seasonal) branch of Maison Chevillard for takeaway sandwiches. For other places to stay and eat, see p. 135 and p. 140.

Grande Plage, Ile aux Moines
★ ★ FIND

For tourist office, see p. 102.

Follow the easy-to-miss 'Les Plages' sign after disembarking from your boat around the Golfe du Morbihan (p. 112) and follow the twisting little path (just about do-able with a buggy) past the 'Wood of Love' to reach this superb beach with its candy-striped bathing cabins in the Baie du Drehen. There are no facilities here, and the spot has a rather wild feel—you'll find lots of seaweed and all kinds of shells, plus, if you're lucky, starfish and live crabs too (bring a net if you want to hook some supper). The island does attract a lot of tourists in high summer, so come off-peak to make the best of this charming spot.

If you don't bring a picnic, the **Hôtel San Francisco** (p. 141) is the island's best place to eat. If you're just looking for snacky fare, **Chez Jeannette**, back by the boat jetty, offers good sandwiches, panini, waffles and Breton and Italian ice creams and sorbets at very fair prices given its location, or there's **L'Ilot Gourmand** (☎02 97 26 35 62) a little further along the harbour at Rue Benoni Praud, for grills and crêpes.

Grande Plage, Quiberon
★ ★ ★

For tourist office, see p. 103.

Quiberon is off the beaten track at the top of its long peninsula. Superbly child-friendly, with swathes of impeccably clean, pale silver sand interspersed with rockpools for kids to dabble in and backed by a long promenade affording wonderful views across to Belle–Ile (p. 110). It's rare to hear English spoken there, but it's popular with the French in summer, when entertainments include Festival Place aux Mômes (p. 57) and beach clubs for different ages. The seafront is lined by decent restaurants and ice cream parlours—**Le Colbri** (1 Boulevard Chanard, ☏02 97 30 49 98) café, brassiere, pizzeria and ice cream counter is a handy all-day option, while **Quai des Glaces** (1 Place Hoche) stands out for its vast choice of ice cream and sorbet flavours. Wander back across Place Hoche to find more amenities, including a merry-go-round and mini-golf course, the **Joué Club** toys/beach-gear shop (☏02 97 50 15 33), a good supermarket (Carrefour City) and several kid-friendly crêperies, some with play areas. A mini-train does the rounds of the town, while at the Pôle Artisanal Plein Ouest, **La Cour d'Orgères** (☏02 97 29 55 62, *www.confiture.net*) is a traditional jam manufacturer where you can see it being made as well as buy some of the scrumptious wares (which also include chocolate and caramel products, honey, mustards and various coastal items including fish soup and sea-salt).

For Quiberon's **Hôtel Bellevue** with its family-friendly restaurant, see p. 142.

Lac au Duc ★★ FIND

For Ploërmel tourist office, see p. 103.

Brittany's largest natural lake, stretching north from Ploërmel, offers beaches (supervised in high season), a mini-aquapark and watersports such as sailing, canoeing and water-skiing at the Club Nautique. The best time to come is for the annual countrywide Fête du Nautisme (p. 196). This being Brittany, the site is shrouded in

myths and legends—Welsh monk Saint Armel is said to have slain a dragon that lurked in the water's depths (you might learn more on an evening boat-trip with storytelling). You can fish at the reserve on the Lézonnet site, and there's a marked 'vélo promenade' bike-track that takes in surrounding villages (the Voie Verte from Questembert to Mauron— p. 131—passes by the lake).

For the Hôtel Le Roi d'Arthur right on the lake, see p. 146; there's also a campsite, **Camping du Lac** (☏02 97 74 01 22), with both pitches and mobile-home rental, a snack kiosk, and some shaded picnic tables beside a play area and table-tennis tables.

INSIDER TIP ⟫

Look out for the 30 species of hydrangea (blooming May–Oct) on the 3km Circuit des Hortensias that links with the larger path (16km) around the Lac au Duc, ranging in colour from mauve and blue and bright pink.

Plage de la Mine d'Or/Pénestin ★★

45km (28 miles) southeast of Vannes on D34. For tourist office, see p. 103.

The 3km (2 mile) beach and listed geological site of La Mine d'Or just south of the Vilaine estuary, unique in Europe, takes its name from a short-lived and unsuccessful gold mine here, but it's entirely apt—at sunset its sandstone and clay cliffs glow the colour of the precious metal. The Mine d'Or is part of a 25km (15½ mile) stretch of

Plage de la Mine d'Or

lovely coastline around Pénestin with pretty, safe, toddler-friendly beaches and wilder creeks, walking, mountain-biking and riding tracks. Nearby, find the **Maison de la Mytiliculture** (☎02 23 10 03 00; admission 3.60€ adults, 2.65€ child 7–12), a small mussel-farming museum in an old lighthouse (Pénestin is a good place for shellfishing on foot; the tourist office can provide guidelines and rules). There's a great hostel and campsite here, plus a small hotel; see p. 144.

Pénestin itself, a 'Station Famille', has new cycle-paths allowing families to bike between the beach and town and around the town in traffic-free safety. It also has a yachting school (☎02 99 90 32 50) offering tuition to adults and kids, as well as a Jardin des Mers crèche for younger kids, a skate park, good markets (Sunday, plus Wednesday in high season), and great childrenswear at Framboise et Chocolate (15 Rue de l'Eglise, ☎02 99 90 31 54).

INSIDER TIP ⟩⟩

If you don't bring your own picnic to the Mine d'Or, stop by at **Le Caprice** (☎02 99 90 45 76) a few seconds' stroll from the car park on Rue de la Plage, for a picnic basket, or home-made pizzas, hot panini, filled baguettes, ice creams, and bottles of ice-cold Breton cider. There are also a couple of small shops selling beach toys and the like.

Museums

For the **Musée de Prehistorie J. Miln−Z. le Rouzic** about Carnac's megaliths, see p. 107. For Lorient's **Tour Davis** and **La Flore** submarine museums, see p. 106.

See also the **Towns & Cities** section (p. 105) for small municipal museums.

Le Cartopole ★ AGE 7 & UP

Bibliothèque Municipale, Rue d'Auray; ☎*02 97 51 15 14; http://www.cartolis.org/contact.php. 34km (21 miles) northeast of Lorient on D768.*

At any one time, this exhibition space in a town library displays around 2,000 postcards in rooms designed to resemble an early 20th-century local village. Part of a collection of around 60,000 belonging to the Conservatoire Régional de la Carte Postale, they provide a wonderful insight into traditional and modern Brittany and the art form as a whole. In the section on the Morbihan, have fun identifying sights you've been to—perhaps the Grand Menhir Brisé (p. 109) or the resort of Carnac (p. 121). A room on unusual postcards includes transparent versions of some with optical illusions (a few are rather risqué). A multimedia area lets you zoom in on a huge choice of cards on its database, often revealing unexpected details.

Time 1hr. *Open* mid-June and mid-Sept daily 10am–12.30pm and 2–6pm; July and Aug daily 10am–12.30pm and 2–7pm; mid-Sept–mid-Nov Wed, Thurs, Sat and Sun 2–6pm. *Admission* 5€ adult, 2.50€ child 8–15. *Amenities* 🅿 ♿

Cité de la Voile Eric Tabarly
⭐ AGE 3 & UP

Base des Sous-Marins de Keroman, Lorient; Cité de la Voile: 📞 02 97 65 45 23; *www.citevoile-tabarly.com.*

This futuristic-looking museum dedicated to the memory of the famous distance racer and to sailing in general opened beside Lorient's monstrous former Nazi submarine base (p. 106) in 2008. As befits the architecture, it's a hands-on modern attraction, with the themes of sailing,

boat-building and navigation explored through all manner of simulators, gadgets, contraptions and moving imagery that your kids will enjoy trying out. Those with kids aged 7 and up can also pay extra to go out in the Rade de Lorient on an actual boat; younger kids will be happy with the model boats to sail. There's a rather grown-up restaurant and a snack bar, plus a good gift shop with a fun selection of toys and books, including the sea-related children's books of Philip Plisson (p. 132).

Time 2hrs. *Open* school holidays daily 10am–6pm; Feb, March, Nov and Dec Tues–Sun 10am–6pm; May, June, Sept and Oct Mon 2–6pm, Tues–Sun 10am–6pm; July and Aug daily 10am–7pm. *Admission* 11.50€ adult, 8.40€ child 5–17, 37.50€ family ticket (2+2). Boat trip (Apr–Sept weather permitting) 13€ adult, 11€ child over 7, 42€ family. *Amenities* 🍸 ☕ 🅿 🍽 🛍 ♿

> **INSIDER TIP** ››
> Get combined tickets to the Cité de la Voile plus all venues at Lorient's former submarine base (p. 106) for a thought-provoking family day out.

Moulin à Papier de Pen-Mur AGE 7 & UP

Muzillac; 📞 02 97 41 43 79; *www.moulin-pen-mur.com. 25km (15.5 miles) southeast of Vannes on D765.*

This restored 15th-century lakeside mill makes paper according to traditional techniques, just as it did in the 1940s, before it was abandoned; a 1hr French-language guided tour of the workshops, followed by practical demonstrations and a visit to the exhibition room tells you all about it.

Time 2hrs. **Open** July and Aug Mon–Fri 10am–12.30 (last tour 11am) and 2.30–7pm (last tour 6pm), Sat, Sun 2.30-7pm (last tour 6pm). **Admission** 6€ adult, 4€ child 4–17. **Amenities** 🅿 🛍 ♿

INSIDER TIP

The Moulin à Papier's shop is a great place for reproductions of quirky old postcards (from a choice of nearly 400,000), plus other paper-based crafts.

Musée des Châteaux en Allumettes AGE 4 & UP

12 Rue du calvaire, Bizole; 📞02 97 43 03 20; http://armel.caro.free.fr/. 8km (5 miles) east of Vannes on D104.

The result of one man's obsession over the last quarter-century, this collection of scale models of some of France's most famous castles and other monuments built from matches counts close to 30 works, each of which takes about a year to complete. Among them you may recognise the nearby Château de Josselin (p. 105), which consists of 26,600 matches, and the Mont-St. Michel (p. 68). There are even buildings from further afield, such as Bavaria's famous Schloss Neuschwanstein. The creator, or sometimes his wife, leads the free guided tours (French only).

Time 1hr. **Open** May–Oct Mon and Tues 2–7pm, Wed–Sun 9am–noon and 2–7pm. **Admission** free. **Amenities** ♿

Musée de la Résistance Bretonne AGE 3 & UP

Les Hardys Béhelec, St. Marcel; 📞02 97 75 16 90; www.resistance-bretonne.com. 37km (23 miles) northeast of Vannes on N166.

The area around St. Marcel was well suited to Allied and French Resistance parachuting expeditions due to its wooded scrubland—easy to land on and hide in—and a famous battle took place on this spot in June 1944. Over July and August on weekdays, you can take a guided tour of the terrain in an old US army vehicle. The wooded park also has space to run around in and a kids' play area, plus space for picnicking and a crêperie/bar. Inside, the museum contains various hands-on displays plus a re-created shopping street under Occupation.

Time about 2hrs. **Open** mid-June–mid-Sept daily 10am–7pm; mid-Sept–Nov and Feb–mid-June Wed–Mon 10am–noon and 2–6pm. **Admission** museum 7.20€ adult, 5.70€) child 5–16. **Amenities** 🍷 ☕ 🅿 🛖 ⛰ 🍽 🛍 ♿

La Thalassa AGE 4 & UP

Quai de Rohan (Port de Plaisance), Lorient; 📞02 97 35 13 00; www.la-thalassa.fr.

Not a seawater spa but an 'oceanology discovery centre', La Thalassa is set partly inside a 67m (220ft) ship that covered the equivalent of 38 trips around the world over 252 missions to gather scientific data on fishing and the conservation of fish stocks. Inside the centre find models of Atlantic fish species, sections conserved as they were to give you a flavour of life on board, and displays on fishing techniques and marine biology, some of them hands-on. After looking round the boat, hop back on land to see displays on

Musée de la Résistance Bretonne

the role of Lorient (p. 106) as France's second-largest fishing port, plus temporary exhibitions.

Time 2hrs. **Open** *July and Aug daily 10am–7pm; May, June and Sept Mon, Sat and Sun 2–6pm, Tues–Fri 9.30am–12.30pm and 2–6pm; French Easter holidays and autumn half-term Mon–Fri 9.30am–12.30pm and 2–6pm, Sat and Sun 2–6pm. Last Admission 90mins before closing time.* **Admission** *6.90€ adult, 5.30€ child 5–17, 20.30€ family ticket (2+2).* **Amenities**

L'Univers du Poète Ferrailleur ★ AGE 3 & UP

La Ville Stéphant, Lizio; ☎ *02 97 74 97 94; www.poeteferrailleur.com. 20km (12.5 miles) southeast of Ploërmel on D174.*

Another extraordinary labour of love, this little world of animated, musical and aquatic sculptures, automats and kinetic machines was created from scrap metal objects over nearly two decades by a filmmaker whose imagination is clearly on the wild side. Visitors can bring the contraptions to life by pressing buttons, pedalling and turning handles— kids are naturally in their element. If you don't want to break the spell, there are two 20-minute films to watch: *Bricoleur de Lune* ('Moon Maker'), about a child so fascinated by a carousel he decides he wants to make one, and *Le Secret de Mermoz*, about an outsider whose meeting with a little girl reawakens his dreams of becoming a pilot. On a more sober note, there's a 'maison écologique' here too, demonstrating the use of renewable energy in homes.

Time 2hrs. **Open** *July and Aug daily 10.30am–7pm; mid-Sept daily 2–6pm; early Apr–June and mid-Sept–Oct Sun and hols 2–6pm.* **Admission** *6€ adult, 5€ child 4–14 (3rd child in family free).* **Amenities**

Parks & Gardens

For the modern sculpture garden and botanical trail at the **Domaine de Kerguéhennec**, see p. 111. For the dinosaur-inhabited **Parc de Préhistoire de Bretagne**, see p. 115.

Parc Aquanature de Stérou ★★ ALL AGES

Priziac; ☎ *02 97 34 63 84; www.parc-aquanature.com. 35km (22 miles) northwest of Lorient on D132.*

Nearly 150 red and fallow deer roam this 70 hectare (174 acre) nature park spread across six valleys and boasting three waterfalls. You'll share their sense of freedom as you choose from the huge range of activities, which include a nature school with school-holiday courses for children 4 to 14, five walking circuits covering 1 to 15km (½–9 mile), horse rides, pony and trap rides (in high season), treasure hunts and half an hour 'Breton safaris' in a 4x4 vehicle. There's also a mill with an aquarium, two legend-shrouded sites, the Trou du Biniou and Clos des Roches de l'Aër, fishing and displays on local plants and animals. You can picnic here, or there's a restaurant with local products such as deer terrine or stew (maybe a bit close to home for some), plus a two to four person and a six to eight person gîte. On-site activities run by third parties include kayaking, karting, archery and mini-golf.

Time half to 1 day. **Open** Apr–Oct daily 11am–7pm. **Admission** (including Breton safari) 9€ adult, 5.50€ child 4–12. **Amenities** 🅿 🎍 ¶¶¶ Ⓥ ♿

> **INSIDER TIP** ▶
> October can be a surprisingly good time to visit Parc Aquanature, for the stags' autumnal rut.

Tropical Parc ★ FIND ALL AGES

Laugarel, Saint Jacut Les Pins; ☎ *02 99 71 91 98; www.tropical-parc. com. 50km east of Vannes on D14.*

This park will transport you to more exotic climes, if only for half a day or so, with its hothouses full of banana trees, orchids, cacao and carnivorous plants, bonsai trees, giant cacti and other fabulous flora from around the world. They're set in the midst of several equally exotic gardens: Thai (complete with Buddha statues and pagodas, lanterns, carp and a 'house of music' with Far-eastern percussion instruments), Mexican, African, rose, and water. Completing the picture is a small zoo with free-roaming kangaroos, dwarf goats, peacocks, Vietnamese potbellied pigs, parrots and more (some of whom feature in daily shows in summertime), and a little museum of minerals.

Time half a day. **Open** early Apr–June, Sept–late Oct daily 10am–noon and 2–7pm; July, Aug and public hols daily 10am–7pm. **Admission** 11.50€ adult, 5.80€ child 4–10. **Amenities** 🍷 ☕ 🎍 🛍 ♿

For Active Families

See also **Fun Days Out** (p. 107–p. 116) and **Best Beaches** (p. 121–p. 124).

Centre Nautique de Kerguelen ★ AGE 4 & UP

Parc Océanique, Larmor-Plage; ☎ *02 97 33 77 78; www.sellor-nautisme.fr. 6km (4 miles) south of Lorient on D152.*

Run by a firm with an excellent reputation for watersports and diving tuition at its seven bases, this year-round centre leads canoeing trips on local rivers or on the sea, sailing in the Rade de Lorient and diving around the Ile de Groix (p. 113). Set in a

Rainy Days: Indoor Activities in the Morbihan

When rain strikes in the Morbihan and you've exhausted the *département's* many interesting museums, there are several appealing options:

Aquatic Club, Vannes. See p. 117.

Bowling du Lac (1 Rue du Lac, Ploërmel, ☏*02 97 72 03 82*) *www.bowlingdulac.fr*). An inland bowling club, with other games such as billiards and table football, plus a family-friendly restaurant. There's a cinema, Cinélac (*www.cinelac.fr*) right next door, showing films mainly dubbed into French.

Cinéville (*www.cineville.fr*)—2 cinemas in Vannes (12bis Rue Alexandre Le Pontois, ☏*08 92 70 21 31*, and Rue Aristide Boucicaut in Parc Lann, ☏*08 92 70 21 31*) and one in Lorient (Bd Marechal Joffre, ☏*08 92 70 21 31*) showing films for adults and kids (most of the latter are dubbed rather than *version originale*, unfortunately). For the Atlanville restaurant village with play area near Vannes' Parc Lann cinema, see p. 136.

Océanis (Bd François Mitterrand, Ploemeur, ☏*02 97 86 41 00*, *www.ploemeur.com*)—an indoor water complex including water jets, a 57m slide and a paddling pool, plus family sessions each Saturday morning.

Le P'Tit Délire Kergo (Ploemel, ☏*02 97 56 73 51*, *www.parc-jeux-petit-delire.com*)—a leisure park with a covered section with lots of inflatables and a big softplay structure, not far north of Carnac.

Parc Super Bowl de Saint Avé (1 Rue Marcel Dassault, Saint Avé, ☏*02 97 60 62 89*, *www.superbowl-vannes.com*)—a family-oriented bowling club just a few minutes from Vannes.

Patinium (6 Rue Georges Caldray, Vannes, ☏*02 97 40 91 23*, *www.patinium.com*)—an all-year skating rink, with skate hire and free entry for non-skating parents or grandparents.

protected natural site with sandy beaches, it offers five-day 'Classes de Mer' for ages 8 and up, which include sailing and windsurfing tuition and 'nature discovery' outings—explorations of the seashore and a museum trip, perhaps to La Thalassa (p. 126) or the Ecomusée on Groix (p. 114). Accommodation and food can be provided in a neighbouring *residence*, or there are gîtes and campsites nearby (see p. 123 for a recommended campsite).

In the Easter and summer holidays, kids aged 4 to 5 can enrol in the Jardin des Mers week-long programme of shell-fishing, aquarium-making and other seaside activities, while 5 to 7 year olds can sign up for the Moussaillons programme of sailing tuition; maximum group size is six, meaning children are kept

Time Travel: The Nantes–Brest Canal

It may begin in the Loire-Atlantique (p. 148) and end in Finistère (p. 223), but this winding 360km (224 mile) chain of Napoléon-era canals and rivers—now a thriving tourist waterway—finds its central junction at Pontivy in the Morbihan. In whichever direction you choose to navigate it and by whatever means (foot, bike or houseboat), you'll discover ancient abbeys, medieval fortresses, granite villages, woods, wildflowers and hiking trails leading off into the local countryside. You can also canoe and fish at certain points.

Pontivy itself, a cheerful market town with narrow medieval streets and wide riverside promenades, is a good place to stop off to admire the 15th-century Château de Rohan, slowly being restored, and stay the night in the chic old-fashioned **Hôtel de l'Europe** (☎ **02 97 25 11 14, www.hotellerieurope.com**) with its triple and family rooms. You can also hire canoes to take out on the water. Other old towns worth a wander along the route include Josselin (p. 105) and Malestroit.

For Pontivy tourist office, see p. 103. For boat hire (with the need for a navigation licence, try **Nicols** (☎ **02 41 56 46 56, www.boat-renting-nicols.co.uk**), which has some models with a *piscinette* or mini-pool. Cycling-mad families should note that **Breton Bikes** (p. 37) has routes that use some of the Canal's towpaths; otherwise, local tourist offices will give advice on bike hire. The book *The Nantes–Brest Canal, a Brittany Guide* (Red Dog Guides) comes highly recommended.

on a very firm rein, and they need to bring snacks.

Time half a day. **Open** *all year.* **Fees:** *119€–122€ for five morning/afternoon Jardin de Mer or Moussaillons sessions.*

Parc Celt'Aventures
FIND **GREEN** **ALL AGES**

La Maison Neuve, Route du Menez Penvins, Sarzeau; ☎ *06 13 08 87 00;* **www.celtaventures.com***. 23km (14 miles) south of Vannes on D780.*

This treetop adventure park near the Château de Suscinio (p. 111) charms more than most, themed as it is on local legends, with course titles named after species of Breton gnome or fairy. Discover trails in the surrounding 'magic forest' on different ecological themes, a Village à Lutins with tots' adventure course featuring huts on stilts and a ball pool, 'elastico-trampolines', hammocks in which to relax and dream, a snack bar and a giant communal picnic table, the Table des Druides.

Time half to 1 day. **Open** *Easter–early Nov daily 10am–7pm; outside school holidays Wed, Sat and Sun 10am–7pm.* **Admission** *3€ adults, free under 3; treetop courses 17€ adults, 3€ child 5–6, 7€ child 7–10, 12€ child 11–15. A 5% discount for families of 5 or more is offered.* **Amenities** ⛾ ☕ 🅿 ⛺

Parcabout Chien Noir

★ **FIND** AGE 3 & UP

Bois du Grao, Ile de Groix; ☎*02 97 86 57 61; www.parcabout.fr.*

Another treetop adventure course offering an original spin on the trend—instead of walkways and zipwires between trees, it has stringed up vast fishing nets that you can crawl about on more freely, several metres above the ground. Though it's open to all, some younger kids and even adults with a fear of heights may find it a little scary. For a truly far-out experience, book one of the little 'nests'—wood and canvas spheres in the trees/nets, which you can sleep in (up to two adults and two small children). Breakfast is served in Parcabout's on-site bistro (otherwise serving Thai cuisine and sometimes hosting live music).

At the time of writing, a second Parcabout had just been installed in the Parc de Branferé (p. 119).

Time half a day or more. **Open** *July–Sept and all school hols daily 10am–7pm; Apr–June and Oct Wed, Sat and Sun 10am–7pm.* **Admission** *free to park; nets (all day) 19€ adult, 14€ child 12–17, 11€ child 4–11, 6€ child under 4, family ticket for 4 or more at 10% discount. Nest 69€ per night, breakfast 8€pp.* **Amenities** 🅿 ⑪

INSIDER TIP »

Other treetop adventure courses in the Morbihan, both offering courses for ages 2 and up, are **Fôret Adrenaline** (☎ *02 90 84 00 20, www.foretadrenaline. com*) at Carnac, and **Camors Adventure Forest** (☎ *02 97 39 28 69, www.camors-adventure-forest.com*) at Camors 38km (24 miles) inland of Lorient.

Les Passagers du Vent

★ ★ **FIND** AGE 7 & UP

Centre Les Dunes and (summer only) Parking du Mané Guen, Plouharnel; ☎ *02 97 52 40 60; www.aeroplage. com. 3km (2 miles) northwest of Carnac on D781.*

Whether you're a total novice or have some experience on a char à voile or a *planche* de surf, this club will get you sand-yachting or surfing at the exhilarating Grande Plage of Plouharnel in no time. Prices start at 18€ for a 1hr sand-yachting lesson, including all equipment, but week-long and weekend courses are available, as well as multi-activity courses combining sand-yachting and surfing. Accompanied children can learn to sand-yacht from age 8, on special Smarty yachts, as long as they're not afraid of wind or speed, and to surf from age 7. Note that Plouharnel's youth hostel (*www.fuaj. org*) offers great-value summer packages including sand-yachting and/or surfing.

Time 1hr to a week. **Open** *Year-round, by reservation.* **Fees** *call or check website.*

Voie Verte Questembert-Mauron ★ ★ ALL AGES

www.voiesvertes.com

The main 'Green Way' cycle track (p. 54) in the Morbiban is suitable for all levels of abilities. Taking you about 50km through beautiful wooded countryside from the far northeast of the department almost as far as the Golfe du Morbihan (p. 112), it passes many charming villages

Shopping in The Morbihan

The six branches of **Comptoir de la Mer** (p. 176) in the département include Lorient (p. 106), Vannes (p. 107), Quiberon (p. 122) and Belle-Ile (p. 110). Vannes also has **Escale Marin** (Rue Gontran Bienvenu, Zone du Prat, ☎ *02 97 47 86 63*) for both practical sailing and watersports attire and nautical fashion, plus fishing gear; there's a second branch in Muzillac. For childrenswear in nautical hues and patterns, head for **Elle Est Où La Mer?** with branches in Port du Crouesty (p. 144; 6 Quai des Cabestans, ☎ *02 97 49 46 05*) and overlooking the Grande Plage at Quiberon (p. 122; 6 bis Boulevard Chanard, ☎ *02 97 30 30 60*). The range is also sold at Boutique Coudémail in Vannes (7 Rue St. Salomon, ☎ *02 97 42 74 75*).

If you've fallen in love with the local landscape, make a beeline for **Galerie Plisson** in La Trinité-sur-Mer (☎ *02 97 30 15 15, www. plisson.com*), where you can buy the works of Philip Plisson, world-renowned for his seascape photographs, taken all over the world but particularly in Brittany (he moved to La Trinité at the age of 4), in a range of formats, from calendars to giant 2m posters. Plisson has also co-written several children's books in French, available here: *Les bateaux racontés aux enfants*, *Les phares racontés aux enfants*, *La mer racontée aux enfants* and *La pêche racontée aux enfants*, on boats, lighthouses, sea and fishing respectively. There's also a Plisson showroom nearby at Crac'h, and another Galerie in St. Malo in the Ille-et-Vilaine (p. 64), plus Pêcheur d'Images stores selling Plisson images in Lorient and Port du Crouesty.

Other local goodies are the famous biscuit and cakes made by the **Biscuiterie La Trinitaine** (☎ *02 97 55 02 04, (www.latrinitaine. com*), based at St. Philibert near Vannes but with shops in Vannes itself, Lorient, La Trinité-sur-Mer and several other points in the Morbihan, as well as further afield. Try the speciality Breton butter biscuits—*galettes*, *palets* and 'cigarettes'—plus traditional Breton madeleines. Some are individually wrapped, making them perfect for picnics or car journeys; others make great gifts in their limited-edition tins. You'll also find other Breton specialities: jam, caramels, cider and liqueurs, fish soup, salt, crêpes and earthenware.

where you can stop off for a meal or to spend the night. Note that at its northeastern end, it joins up with other Voies Vertes taking you as far as St. Malo (p. 61) in the Ille-et-Vilaine. See the website for bike-hire/repair and eating/sleeping/sightseeing recommendations en route.

Time *several days.*

For more local gourmet treats, seek out **La Maison d'Armorine** (*02 97 50 24 25*, ***www.maison-amorine.com***), purveyor of salted-butter caramels and *niniches* (lollipops). It has stores in Carnac, Le Palais (Belle-Ile), and Quiberon, and also a visitors' centre at its factory in Quiberon, where you can learn about the making of sweets and even sample a few.

Foodies should also head for **Rochefort en Terre**, a pretty inland village listed as Petite Cité de Caractère, with lots of traditional food shops, tea-rooms, crêperies and restaurants, and a very good market on Wednesday and Saturday afternoons. Among the shops are **Le Rucher Fleuri** (*02 97 43 35 78*) for honey and products made from honey, including *chouchenn* (p. 236), and ginger-bread, and Breton galettes, **Le Puits des Gourmandises** (*02 97 43 35 78*) for hand-made biscuits such as *kouign amann* and *sablé breton*, plus *far breton*, and **L'Art Gourmand** (*02 97 43 46 69*) for old-fashioned chocolates preserved fruits, cakes and ice creams, some of which you can sample in its *salon de thé*. Rochefort also has lots of craft shops and galleries, selling everything from hand-made candles to figurines of *korrigans* and other figures from Breton legend. One of the best is **L'Orée de Bois** (*02 97 43 36 12*), selling hand-crafted wooden toy, games and decorative items for kids' bedrooms.

Other **markets** in the Morbihan include:

Auray	Mon morning, plus organic market Thurs evening.
Carnac	Wed and Sun morning.
La Gacilly	Sat morning.
La Roche-Bernard	Thurs morning.
Malestroit	Thurs morning.
Muzillac	Fri morning.
Questembert	Mon morning and Wed afternoon.
Quiberon	Sat morning.
Vannes	Wed and Sat morning.

If you need English-language books and magazines, or other media items, your best bet is **Fnac** (p. 60), with branches in Lorient and Vannes.

FAMILY-FRIENDLY DINING

As elsewhere in Brittany, eating out in the Morbihan is usually a great pleasure, especially beside the sea. Look out for flat Quiberon Bay oysters and sardines grilled with butter or marinated and served in salads, and, inland (but served everywhere), the famed *andouille de Guémené* (pork and chitterling sausage). Parents should also try out the local beer—Morgat, brewed on Belle-Ile (p. 110).

Lorient & Around

This is not the best area for eating—if you're just visiting the former submarine base at Lorient, it's best to stick to the snack bar or restaurant at the **Cité de la Voile Eric Tabarly** (p. 125).

EXPENSIVE

Le Vivier ★

9 Route de Beg-Er-Vir, Lomener; (02 97 82 99 60; www.levivier-lomener. com. 9.5km (6 miles) southwest of Lorient on D152.

Set on a rocky outcrop with views over the sea to Groix (p. 113), this gastronomic restaurant with rooms (89€–116€, extra beds 15€) has long been fêted for its seafood, served in a light-flooded dining room that makes you feel as if the waves are lapping at your feet. Adventurous younger diners are welcomed with a great value 11.50€ 'gourmet discovery' menu consisting of a starter, a main course (except lobster) and a dessert from the *à la carte* menu, all in smaller portions. Tempting dishes for kids might include an *entrée* of crab and artichoke cake, a main of cod and shellfish stew, and a dessert of banana and coconut tart. You, meanwhile, might be tempted to blow the budget on the 75€ five-course tasting menu, which includes lobster and scallop

tartare, Groix abalone with cider, and Grand Marnier soufflé.

Speaking good French is an asset here, as the place is well off the tourist trail.

Open *daily noon–2.30pm and 7–10pm. Closed late Dec–early Jan.* **Main course** *16€–48.50€.* **Amenities** 🖵 🛆 ⌣

MODERATE

There's a branch of **Hippopotamus** (p. 136) near Lorient, at Rue Dominique Arago in Lanester (02 97 89 32 40).

La Casa Varadero ★

19 Bd Franchet d'Esperey, Lorient; (02 97 64 20 77.

This bright and cheerful Italian with colourful decor, attracts locals of all ages and film-goers from nearby Cinéville (p. 129) for the best pizzas in Lorient (including a monthly special), plus authentic main-course dishes such as *saltimbocca* veal escalope (breaded, with mozzarella and *proscuitto*), carpaccio of beef, pasta dishes and some decent risottos. Staff, though invariably rushed off their feet, are charming. There's a *menu bambino* for under-10s (8.40€), with mini tomato, ham and cheese pizza, *steak haché* or high-quality ham with home-made fries or pasta, and two scoops of ice cream or house chocolate mousse, plus drinks. Prices are very fair given the quality.

Open *Mon–Thurs noon–2pm and 7–10.30pm, Fri and Sat noon–2pm and 7–11.30pm, Sun 7–10.30pm.* **Main course** *6€–15€.* **Amenities** 🖵 🛆 ⌣

O Thon Bleu ★ ★ FIND

52 Rue du Géneral de Gaulle, Groix (Le Bourg), Ile de Groix; 02 97 86 58 86.

The 'Blue Tuna' brasserie is worth seeking out—serving throughout the day, it offers a wide range of foods to suit all moods, from seafood specialities to grilled meats and pizzas, and also doubles as a tea room and a cocktail bar, with free Wi-Fi. The bright, nautically decorated dining room with its artworks opens out onto a large terrace, heated in winter and a sun-trap in summer (when live concerts take place).

Open *daily 10am–11pm, closed Oct–Mar.* **Main course** *5€–10 €.* **Amenities**

INSIDER TIP

If O Thon Bleu is packed out (it's by far the best place on Groix), **Le Safran** 02 97 86 58 72 at Place de l'Eglise offers pizzas, crêpes and galettes, and ice creams, plus colouring materials for kids.

Vannes & the Golfe du Morbihan

This is beach-holiday central, so it's here that you'll find the greatest concentration of family-friendly eateries in the Morbihan, especially beachfront brasseries serving flexible menus throughout the day.

Le Gavrinis ★ ★

1 Rue de l'Île Gavrinis, Baden; 02 97 57 00 82; www.gavrinis.com. 13km (8 miles) west of Vannes on D101.

The kind of restaurant that some customers have felt moved to describe as no less than the gastronomic highlight of their life, Le Gavrinis is an oasis of muted chic behind an ugly modern façade, offering regional specialities with a Mediterranean or Asian twist, with the emphasis on seafood. Younger diners (under 12) get a 14.50€ menu offering fish stew with potatoes or seasonal vegetables, followed by ice cream or sorbet, or they can opt for a reduced-price version of the Menu Terroir (20€/full price 27€), which might include warm sardine tart then *confite* of farm-bred pork with crushed potatoes, followed by jasmine *crème brulée* with gingerbread.

The restaurant is part of a hotel with 18 restful double rooms costing 52€–120€, with a cot provided free or an extra bed for 20€. If you opt for half-board, kids get a 50% reduction.

Open *daily 12.15–1.30pm, 7.15–9.30pm. Closed 3–28 Jan.* **Set menus** *16€ (lunch only)–44€.* **Amenities**

There's a second **A L'Aise Breizh Café** (p. 228) overlooking Vannes's yachting marina, with a fabulous terrace. For family-friendly eateries in **Carnac-Plage** and **Carnac-Ville,** see p. 122; for La Trinité-sur–Mer, see p. 140; for **Quiberon,** see p. 122; for **Port du Crouesty,** see p. 137.

Atlanville FIND

Rue Jacques Rueff, Vannes; www. atlanville.fr.

Vannes' Parc Lann *zone commerciale* may not be the most glamorous of destinations, but if you're here to shop or catch a movie at Cinéville (p. 129), it's worth knowing about this restaurant village with its covered, secure play area for kids. The most child-friendly offerings are a branch of the France-wide grill specialist **Hippopotamus** (*02 97 46 27 00, www.hippopotamus.fr*), and **Brooklyn Café** (*02 97 27 15*), serving snacky fare and coffees and hosting occasional family events such as Easter egg drawing contests and face-painting workshops. There's also **Kergalette** (*02 97 46 27 12*) for crêpes and galettes made from organic flour, **Tablapizza** (*02 97 46 27 03*), an Italian garnering mixed reviews, and **La Taverne du Maître Kanter** (*02 97 46 27 06*), part of a nationwide Alsatian brasserie chain serving average food amidst rather cheesy decors. For big-screen sports fans, **Le Skellig** (*02 97 46 27 09*) is an Irish pub showing international football and rugby, plus live music on Saturday nights.

Open times and prices vary by restaurant. **Amenities** ⋀

Brasserie Edgar

19 Rue Daniel Gilard, Parc du Golfe, Vannes; 02 97 40 68 08.

Though part of a hotel chain (the Mercure at Vannes's leisure complex, including family rooms), this place strives for a 1930s Parisian brasserie feel. Some may find the overall effect a tad cheesy, but it's a welcoming spot for a family meal, perhaps a Sunday lunch. Portions are good and prices fair, with several *menus/formules* helping you to eat very economically. The under-12s menu (2/3 courses 7.50€/10.50€) offers up tomato salad or egg mayo, then Strasbourg sausage or ham with chips, or fish with rice, but there are also omelettes, tagliatelle carbonara and other reassuringly familiar dishes for kids dotted about the wide-ranging menu. Adults might choose brasserie classics such as *andouillette* or duck *magret*, more original creations or super-fresh seafood galore. The chips are superb, as are the main-course salads (including local lobster). Handily, Edgar also serves breakfast and operates as a day-long café and *salon de thé*. In summer, its spacious terrace comes into its own. Free Wi-Fi is available.

Open daily from 7am; lunch served noon–2.30pm, dinner 7–10pm (to 11pm Fri and Sat). **Main course** 7€–27€. **Amenities** 🔲 🎵 📶 ☕

Côte et Saveurs ★ FIND VALUE

8 Rue Pierre-René Rogue, Vannes; 02 97 47 21 94.

On a cobbled street with a wide choice of restaurants, this charming little corner site with its tiny terrace stands out for great prices, a very friendly welcome and exciting food. Its main attraction for families is that while parents (and adventurous older kids) can sample adult fare that might include oysters, *tartare d'andouille* (raw horsemeat sausage—not for everyone!), scallop casserole with turmeric, or even kangaroo marinated in green peppercorns, younger diners can feast on simpler dishes, including pizzas, or choose from a *menu enfant* (8.50€) featuring *steak haché* or ham with chips, ham and cheese pizza, or pollock, followed by ice cream and including a drink. Those with exuberant kids might find the space a little claustrophobic, while art-lovers should ask for a table upstairs.

Open Apr–Aug daily noon–2pm and 7–10pm (to 11pm Sat, Sun and school hols); Sept–Mar Thurs–Tues noon–2pm and 7–10pm. **Main course** 8€–16€. **Amenities** 🚻 ☕

INEXPENSIVE

Crêperie Bara-Breizh
★★★ FIND

35 Route de Penvins, St. Armel; ☎ 02 97 26 46 52. 16km (10 miles) south of Vannes on D780.

Awarded the quality label 'Crêperie Gourmande', Bara-Breizh on the Rhuys peninsula leading up to Port du Crouesty lures in families not only with its great galettes and crêpes but also with the extensive and enclosed outdoor play area where junior diners can run off steam as their parents enjoy an aperitif on the

terrace (book ahead to be sure of getting a place outside). Some of the best dishes—the 'Entre Terre et Mer' galette featuring scallops, Guéméné sausage and cider jelly, and the Mille Sabord with pear and almond jam, chocolate, and caramel ice cream—can be enjoyed as part of the Menu Gourmand, but everything here is good. Take pleasure in spotting unusual ingredients and combinations such as seaweed with smoked salmon or with Swiss charcuterie, goat's cheese and melon jam—let yourself be swayed to try something that challenges your boundaries. Kids get their own menu of ham and chips or a mini-galette with cheese and either ham or egg, followed by a Mini Milk ice cream or mini-crêpe with butter and sugar, chocolate or Nutella, plus a drink for 7.10€.

Open Tues noon–2pm, Thurs–Mon noon–2pm and 7–9pm (plus Tues eve in July and Aug). **Main course** 2.50€–14.20€. **Amenities** 🎆 🚻 🎪 ⚠ ☕

Crêperie Chez Renée ★★★

Route de Grand Village, Le Bourg, Bangor, Belle-Ile; ☎ 02 97 31 52 87.

Renée retired years ago, and Président Mitterrand, who used to fly over by helicopter for a simple buckwheat pancake in this charming traditional house, is no more. Yet this local institution keeps on and on, and if you come after 8pm you'll have to wait ages for a table. The galettes and crêpes—fine, crispy yet soft in the middle—make the wait worthwhile. The choice of fillings, from the simple to the elaborate, should please everyone, from fresh tomato compote, thick local bacon, and local cheese and honey (the latter a surprisingly winning combination) to banana and *crème fraîche* crêpe flambéed with rum. On a balmy evening, it's worth trying to get a table in the garden with the giant flowerpots, although you can't reserve these so it's a case of luck. The interior, which sparkles with fairylights, candles and a real fire, has a children's corner with books and toys on an old school desk.

Open *Apr–Sept daily noon–2pm and 7–9.30pm; Oct–Mar Sat and Sun noon–2pm and 7–9.30pm.* **Main course** *3.95€–10.50€.* **Amenities** 🍴 ✻ ↻

Inland Morbihan

It's harder but not impossible to find good child-friendly eateries.

MODERATE

Les Enfants Gat'thes ★ FIND

24 Rue Lafayette, La Gacilly; ☎ *02 99 08 23 01. 32km (19 miles) southeast of Ploërmel on D8.*

The name of this delightful tea-room and lunchtime restaurant (located in an old schoolhouse), is an untranslatable pun involving spoilt children and tea. On top of organic coffee, speciality brews, home-made pastries and ice creams, there are some inventive dishes on the menu, utilising less common seasonal and local vegetables. Both the dining room with its exposed stones and beams and the flower-filled

terrace are wonderful spots to relax, perhaps after a donkey trek with the nearby Clos du Tay (p. 117). On a chillier day, warm up with a hot chocolate scented with vanilla, hazelnut or caramel; on a hot day, there's iced chocolate and delicious home-made lemonades to refresh you. Lunch sees three adventurous daily menus to choose from, with kids under-11 invited to select three courses from the Menu du Jour for 8.40€.

Open *tea-room Thurs–Sun 2.30–6pm (plus Mon and Tues in high season); restaurant Oct–May Tues and Thurs–Sun 12.15–2.30pm (plus Mon rest of year, but may vary so call ahead to check).* **Set menus** *12€–35 €.* **Amenities** ☐ 🍴 ↻

> **INSIDER TIP** ⟩⟩
>
> La Gacilly is also home to the child-friendly **Végétarium** organic brasserie (☎ *02 99 08 35 84*; open June–mid-Sept), within an exhibition space dedicated to the botanical beauty products company Yves Rocher (Rocher himself, who died in 2009, was born in the town and was once also its mayor). Nearby you can also visit Rocher's botanical gardens and stay in his 'eco-hotel', La Grée des Landes, with its spa. Each year also sees an open-air summer photographic festival in La Gacilly.

Le Jardin des Saveurs ★ FIND

4 Rue des Francs Bourgeois, Ploërmel; ☎ *02 97 72 12 71.*

Easy to find in the heart of old Ploërmel by virtue of the tall metal sculptures of ants outside, the 'Garden of Flavours' really does pack a taste punch, serving as a traditional Breton restaurant (with the odd more exotic dish for good measure) and as a crêperie and pizzeria too—ideal for families who can't agree on what to eat! There's a great-value 8.90€ kids' menu, but younger diners will probably appreciate the wider scope of the various menus. Sample dishes include five-spice prawn brochettes, mussels in various guises (including in a curry and coconut milk sauce), the 'Seguin' galette (honey-roast goat's cheese, grilled pork and nuts) and even just plain steaks or pasta dishes. The dining room with its quirky log-cabin décor is a delight, but there's outdoor seating too.

Open July and Aug daily noon–2pm and 7–10pm; Sept–mid-Feb and early Mar–June Tues noon–2.30pm, Thurs–Mon noon–2.30pm and 7–10pm. **Main course** 2.90€–18.50€. **Amenities** ☐ 🎧 ♨

Pizzeria de Pont Kerran

While waiting for your food, you can challenge your kids to a game of Breton *boules*, table football, billiards or darts. Some evenings there's live music so the place can get a little raucous.

Open Wed–Mon noon–2pm and 7.30–10pm. **Main course** 5.50€–10.90 €. **Amenities** ▨

Crêperie des Forges ★ FIND

Moulin de Cadoret, Les Forges; ☏ 02 97 75 38 49. 12km (7.5 miles) north-west of Josselin on D778.

Worth visiting for its setting alone (an 18th-century mill beside the Brest-Nantes canal, with wooden floor and beams and a kids' corner), this crêperie serves up great pancakes made from batter created the old-fashioned way, by hand. Among the speciality galettes are 'Bord de Mer' ('Seaside', with scallops and leek fondue) and Grande Doudouille (Guémené sausage with onions, apples and *crème fraîche*) but you can also get salads in summer, steak or ham and *frites*, and various delicious fish soups. Crêpes worth singling

INEXPENSIVE

Bar–Pizzeria de Pont Kerran FIND

Kerspernen, near Languidic (road to Pluvigner); ☏ 02 97 65 58 33 24km. (15 miles) northeast of Lorient on D102.

On a middle-of-nowhere country lane inland of Lorient, this eaterie proves a popular stop-off for kids due to the giant shark's mouth that constitutes its entrance. Inside, find a quirky all-wood interior and a simple range of dishes from pizzas to steak or omelette with chips.

Best Picnic Spots

Aside the Morbihan's many glorious coastal beaches—among them the stunning Mine d'Or—the following are wonderful places to picnic:

Alignements de Carnac, p. 107.

Parc de Préhistoire de Bretagne, p. 115.

Parc Aquanaturee de Stérou, p. 127.

L'Odyssaum, p. 119.

Lac au Duc, p. 123.

Beside the Nantes–Brest Canal, p. 130.

out include Duchesse (pears, pear ice cream, home-made chocolate and grilled almonds). In fine weather you can sit on a terrace overlooking the canal, watching the barges float peacefully by.

Open July and Aug daily noon–10pm; Sept–June Wed–Sun noon–2pm and 7–10pm (plus Mon and Tues if public hol or eve of public hols). ***Main course*** *5€–11€.* ***Amenities*** 月 ❀ ↝

FAMILY-FRIENDLY ACCOMMODATION

Lorient & Around

You're unlikely to base yourself in this neck of the woods, with most good seaside accommodation clustered further south around Carnac and the Golfe du Morbihan.

If you do need to stop over in Lorient, your best bet is the **Hôtel Mercure** (☎ 02 97 21 35 73, *www.accorhotels.com*), part of a reliable chain, offering four family rooms, eight connecting rooms, or one extra bed per double room. Doubles start at 74€.

MODERATE

For **Le Vivier** hotel and restaurant at Lomener just under 10km (6 miles) west of Lorient, see p. 134.

INEXPENSIVE

Also at Lomener, Camping Qualité (p. 93) recommends **Camping Pen Palad** (☎ 02 97 82 94 56, *www.camping-pen-palud. com*), a peaceful seaside site with mobile homes and cottages, plus spaces for tents and caravans, plus a heated outdoor pool. The site is handy for the **Centre Nautique de Kerguelen** p. 124.

Vannes & the Golfe du Morbihan

MODERATE–EXPENSIVE

Le Lodge Kerisper ★ ★ ★ **FIND**

4 rue du Latz, La Trinité-sur-Mer; ☎ *02 97 52 88 56; www.lodge-kerisper.com. 12km (7.5 miles) southwest of Auray on D781.*

For parents who don't want to compromise on style, this intimate hotel in a renowned yachting town has a beautiful, if tiny, outdoor pool edged with decking,

Le Lodge Kerisper

floored bathrooms. Some rooms have clawfoot baths and coffee machines. Buffet breakfasts are served on the stilted veranda (15€; 8€ for children) or in your room (3€ extra). Staff will rustle up seafood platters on request, though there are plenty of places to eat within walking distance.

20 units. Rates 95€–155€, suite for four 160€–290€. Extra bed €40, or €25 for children 2–11. Cot free. Amenities ▼ 🍷 🖥 🚲 📷 🎒 🖼 📶 *In room* ☐ 🖊 📶

INSIDER TIP

Ask staff at Le Lodge Kerisper for their tips on the best local eateries with kids. Among the tried-and-tested options are the **Crêperie Saint François** (☎02 97 55 75 80) on the same street as the hotel, with a gorgeous garden bursting with blooms in which to enjoy its organic pancakes; the extremely welcoming **La Plancha** (8 Rue de Carnac, ☎02 97 55 71 63) with its grilled meats, fish and vegetables, and the slightly scruffy, boho-chic **Le Quai** (Cour des Quais, ☎02 97 55 80 26), offering seafood in traditional but also more eclectic guises (in a Moroccan stew, for instance).

loungers and parasols and equipped with games and waterwings; trendy 'beach hut' decor; a space for massages; and a baby-sitting service—though you may be happy to stay put once you've clocked the gorgeous zinc bar (open all day) and the library with its cosy hearth and stone walls. In fact, the charming couple who opened the place in 2005 had children very much in mind, having often been disappointed by hotels when travelling with their own. As a result, you'll also find beach games, waterproof coats and boots to borrow, children's books, and children's films to watch in your room.

Bikes (and child seats) can be hired here, and staff will organise outings, including sailing trips to nearby islands. Or you can simply doze in the old curate's garden beneath the fruit trees while the kids play. Rooms are tucked away and private, linked by a series of walkways and footbridges. Light and airy, they include three spacious suites with three or four beds, and four connecting rooms, with wooden

Le San Francisco ★ FIND

Le Port, Ile aux Moines; ☎02 97 26 31 52; www.le-sanfrancisco.com.

For those looking for an escape, this hotel on the Ile aux Moines, a few minutes' walk from the island's Grande Plage (p. 122) makes for a blissfully peaceful retreat provided you come out of high season. It offers only eight quite plain, wholly unostentatious rooms with a hint of maritime spirit; two can inter-connect, another is a good value attic room with a double bed and a lounge with two armchairs convertible into single beds, and there's also a double with one convertible armchair. The hotel's restaurant is the island's best place to eat, offering the freshest of local seafood including wild blue lobster and oysters, often cooked in quite original ways using spices or unusual ingredients such as Tunisian fig brandy. Kids' favourites include the huge langoustines served simply, with mayonnaise, and the home-made rice pudding with citrus jam. In fine weather you can spread out on the large terrace with its wonderful Gulf views to enjoy lunch or dinner, or just fruit or alcoholic cocktails and ice cream. Breakfast (10€; 8€ for kids aged 4–10) can also be taken on the terrace, or in the dining room or your own room. The hotel is closed from November to March.

8 units. **Rates** *85€–140, family room for 4 120€, connecting rooms 230€. Extra bed 10€.* **Amenities** ▼ ¶¶ *In room* ⬜

MODERATE

For the **Mercure** in Vannes, see p. 136.

Dihan

Kerganiet, Ploemel; ☎ *02 97 56 88 27;* **www.dihan-evasion.org.** *8km (5 miles) north of Carnac on D119.*

If you're looking for something leftfield, this spot near Carnac offers several interesting options: Mongolian yurts, a roulotte

(Romany caravan)—both inexpensive—and several treehouses. Mountain-bikes are available to hire (the hosts will give you info on local routes) or you can even take kite-surfing tuition with the owner. Parents can indulge in the sauna and even book a massage (including Shiatsu and Thai).

Breakfast (organic/local ingredients) is included—if you're in a treehouse, kids will love raising it up by pulley. Dinner can feature Breton, Mauritian or Indian specialities and is sometimes accompanied by live music/cabaret; otherwise, you can order a picnic basket in your accommodation, including a hot main course, or use the communal kitchen or BBQ. My sole gripe at Dihan is the late check-in time (5–7pm, or 6–7.30pm in high season).

11 units. **Rates** *treehouses 120€–140€, yurts 80€ –90€, roulotte 90€–100€, extra person under 16 30€, rooms 60€–80€.* **Amenities** ⚲ 🆚 ✕ ♨

INSIDER TIP ▶

With several older kids, you might consider getting them their own yurt or treehouse while you snuggle up in one of Dihan's three cosy B&B rooms (the most romantic is the snug lovers' lair of the Chambre Bihan) and order a bottle of champagne!

Hotel Bellevue ★ VALUE

Rue de Tiviec, Quiberon; ☎ *02 97 50 16 28;* **www.bellevuequiberon.com.** *18km (11 miles) south of Carnac on D768.*

This unpretentious, friendly, and relaxing little seaside hotel admittedly has some shabby elements but is a bargain given the outdoor pool and the close proximity (10-minute walk) to Quiberon's Grand Plage (p. 122; there's a smaller rocky beach on the doorstep). Rooms come in four categories, of which three include family rooms for three or four (some with separate bedrooms for kids, sharing a bathroom with parents). Most rooms also have a balcony or large decked terrace where you can eat a decent Continental breakfast (9.50€, children 3 and over 5€) if you wish (you can also sit by the pool in high season). There's a large, light-flooded but somewhat stuffy restaurant offering fancier food than you'd generally expect in this price category, including a decent kids' menu; at lunch you can get the dish of the day either in the dining room or beside the pool.

38 units. 60€–120€, family room for four 95€–123€. Extra bed 10€. Cot free. **Amenities** ▼ ☐ 🖼 🍽 **In room** ☐ ⏷ 📶

INSIDER TIP ❯❯

Staying at the Hôtel Bellevue is a good-value way of enjoying treatments at the well-reputed thalassotherapy centre of the Sofitel Thalassa (www.sofitel.com) a 20-minute walk away along the seafront.

Villa Mine Lann ★ FIND

Chemin de Mane Lann, Plouharnel; 📞 *02 97 58 31 99, www.villamane lann.com. 3km (2 miles) northwest of Carnac on D781.*

This remarkable B&B goes beyond the usual remit to offer luxury modern décor including contemporary artworks, flatscreen televisions, an outdoor pool and a Jacuzzi—things that will please parents who like their family accommodation to come with some style. The large pine-shaded grounds, meanwhile, mean that kids can lope around at will, as you enjoy the views of Quiberon bay, over a seafood platter and a bottle of wine if the mood takes you. You might also indulge in an in-room Shiatsu or Thai massage.

The six rooms all look out over the pool; one is a family room with a double bed and a bunkbed in an alcove (plus the possibility of adding an extra bed), another is a duplex with a main and a children's bedroom, two bathrooms, a kitchen, and two private terraces. The latter's normally available only by the week, but out of high season, short breaks of two or more nights might be available. The Villa is well-sited for learning to kite-surf (p. 142).

Rates 72€–110€, family room 72€–99€ (plus extra bed 10€), duplex 110€–130 € (min 2 nights) or 990€/wk in July and Aug (min booking 1wk). **Amenities** 🧖 🖼. *Closed Feb–Nov.* **In-room** 📶 ❎ ⏷

INEXPENSIVE

In terms of campsites, Keycamp, Canvas Holidays and Thomson Alfresco (p. 38) all offer La Grande Metairie near Carnac, which has mixed feedback but usually goes down well with those who prefer larger, more lively sites with aqua complexes, kids' clubs and a large Brit contingent. As well as mobile homes and space for camping, it offers Celtic treehouse cabins and 'exotic huts' (new for 2010).

La Grande Metairie

You can book direct on its website **www.lagrandemetairie.com**.

For quieter campsites in the area, refer to the reliable Camping Qualité (p. 93). They include the flower-filled **Ferme de Lann Hoëdic** at Sarzeau (02 97 48 01 73, **www.camping-lannhoedic.fr**), near the Château de Suscinio (p. 111).

For the **youth hostel at Plouharnel** just northwest of Carnac, see p. 131.

CLAJ La Mine d'Or ★

Pénestin; 02 99 90 30 22; http:// clajpenestin.free.fr. 45km (28 miles) southeast of Vannes on D34.

This super-friendly independent youth hostel encourages everyone to muck in together and socialise and is centred around a quaint thatched Breton cottage by the sea, surrounded by pine trees and cypresses. Its accommodation options are varied—you can stay in a dorm (for four to nine people), in one of three bungalows in the grounds sleeping five people, in a four-person tent supplied by the hostel or in your own tent as

long as it's not huge. As you'd expect, rooms are basic but entirely acceptable, with clean shared facilities. If you opt for half or full-board, traditional meals are enjoyed together in the dining room or outdoors, followed by frequent musical gatherings. There's a great beach (p. 123) two steps away, with a seawater tank where children can bring any crabs, prawns or little fish they have caught for inspection. Hostel staff will fill you in on other local activities, including sailing, cycling, horse-riding, canoeing on the Vilaine, *pétanque* and volleyball.

60 spaces. **Rates** *9€ per person per night, including breakfast; ask about family rates.* **Amenities**

INSIDER TIP

For a night or two right by the Mine d'Or beach, the unpretentious **Hôtel L'Ancre d'Or** (Rue de la Plage, 02 99 90 38 92, **www.hotel-penestin.com**) is also good value, with doubles and twins for 65€–80€, or for longer stays a couple of nearby apartments for three or four people.

Pierre & Vacances Port du Crouesty ★ VALUE

Arzon; 0870 0207 145 (UK only); 01 58 21 55 84; www.pv-holidays. com. 33km (20 miles) southwest of Vannes on D780.

Pierre & Vacances has long been a major player on the French holiday market but only in the last few years has the firm appeared on the British radar. Visitor feedback on its 100-or-so residences and holiday villages in

France in Internet forums and the likes is mixed, but once you know that P&V also owns Centerparcs Europe, you'll know the kind of thing to expect—rather basic accommodation compensated by lots of family amenities (particularly in the case of holiday villages). Port du Crouesty, part of the town of Arzon at the tip of the Rhuys peninsula bordering the Golfe du Morbihan (p. 112), is the firms only holiday village in Brittany (there are several residences) and boasts four pools (two for toddlers), tennis courts, table tennis, a playground, bike hire, kids' clubs, a minimarket and an multimedia centre with Internet, a kids' activity corner, newspapers, and tourist information/day-trip bookings (such as excursions in the Golfe du Morbihan; p. 112). Some amenities incur an extra charge but nothing is unfairly priced; note also that kids' clubs are sometimes free if booked in advance. The resort also has direct access to Le Fogeo beach; it's not one of Brittany's best but does have a sailing school for ages 7 and up.

Most families go for the one bedroom apartments suited to four or five—an economical if slightly cramped option (there's a double bedroom and two sofabeds sleeping a total of three in the living room/kitchenette—it's tiny but ingenious use has been made of the restricted space). Studios for four to five people are an even cheaper, smaller option, or there are larger apartments and

houses for those prepared to pay for more space. The options are complex and rather confusing, so be sure to specify your exact requirements, such as a sea or garden (as opposed to car-park) view or ground-floor lodgings, and to contact your holiday village directly a couple of weeks' before arrival to make sure all your needs have been taken on board. The 'village' itself is surprisingly attractive, with clusters of apartment buildings built in the local style and stone around a large lawned area where kids can play ball and fly kites.

385 units. **Rates** *studio for 4/5 without sea view one week stay 530€– 2410€.* **Amenities** 🍴🏧 🚲 📶📺 📷🎿♥🔒🎣🔥📷🧺 **In room** 📺 🍴🛒❌🎽▭

For lunchtime or evenings when you've had enough of self-catering at P&V, there's a string of eateries around Port du Crouesty's pleasant harbour, including **L'Equinoxe** (7 Quai des Cabestans, 02 97 53 98 30), a flexible brasserie, pizzeria and crêperie (takeaway pizzas are also available). Alternatively, a short distance away at Port-Navalo, where some boats leave for tours of the Golfe du Morbihan (p. 112), you'll find **L'Escale** (20 Rue du Général de Gaulle, 02 97 53 63 67), an unpretentious quayside spot serving all day in July and August. There's everything from breakfasts and sandwiches on offer to pizzas and pasta dishes plus main-course salads and seafood.

Water, Water, Everywhere

Treat yourself without leaving the kids at home—the Morbihan is great for **thalassotherapy** centres offering childcare. The **Miramar Crouesty** (☎02 97 53 49 13, www.miramarcrouesty.com) at Port du Crouesty/Arzon on the Rhuys peninsula resembles an ocean liner in its own artificial seawater lake. While you're being pummelled in its Institute of Thalassotherapy or pampered in its spa, kids aged 3 months to 3 years are kept occupied in the nursery (year-round, from 11€ hr), while those aged 3 to 12 can attend the kids' club (school holidays only, from 22€ per half-day), which offers treasure hunts, shellfish hunts, shore explorations, beach and water games, sailing and mini-golf. If you come with a baby, a cot, bottle-warmer, steriliser, highchair and baby bath are provided, and there's a six-night Mother and Baby programme. There's also a pool complex and family rooms for up to two adults and three kids. Pricing is complex due to the range of options and treatments and to seasonal shifts, but expect to pay from about 250€ per night for accommodation only. It's best to speak to an operator as the website booking system can be haphazard and confusing. Note that you might also stay at the neighbouring P&V Village Port du Crouesty (p. 144) and make use of the kids' clubs there while you pop over and enjoy a discounted treatment at the Miramar.

Inland

MODERATE–EXPENSIVE

For the **Hôtel de l'Europe in Pontivy**, see p. 130.

Hôtel Le Roi Arthur FIND

Lac au Duc, Ploërmel; ☎02 97 73 64 64; www.hotelroiarthur.com.

The only hotel option for those wanting to stay by the Lac au Duc, the 'King Arthur' which is well known as a spa and golfing complex, and despite the modern buildings, has an old-fashioned feel to it. For all that, it's surprisingly family-friendly, with several cottage-apartments for up to five, with kitchenettes, and junior suites (connecting rooms) for four, with small balconies, some with lovely lake views. The wellbeing centre has an indoor pool, and there's a lounge where storytellers and entertainers come to share the legends of the forest of Brocéliande (p. 67) not far from here. Meals in the restaurant can be hit-and-miss, although your kids will be entertained by occasional quirky touches such as swan-shaped profiteroles.

86 rooms. 96€–199€, Junior Suite 230€–408€, cottage for 4/5 153€–172€, with discounts for stays of over four nights. Extra bed (in superior doubles only) 21€. **Amenities** ⬜ 🖼 🍴 🔊 **In room** ⬜ ☒

For a cheaper thalasso experience, the **Carnac Thalasso & Spa Resort** ★★ (℡02 97 52 53 54, *www.thalasso-carnac.com*) at Carnac-Plage (p. 147) has three hotels: the **Résidence** with 34 apartments with kitchenettes and balconies, let by the week; the **Hôtel Novotel** with interconnecting rooms with X-Boxes and an outdoor play area; and the **Hôtel Thalasso Ibis** with both interconnecting rooms and 23 duplex rooms for two to four, some set up for new mums (cots, baby baths, bottle warmers and a laundry service). Of the three on-site eateries, the Fleur de Sel and the Transat Bar are the best for families, with kids' menus and highchairs. Guests have access to all the Resort's amenities, including the thalassotherapy centre, beauty spa and marine spa, the pools, the tennis courts, table tennis and table football, and bike loan, as well as the wider offerings of Carnac itself, including watersports. There's also a kids' club for ages 3 to 12 on weekdays in the French school holidays (16€ per half-day). Accommodation-only costs about 500€–1110€ per week for a four person apartment (double and two single beds) in the Résidence, according to season. The Novotel (125€–230€ per room) and the Ibis (75€–145€ per room) both offer free accommodation and breakfast to two under-16s sharing a room with parents.

Auberge des VoyaJoueurs
★★★ FIND VALUE GREEN

Rue du Chaperon Rouge, Monteneuf; ℡*02 97 93 22 18, www.auberge-des-voyajoueurs.com. 24km (15 miles) from Ploërmel on D776.*

Utterly unique, the 'Inn of the Travelling Players'—open since 2009—is based on games from around the world, from Finland to Nepal. You not only stay in rooms themed on different games; two friendly experts will also instruct you in around 400 games on offer inside the inn or in its grounds, from giant chess and Connect 4 to Wii via marbles, cards and other obscure amusements you may not have heard of before. Storytelling walks and guided mountain-bike outings are also available, or there are plenty of walks and horse-riding trails in the area.

There's snacky fare available plus hot and cold drinks (cold meats, tarts, hot chocolate, cider), and staff order in dinner from local restaurants with advance notice. Accommodation, including two family rooms for three to four or interconnecting doubles (only the latter have bathtubs), are restful and clean, and the building and furnishings were conceived along green lines, from the solar panels to the bamboo bedding. For

The Loire-Atlantique: The Brittany That Was

If you access Brittany via the airport at Nantes (p. 103) in the Pays de la Loire the south, you'll be interested to learn that many people still consider this city to be Brittany's capital, even though the *département* in which it lies, the Loire-Atlantique, was taken out of the region in 1941! (A campaign is still being waged to have it reintegrated.)

With an international airport scheduled for Nantes by 2015, this is the time to explore the untouristy, relatively little-known Loire-Atlantique with its many low-key delights to offer families. They include **La Baule,** a chi chi seaside resort with an 8km beach, where the luxurious Lucien Barrière chain (p. 90) has four hotels, three with kids' clubs and one with a thalassotherapy centre and baby-minding centre. Camping is also popular here—Siblu (p. 138) has a holiday park at St. Brévin-les-Pins south of the Loire estuary.

Nantes itself is worthy of at least a day or so, especially the Ile de Nantes or 'Nantes island'—home to, among other things, the amazing **Machines de l'Ile** (*www.lesmachines-nantes.fr*) an ongoing artistic project involving the creation of giant mechanical 'living machines' based on the imaginings of Jules Verne, Leonardo da Vinci and more, some of which you can 'test' or even ride, including the 12m-tall Great Elephant. You can also observe ongoing creations in the workshop. Also in Nantes, check out the **Musée Jules Verne** (*www.nantes.fr/julesverne*) with its multimedia trail on the science-fiction author who was born in the city. And don't miss the **Château of the Dukes of Normandy,** which contains the city's impressive new history museum (including displays on

those with babies, just about everything has been thought about, from baths and sterilisers to monitors.

You can come and play games at the hotel without staying here (5€pp for families of two adults and two or more children).

10 units. **Rates** *59–62€, triple/quad* *89€.* **Amenities** 🐾 💼 ♥ 🍽 🏊 *In room* 📶

Fans of local folklore should ask about the three-night Dragon **VoyaJoueur** package, which includes half-board and a local trail taking in 88 legendary sites described in a booklet. In Monteneuf itself, the Association Les Landes (1 Rue des Menhirs) will give you a 'Korricarte' or 'Fairy Map' to follow Sentier d'Ozegan, a nature trail dotted with works of natural art.

Nantes's role in the slave trade) and lovely ramparts and gardens. The city's natural history museum has also had a big revamp.

Other particularly child-friendly resorts are **Piriac-sur-Mer and Pornichet,** while Le Croiset has an **Ocearium** (*www.ocearium-croisic.fr*) where you can marvel at Atlantic and tropical sea-life. But it's also worth popping inland, to the **Parc Naturel Régional de Brière** (*http://uk.parc-naturel-briere.fr*) where you can ride in traditional barges, spot birdlife, explore the marshes and islands by bicycle or on foot, and stay in a thatched cottage. Nearby **Guérande** is a charming medieval town famous for the salt harvested from its marshes.

Further south, not far from Nantes airport is **Planète Sauvage** (*www.planetesauvage.com*), a large safari park with a mock African village with a jungle bridge, plus a special encampment for overnight stays. Not far away, at Frossay, **Le Grand Parc des Légendes** (*www.sentierdesdaims.com*) is an off-the-wall theme-park of myths, legends and superstitions, with a magic forest, an elves' village, Father Christmas's summer home, reindeer and scores of forest and farm animals; costumed events take place on a regular basis.

If you need to stay over in Nantes, the **Novotel Centre Cité des Congès** (℡*02 51 82 00 00, www.novotel.com*) has modern rooms sleeping for up to four, with under-16s staying in a parent's room. It also offers welcome gifts for young guests, a children's menu and an indoor playground.

Château de Trédion 〖FIND〗

Trédion; ℡*02 97 67 12 37 www.chateau-tredion.fr. 27km (17 miles) northeast of Vannes on D1.*

Looking like something out of a fairytale, this manor house built in the 14th century once belonged to the Dukes of Bretagne themselves, who liked to hunt in the surrounding forests. Previous guests over the centuries have including François I and Catherine de Médici. Today the stately building, surrounded by large grounds housing several themed gardens (including one dedicated to korrigans), sculptures and plenty of animals, offers 26 apartments sleeping from four to eight people. Most have mezzanines accessible by ladder—great for older kids, but roomy enough for adults should your children be too young for such a set-up. Some rooms have showers rather than baths—ask when booking. Guests also have access to an unheated outdoor pool, a tennis court and several fishing lakes. Breakfast is included in the prices.

26 units. **Rates** *Studio apartment for 4 130€–190€ per night, 310€–640€ per week, two-room apartment for four 205€ per night, 500€–700€ per week, 3-room apartment for up to six 260€ per night, 600€–900€ per week. Electricity extra (meter).* **Amenities** 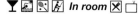 *In room*

INEXPENSIVE

The smallish, tranquil **Camping Le Clos du Blavet** (℡*02 97 51 83 07, www.closdublavet.com*), close to the Nantes–Brest Canal at Pontivy (p. 223), is recommended by Camping Qualité (p. 93). It offers tent pitches and wooden cabins.

Ty Louisette FIND

Kergouet, Saint Gérand; ℡*02 97 51 42 54, www.tylouisette.com. 12km (7.5miles) northeast of Pontivy on D125.*

Extremely for the Nantes–Brest Canal (p. 223), this single-level, four-bedroom gîte sleeping up to seven (plus a baby/toddler in a cot) offers a rare level of luxury and stylishness that sets it apart in an overcrowded market. Parents will appreciate the sunny breakfast table clad in wisteria and clematis, whilst kids will love the enclosed back garden and play equipment. Unlike in many gîtes, lots of basics are provided for you, and you'll be welcomed with two bottles of wine, fresh flowers, and a local newspaper.

Rates *420€–830€ per week.* **Amenities**

INSIDER TIP ⟩⟩

For more gîtes in the area, see *www.gites-de-france-morbihan. com*.

5 Côtes d'Armor

CÔTES D'ARMOR

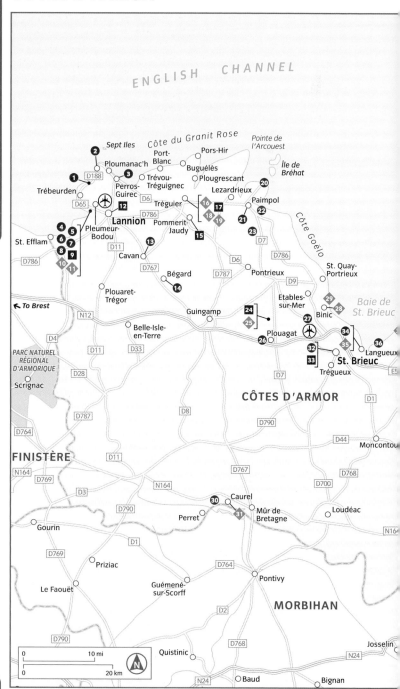

ENGLISH CHANNEL

Côte du Granit Rose

Sept Iles

Pointe de l'Arcouest

2

Ploumanac'h

Port-Blanc

Pors-Hir

Buguélès

Île de Bréhat

1 D188

3

Trévou-Tréguignec

Plougrescant

20

Trébeurden

Perros-Guirec

Lezardrieux

Paimpol

D65

D6

Tréguier

16 **17**

22

Côte Goëlo

12

Lannion

D786

18 **19**

21

4 **5**

Pleumeur-Bodou

Pommerit-Jaudy

15

23

6 **7**

D11

13

D6

D7

St. Efflam

8 **9**

Cavan

D786

D786

10 **11**

D767

Bégard

D787

Pontrieux

St. Quay-Portrieux

D786

14

D9

Plouaret-Trégor

Guingamp

Etables-sur-Mer

29 **28**

Baie de St. Brieuc

← To Brest

N12

24

27

Binic

D4

25

Plouagat

34

Belle-Isle-en-Terre

26

32

35

Langueux

D11

D33

33

St. Brieuc

36

PARC NATUREL RÉGIONAL D'ARMORIQUE

D28

Tréguex

E...

Scrignac

CÔTES D'ARMOR

D1

D787

D8

D790

D44

Moncontou...

FINISTÈRE

D11

D764

N164

D767

D768

D700

D769

D3

N164

Caurel

30

D790

Perret

31

Mûr de Bretagne

Loudéac

N16...

Gourin

D1

D769

D764

Pontivy

Priziac

Guémené-sur-Scorff

Le Faouët

D2

MORBIHAN

D790

D768

Josselin

0   10 mi

Quistinic

N24

0   20 km

N24

Baud

Bignan

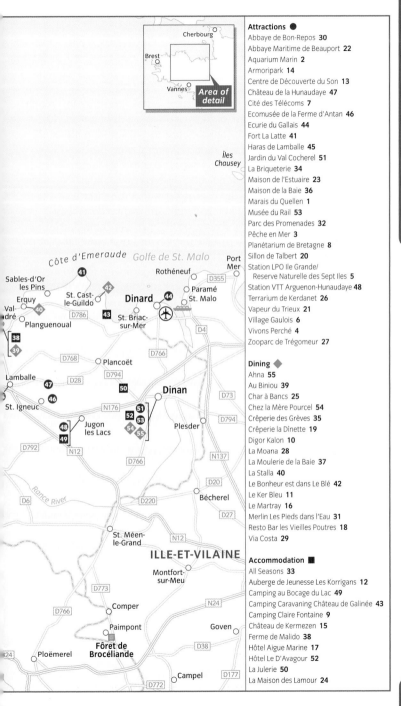

Cherbourg

Brest

Vannes **Area of detail**

Îles Chausey

Côte d'Emeraude *Golfe de St. Malo*

Rothéneuf
Port Mer

D355

Sables-d'Or les Pins ❹❶

St. Cast-le-Guildo ❹❷
Paramé
O St. Malo

Erquy ❹❶
Dinard ❹❹

Val-dré ❹❶
St. Briac-sur-Mer ❹❸
D786

Planguenoual
D4

❸❽
❸❾
D768

Plancoët
D766

Lamballe ❹❼
D794

St. Igneuc ❹❻
Dinan ❺❶

D28
❺❶ ❺❶
D73

❹❽
Jugon les Lacs
❺❷ ❺❸
Plesder
D794

❹❾
❺❹ ❺❺
N176

D792
N12

Rance River
D766
N137

D6
D220
D20

Bécherel

St. Méen-le-Grand
D27

N12

ILLE-ET-VILAINE

Montfort-sur-Meu

D773

Comper
N24

D766

Paimpont
Goven O

Fôret de Brocéliande
D38

❷❹
Ploëmerel

Campel
D177

D772

Continuing the sparkling Côte d'Emeraude that began in the Ille-et-Vilaine (p. 49) and then swooping round the awesome Baie de St. Brieuc, the Côtes d'Armor becomes the jagged, rocky coast for which Brittany is renowned on the Goëlo coast up to Paimpol. But it's at the Côte du Granit Rose west of here that the real fun starts, with its famous boulders twisted by the elements into all manner of odd shapes—and stained pink, according to legend, by the blood of persecuted saints. Here, too, signs begin appearing in French and Breton, giving you a sense of having entered a different world.

Most tourists, French and English, head for this 'pink granite coast', and the Côtes d'Armor is indeed prime Breton beach holiday territory, with some fabulous boat trips out to nearby islands. You might even like to try scouting out likely locations for Astérix's village, which some claim to be the Cap d'Erquy towards the eastern end of the Côtes d'Armor. Yet there are many charming inland spots that might lure you away from the sea, especially medieval Dinan, the pretty Lac de Guerlédan with its lake resorts, and two more lakes and fantastic cycling at Jugon Les Lacs. In summer, the town of Guingamp is a great place for family-oriented entertainment. St. Brieuc, the Côtes d'Armor's capital, is within good striking distance of the Côte du Granit Rose, Côte d'Emeraude and the inland attractions, but you're most likely to base yourself on or near the coast.

VISITOR INFORMATION

Information Centres

The CDT website, *www.cotes darmor.com*, which has an English translation, is an excellent source of info on the region.

Binic: Avenue Général de Gaulle, 📞*02 96 73 60 12, www. ville-binic.fr.*

Dinan: 9 Rue du Château, 📞*02 96 87 69 76, www.dinan-tourisme. com.*

Erquy: 3 Rue du 19 Mars 1962, 📞*02 96 72 30 12, www.erquy-tourisme.com.*

Guingamp: 2 Place du Champ-au-Roy, 📞*02 96 43 73 89, www. ot-guingamp.org.*

Ile de Bréhat: Le Bourg, 📞*02 96 20 04 15, www.brehat-infos.fr.*

Jugon Les Lacs: Place du Martray, 📞*02 96 31 70 75, www. jugon-les-lacs.com.*

Lancieux: Square Jean Conan, 📞*02 96 86 25 37, www.lancieux-tourisme.fr.*

Le Val-André (Pléneuf): Rue Winston Churchill, 📞*02 96 72 20 55, www.val-andre.org.*

Mûr-de-Bretagne (Lac de Guerlédan): 1 Place de l'Eglise, 📞*02 96 28 51 41, www.guerledan.fr.*

Perros-Guirec: 21 Place de l'Hôtel de Ville, ☏ *02 96 23 21 15*, *www.perros-guirec.com*.

St. Brieuc: 7 Rue St. Gouéno, ☏ *02 96 33 32 50*, *www.baiedesaint brieuc.com*.

St. Cast Le Guildo: Place Charles de Gaulle, ☏ *02 96 41 81 52*, *www.ot-st-cast-le-guildo.fr*.

Sables-d'Or-les-Pins (Plurien): Manoir Montangué, ☏ *02 96 72 28 52*, *www.plurien-tourisme.com*.

Trébeurden (Marais du Quellen): Place de Crec'h Hery, ☏ *02 96 23 51 64*, *www.trebeurden.fr*.

Orientation

The major road in the region is the **N12** running northwest from **Rennes** in the Ille-et-Vilaine (p. 49), which just bypasses the Côtes d'Armor capital **St. Brieuc** (99km/62 miles from Rennes) then travels parallel to the Côte du Granit Rose, past **Guingamp** (35km/22 miles from St. Brieuc) and into northern Finistère, with Brest (p. 196) 146km/91 miles from St. Brieuc.

Just past Guingamp, the **N767** is the fast track up to **Lannion** (68km/42 miles) from St. Brieuc), **Perros-Guirec** and the Côte du Granit Rose as a whole, but it's not scenic—take the coastal route if you have time. Otherwise, the département is a network of minor roads.

Arriving

By Boat There are no cross-Channel ferries to the Côtes d'Armor: the nearest terminals are **St. Malo** in the Ille-et-Vilaine (92km/57 miles from St. Brieuc) and **Roscoff** in Finistère (115km/71 miles from St. Brieuc).

By Train TGVs on the Paris–Brest line pass through **Lamballe, St. Brieuc** (about 3 hours from Paris), **Guingamp** and **Plouaret-Trégor,** but not all trains stop at every station. There is also a branch line to **Lannion.** For the SNCF, see p. 30.

By Air The nearest airport receiving flights from the UK is Dinard in the Ille-et-Vilaine, about 76km (47 miles) east of St. Brieuc.

By the Côte du Granit Rose, **Lannion** has daily 1hr 20min flights to and from **Paris (Orly)** on Airlinair (☏ *02 96 05 82 22*; *www.airlinair.com*), plus links with various other French cities. At the time of writing, St. Brieuc's airport had no scheduled flights.

Getting Around

As with all of Brittany, public transport is scarce (even non-existent in many places) and a car is the only means of properly exploring this area, especially the regional highlight—the Côte du Granit Rose with its winding coastal 'circuit' (p. 161).

For those arriving by train or air and needing to hire a car, Easycar (p. 103) offers pick-up from St. Brieuc, Guingamp and Lamballe train stations and from Lannion airport or train station.

WHAT TO SEE & DO

Children's Top 10 Attractions

❶ **Spotting** witches, crêpes, tortoises and other shapes in the contorted rocks of the Côte du Granit Rose. See p. 161.

❷ **Visiting** the LPO seabird clinic and sailing to the Sept Iles bird reserve, looking for seals en route. See p. 165.

❸ **Playing** Celtic-themed games in a setting out of an Astérix book at the Village Gaulois. See p. 166.

❹ **Watching** 1,000 local children dance in traditional costume at the Bugale Breizh. See p. 156.

❺ **Being outdoorsy** at Jugon Les Lacs with its wonderful cycling, fishing and other activities. See p. 159.

❻ **Taking** an illuminated night walk at the atmospheric ruined Abbaye Maritime de Beauport. See p. 159.

❼ **Steaming** through woods and valleys on the Vapeur du Trieux, stopping off to canoe in the estuary. See p. 166.

❽ **Seeing** snow leopards at the newly reopened Zooparc de Trégomeur. See p. 170.

❾ **Staying** at the eccentric but stylish Maison des Lamour and lunching on pork hotpot and rhubarb crêpes. See p. 186.

❿ **Exploring** the string of family-friendly resorts on the Côte d'Emeraude. See p. 171.

Children-Friendly Events & Entertainment

For Festival Place aux Mômes children's events in seaside resorts, see p. 57 (the Côte d'Armor's 'Stations Famille', are listed on p. 171 and 173). The France-wide Fête du Nautisme (p. 196) sees sailing tuition and events, mainly free, in Perros-Guirec (p. 173) and other resorts.

For the *son-et-lumiere* history spectacular at the Abbaye de Bon-Repos, see p. 172.

Bugale Breizh ★★★

Guingamp; contact Guingamp tourist office (p. 154).

The one-day 'festival of children in Brittany' brings together most of the region's children's traditional dance groups in a town famous for Breton dancing. All 1,000-or-so performers, some as young as 5, dress in historical costume—elaborate white headgear for the girls, cute waistcoats for the boys. The event begins with a procession to the Jardin Public, where the shows take place, as do the free children's dance embroidery, make-up and traditional games workshops.

Date early July. **Tickets** Jardin Public 10€, free under 12.

Festival de la Danse Bretonne et de la Saint Loup ★

Guingamp; contact Guingamp tourist office (p. 154); www.dansebretonne. com.

An outstanding gathering of musicians and dancers from all over the Celtic world, this nine-day festival has attracted performers as high-calibre as Ireland's *Clannad*. More than 2,500 people perform and compete in the Jardin Public and on the Place du Vally, and there are also processions through the streets. Watch out especially for the Dérobée de Guingamp, an energetic dance native to the town, and the *gouren* (Breton wrestling) tournament. Free classes in Breton dance are held on some days, and the event culminates in a huge free *fest noz* (p. 16).

Date Aug. **Admission** free.

Les Jeud'his de Guingamp ★★★ FIND

Place du Centre and Jardin Public, Guingamp; contact tourist office (p. 154).

Guingamp's quest to lure summer visitors away from the sea-side resorts includes an annual programme of free family-oriented street events and entertainment on a different theme each week. From 3pm each Thursday you can come and join in all kinds of fun: anything from giant chess, Breton games and kids' painting, crêpe-making and circus workshops to hip hop or

Breton dance lessons, canoeing tuition and pony rides, together with rock, jazz and folk concerts, dance shows and alfresco cinema screenings in the Jardin Public.

Date mid-July–early Aug. **Admission** free.

Festival Les Marionnet'Ic ★

Binic (and around); ☎02 96 73 60 12.

Binic's week-long marionette festival offers both indoor and outdoor shows and related exhibitions by puppetry artists from all over Europe and sometimes further afield, giving you the chance to see how puppets have evolved in different countries—witness the similarities between the Italian Pulcinella, English Punch, French Polichinelle, Spanish Don Cristobal and Russian Petrouchk, for example. The 12-year-old festival has now overspilled the resort of Binic itself, with some events held in nearby towns, farms, château grounds and so on. Ask about related workshops.

Date late April/early May. **Tickets** vary; some shows free.

Les Mediévales de Moncontour de Bretagne ★★

Moncontour; ☎02 96 73 49 57 (tourist office); www.moncontour-medievale. com. 25km (15.5 miles) southeast of St. Brieuc on D1.

Held every other year, this festival celebrates the fortified town of Moncontour's medieval heritage with a mass in the church of St. Mathurin followed by all kinds of costumed fun and frolics—fire-eaters, jugglers, stilt walkers, dancing, archery, horse-back jousting, plays, falconry displays, a procession and much more, culminating in an open-air ball in the evening. You can try some medieval recipes too, though you need to book ahead of time. Many visitors dress in medieval attire (the website gives a number for costume hire).

Date bi-annually in Aug (odd-num-bered years). Tickets 8€, 2€ child 6–12; extra fee for jousting tournament.

Mille Sabots ★ FIND

Parc Equestre de Lamballe (Haras National); 02 96 50 06 98); www. mille-sabots.fr.

Ten years old in 2011, 'A Thou-sand Hooves' takes over the horse-loving town of Lamballe, or more specifically the horse park surrounding Lamballe's Haras National (p. 168), for one day each September. The event starts with a parade from the Haras through town just before noon and continues until early evening, with equestrian shows, demonstrations and related activities. Kids especially love the fancy dress contest (human and animal!) and the 'Donkey Vil-lage', but this is also a great opportunity to find out about horse, pony and donkey riding in the area, with stalls by local equestrian businesses, as well as food and drink stands.

Date late Sept. Admission free.

Tournoi de Lutte Bretonne ★

Belle-Isle-en-Terre; 06 78 16 58 35. 23km (14 miles) west of Guingamp off N12.

Breton wrestling (*gouren*) is cele-brated at this day-long tourna-ment, with participants shaking an oath of loyalty before starting combat—the aim of which is to pin both your opponent's shoul-ders to the floor. Very like Cor-nish wrestling, this ancient sport was practised by Breton war-riors. There are also donkey rides, traditional wooden games and music.

Date July. Admission free.

Towns & Cities

See also **Best Beaches,** p. 170, for the *département's* fabulous resorts. The Côtes d'Armor has no cities and few towns that stand out in their own right, although **Guingamp** gets very lively with special events, while **Lannion** and **Tréguier** have some especially pretty medieval architecture.

Dinan ★

For tourist office, see p. 154.

This medieval citadel in a splendid hillside location overlooking the Rance is one of those places you can enjoy visiting just to wander along cobbled streets and through pretty squares, admiring the beautifully preserved timbered houses. You can also stroll along the almost wholly preserved town walls (more than 3km/1.8 miles long), inspect the 14th-century **castle** with its small museum, and investigate the **railway museum** (p. 174) and the **Mai-son de la Harpe** (6 rue de l'Horloge, 02 96 87 36 69, *www. harpe-celtique.com*), a unique museum of the Celtic harp running 1hr 30min Celtic harp discovery workshops for 6- to 12-year-olds (June–Sept and in school hols). Gory older kids may be interested to learn that the **Basilique Saint-Sauveur** contains the heart of Bertrand du Guesclin, the soldier who reclaimed for France much of the ground it lost to the English at the start of the Hundred Years War.

The best time to come here is in July (on an even-numbered year), for the medieval themed **Festival des Remparts,** including jousting and a costumed torchlight procession. For eating and accommodation, see p. 179 and p. 184.

> **INSIDER TIP** >>
> Dinan makes for a good day-trip destination, arriving by boat from St. Malo (p. 61) or by Voie Verte bike route from Dinard (p. 82).

Jugon Les Lacs ★ ★ FIND GREEN
For tourist office, see p. 154.

As the name suggests, this little town west of Dinan—a Station Verte in recognition of its wealth of outdoors activities—boasts more than one lake: there's a south lake, Jugon, and a north lake, Arguenon. Both are great for fishing; the **Maison Pèche et Nature** (02 96 50 60 04) offers courses and family activities, some in English. During autumn months this is a good place for mushrooming, while year round there's superb mountain-biking, with bike hire available along with dedicated tracks and trails (p. 178). You can also walk and horse-ride along more than 200km (124 miles) of trails, and there's an open-air swimming pool with a big slide beside Jugon lake.

In the town itself you'll discover ample medieval buildings to admire. A lively programme of events in and around town, dubbed 'Festilacs' by locals, includes a fair, concerts and barbecues, and a fantastic Christmas market with festive log cabins.

> **INSIDER TIP** >>
> Jugon Les Lacs is a fine place to celebrate Bastille Day (14th July), with lakeside fireworks followed by an open-air dance on the Place du Martray.

St. Brieuc
For tourist office, see p. 155.

The *départemental* capital doesn't have the charm of Rennes but it's chief attraction lies in its location, which is great for both beach-lovers and those venturing inland, and it's good for shopping too (p. 176). In summer (Thurs and Fri evenings), Les Nocturnes is a programme of free Breton, blues and world music concerts in the city's streets and squares.

Fun Days Out

Abbaye Maritime de Beauport ★ ★ AGE 4 & UP
Kérity; 02 96 55 18 58, www. abbaye-beauport.com. 2km (1.25 miles) southeast of Paimpol on D786.

Still undergoing painstaking restoration work begun nearly two decades ago, this ruined Gothic abbey set atmospherically on the coast, with lovely bay views, can be explored freely or by guided tour (in French), taking in the parlour, cellars, kitchen, cloister with abbey church, refectory and more. The best time to come, at least with older kids, is for the Escales de Nuit night walks in July and August (Wed and Sun, 10pm–1am, no reservations needed), when stunning, ethereal depictions of the monks' daily life—images of talking apples, a library illuminated by fireflies and other oddities—are projected onto the abbey walls. In October, the apple festival features demonstrations, a market, kids' workshops, storytelling, an apple-tart contest and more, while at Christmas there's festival storytelling around a cosy hearth, cake decorating and a nativity scene. The rest of the year sees children's creative workshops devised to fit in with the temporary exhibitions.

Abbaye Maritime de Beauport

Time 1hr 30mins for visit. *Open* mid-June–mid-Sept daily 10am–7pm; rest of year daily 10am–noon and 2–5pm. *Admission* 5.50€–6€ adult, 2.50€–3.50€ child 11–18, 1.50€–2.50€ child 5–10, 12€–13€ family (2 + 2), then 1.50€ per child. *Amenities* 🅿 🛍 ♿

Centre de Découverte du Son ★ ALL AGES

Kérouspic, Cavan; 📞 *02 96 54 61 99;* ***www.decouvertesonore.info/centre.*** *11km (7 miles) southeast of Lannion off D767.*

An original concept, the 'Sound Discovery Centre' consists of a 'magic pathway' through a natural setting. On your way along it, you listen to, create and play with sounds of various kinds, from waterfalls to fairy music. Children love the open-air, hands-on installations, which include huge xylophones and musical pulleys. There's a picnic space and snack bar at the end of the circuit, and you can buy various sound devices in the shop if you don't mind the consequences. In summer, watch out for the Centre's 'road-show' of performances in local towns.

Time 2hrs. *Open* Apr–Nov Sun and public hols 3–6pm (daily in school hols). *Admission* 6.50€ adult, 4.50€ child 3–14. *Amenities* 🍸 ☕ 🅿 🪑 🛍 ♿

Château de la Hunaudaye ★★ AGE 4 & UP

Plédéliac; 📞 *02 96 34 82 10,* ***www. la-hunaudaye.com.*** *32km (20 miles) southeast of St. Brieuc on D55.*

Hidden away in marshy country-side, this partially ruined 13th-century castle, rebuilt in the 15th, has created a 4€ French-language children's booklet, 'Y'a pas d'âge pour le Moyen Age' (roughly: 'You're Never too Young for the Middle Ages'), explaining the castle's history from a fun and accessible angle. Additionally, in high summer, kids can take part in creative workshops on medieval themes while their parents tour the castle, and for 8- to14-year-olds there's a Cluedo-inspired mystery tour in search of the castle's ghosts. Other times of year see archaeology workshops for ages 7 to 12, but best of all is the annual children's day (mid-Sept), La Journée des Enfants Rois, with games, workshops and activities. The bookshop has books and games for kids.

Time 1hr 30mins for visit. *Open* Easter hols and Nov half-term daily 2.30–8pm, Apr–mid-June Wed, Sun and hols 2.30–6pm, mid-June–Sept daily 10.30am–6.30pm. *Admission* 5€ adult, 3.50€ child 6–16. *Amenities* 🅿 🏪 ♿

> **INSIDER TIP** ⟩⟩
>
> Handy for the Côte du Granit Rose, **Armoripark** ☎ 02 96 45 36 36, *www.armoripark.com* between Lannion and Guingamp offers low-key fun for kids of all ages, including an aquapark with indoor and outdoor pools and giant slides, pedaloes and bumper boats, inflatables and trampolines, bowling, and a mini-farm. There's a snack bar or you can picnic in the designated areas.

Côte du Granit Rose
★★★ ALL AGES

For Perros-Guirec tourist office, see *p. 155.*

Although only about 15km (9 miles) long as the crow flies, this is one of France's best-known strips of coastline, because of its pinky-brown rocks that have been slowly contorted during

The rocky coastline around Perros-Guirec

Natural Wonder

The Sillon de Talbert on the peninsula north of Lézardrieux is a real oddity—a thin spit of land that curves out almost 3km (2 miles) into the sea, seemingly resistant to the tides that ought to wash it away. In fact, it was created by two converging currents and powerful north-westerly swells, and it stretches northeast, which means it'll eventually break away from the coast. Storms can be so forceful here that pebbles are tossed into the air. This being Brittany, there are numerous legends associated with the spit: according to one, Merlin placed millions of pebbles here to get closer to the fairy Viviane.

Up close, it's difficult to get the measure of the Sillon, though driving down towards it you get glimpses of its spectacular extent. To appreciate its wonder properly, walk out along it, taking care not to tread on the terns' and plovers' eggs at the end (they blend in spookily with the pebbles, so some areas have been marked off for their protection) or the sea kale that grows here.

From the tip you have a good view of the 45m **Phare des Héaux-de-Bréhat** about 10km (6 miles) northwest of Bréhat; four times further out, towards Guernsey, is the **Phare des Roches-Douves** (p. 215).

---

erosion, often into odd shapes. It begins, in the west, around **Tré-gastel-Plage,** where it's fun to spot rock formations named after objects they resemble, including the *Sorcière* (Witch), *Tas de Crêpes* (Pile of Crêpes), *Tortues* (Tortoises) and *Tête de Mort* (Skull). Around the coast at **Ploumanach,** on the old coastguards' path, **La Maison du Littoral** (☎ 02 96 91 62 77) explains how the granite here was formed over millions of years. The spectacular golden-sanded **Plage de St. Guirec** precedes **Perros-Guirec,** the Côte's main resort (p. 173).

Past Perros-Guirec, the pink rockscapes continue up as far as **Pors-Hir.** You can follow a sign-posted driving circuit, the '**Côte des Ajoncs**' ('Gorse Coast'),

around a series of boat-filled bays with breathtaking turquoise waters; highlights are **Trévou-Tréguignec**, **Port-Blanc** and **Buguélès**. At Plougrescant there's a charming brasserie-crêperie, **Le Gouermel** (☎ 02 96 92 55 26), with a seaview terrace. At Buguélès you'll begin to see houses built in-between the boulders, often so closely that they're seemingly wedged in. Walking around on the beaches themselves, children might enjoy trying to see shapes in the boulders, such as hands and faces.

Time *1 day or more.*

Fort La Latte ★ AGE 2 & UP

Cap Fréhel; ☎ *02 96 41 40 31; www. castlelalatte.com. 20km (12 miles) northwest of St. Cast Le Guildo on D16.*

Fort La Latte

One of the most dramatic sights on the Breton coast, this fortified medieval castle looks almost as if it was sculpted from the jagged 70m (230ft) cliffs on which it's perched, against a backdrop of blue sea. Though it's a fair trek from main roads, it attracts tourists by the coachload in summer partly to its fame as a location for the rip-roaring final scenes in the 1958 film *The Vikings*, starring Kirk Douglas and Tony Curtis. Some of the structure dates back to the 14th century—curtain walls, rampart towers, two drawbridges and the dungeon—but most of what you can see now dates back to between 1690 and 1715, and that has been subject to more or less continuous restoration over the past century. Once you've followed the winding forest footpath down to the fort (there's a wider track for those less sure on their feet or with buggies) and crossed its first drawbridge, there's not a huge amount to see inside but the views *are* incredible, especially from the roof of the keep. The 18th-century oven used to 'cook' cannonballs (to set enemy ships on fire) is a thought-provoking remnant.

Time 1hr. **Open** Apr–early July and late Aug–Sept daily 10.30am–12.30pm and 2–6pm, early July to late Aug daily 10.30am–7pm, rest of year Sat, Sun and hols 1.30–5.30pm. **Admission** 5€ adult, 2.80€ child 5–11. **Amenities** ♉ 🍽 🅿

INSIDER TIP

Fort La Latte is on a headland of the Cap Fréhel peninsula; to your left as you look out to sea, you can spot the **Cap Fréhel** itself, an ornithological reserve where cormorants, razorbills (p. 167) gannets and other seabirds nest here. The Cap is also home to the 33m (108ft) high **Phare du Fréhel** (local *mairie* ☎ 02 96 41 43 06), a 1950s lighthouse; climb its 145 steps (Apr–Sept) for views of the western Manche coast in Normandy, the Iles Chausey off it, and the Ile de Bréhat (see below) on very clear days.

Ile de Bréhat ★ ALL AGES

Cruisers: ☎ 02 96 55 70 50; *www.vedettesdebrehat.com. For tourist office, see p. 154.*

Bréhat, a pretty car-free archipelago with a dramatic jagged

Rocky Horror

Travelling away from the Côte du Granit Rose, on your way into Finistère (p. 189), try to stop in the unspoilt Baie de Lannion, particularly at St. Efflam. From the latter you can look across to the Lieue de Grève with its **Roche Rouge**—a rock that looks a bit like a dragon, complete with knobbly spine and tail. Indeed, according to legend this was the place where a monstrous red dragon with a human head, snake's body and fish's tail came to die after being slain by King Arthur and St. Efflam. The dragon had lived inside the nearby **Grand Rocher,** or Roch hr glas, causing such terror among local people that they tried to appease it with human sacrifices, including unbaptised children.

coastline, curiously shaped pinkish rocks and a mild climate, makes for an enjoyable family day out. There's little to do on the Ile de Bréhat, other than walk or cycle among the imported exotic vegetation (eucalyptus, palm trees, mimosa and aloes), look at the restored tidal mill and the **Phare de Paon,** a lighthouse next to a wave-smashed chasm, or sunbathe and picnic on the beaches. Bikes can be hired by the jetty, though they're not allowed on the coastal paths.

Direct ferries leave the Pointe de l'Arcouest north of Paimpol and take just 10 minutes, but there are a number of excursions departing from various ports on the mainland, including a 45-minute cruise around the island followed by unlimited free time to explore it. In summer you need to book well in advance, but it's better (for both you and the island) if you come at a quieter time. Bréhat has a delicate ecosystem and is vulnerable to high-season hordes.

If you want to stay over, there's a moderately priced hotel, the **Bellevue** (☏ *02 96 20 00 05, www.hotel-bellevue-brehat.fr*) with duplex rooms for four or five and a restaurant amenable to children's requests.

Time a day or more. Cost direct crossing 9€ adult, 7.50€ child 4–11.

Maison de l'Estuaire
★ **FIND** AGE 4 & UP

Traou Nez, Plourivo; ☏ *02 96 55 96 79; www.plourivo.fr. 5km (3 miles) south of Paimpol on D15.*

A great place for raising environmental awareness in kids, this little nature centre on the Trieux estuary hosts changing displays of nature-themed arts and crafts (some by local schoolkids) but is best visited for one of its excellent (French-language) activities. These change yearly but might include woodcraft afternoons (with whistle-making, plant-tasting and more), insect-discovery workshops, butterfly walks and lantern-lit storytelling evenings. Note that the Vapeur du Trieux (p. 166) runs trips from Paimpol to the Maison, where ages 8 and over can go canoeing with a nature guide on the estuary.

Time varies by activity. *Open* mid-May–June and first half Sept Sat and Sun, July and Aug Tues–Sun 3–6pm. *Admission* free; activities vary but average about 5€ adult, 3€ child, with family tickets available. *Amenities* 🅿 ♿

Marais du Quellen ALL AGES

Contact Trébeurden tourist office (see p. 155).

Just west of Perros-Guirec (p. 173) and north of Trébeurden (p. 155), this protected area of freshwater marshland, separated from Goas Treiz beach by a string of dunes, is a lovely place for a guided nature walk. Some take as their theme the local population of beautiful white Camargue horses—this ancient breed from southern France is thought to be descended from a Palaeolithic horse crossbred with other races, including Arabian horses. A few of them were brought here in 1989—there are only about 30 herds in the world—and they've had a profound effect on the vegetation. The marsh has a network of paths for walkers, with sections on stilts where the ground is boggy. Observatories allow you to watch the rich birdlife of the marshes.

Time guided walks 1hr 30mins. *Open* pathways open all the time; enquire about guided walks. *Admission* free.

Station LPO Ile Grande/ Réserve Naturelle des Sept Iles ★★★ ALL AGES

Pleumeur-Bodou; 📞02 96 91 91 40; http://bretagne.lpo.fr/dept/22.

7.5km (4.5 miles) northwest of Lannion on D21.

The Station LPO clinic, unique in France, was set up by the Ligue pour la Protection des Oiseaux in 1984 to treat and rehabilitate seabirds that have fallen victim to oil slicks in Brittany—several hundred a year, about half of whom eventually return to the sea. It houses a permanent exhibition on seabirds, including their biology and migration habits, ecological issues and the care of petrol-damaged birds; you can also watch live footage of gannets relayed from a remote-controlled camera on nearby Ile Rouzic; and follow guided walks along the coast to discover its bird and plant life, some specially for children (on Wednesday afternoons, when French kids are out of school).

Time Station 1hr, outings vary. *Open* school hols and June daily 2–6pm; July and Aug Mon–Fri 10am–1pm and 2.30–7pm, Sat and Sun 2.30–7pm; rest of year Sat and Sun 2–6pm. *Admission* 2.50€, 1.50€ child under 12, 6.50€ family. Coastal walks 6€ adult, 2€ child 6–12. *Amenities* 🅿 🔒 ♿

INSIDER TIP ⟫

The Ile Rouzic, the only place that gannets come to mate in France (the presence of up to 20,000 pairs here can make it look like it's covered in snow), is one of the **Sept Iles,** France's most important bird reserve. LPO run boat tours of this stunning archipelago, as do **Vedettes des Sept Iles** (📞 02 96 91 10 00, www.armor-decouverte.fr) from Perros-Guirec, during which you'll see cormorants and razor-bills (p. 167)—plus seals in the surrounding waters.

Vapeur du Trieux
★ ★ ★ ALL AGES

Train station, Avenue du Général de Gaulle, Paimpol; ☎08 92 39 14 27; www.vapeurdutrieux.com.

Accessing parts of the Trieux valley otherwise unseen by visitors, this steam train chugs its way between Paimpol and Pontrieux at a leisurely 30km/h (19mph), leaving you free to enjoy sights such as the 15th-century **Château de la Roche-Jagu,** the Leff–Pontrieux viaduct, a tidal mill and the town of Pontrieux, famous for its old public wash-houses now embellished with flowers. As the costumed guides explain (in French or English), the 104-tonne engine that pulls the carriages with their wooden seats has covered more than a

million kilometres since it was made in 1922. It all makes for a lively family day out, with a magician and storyteller aboard the train on certain days and regular opportunities to canoe on the Trieux (at the **Maison de l'Estuaire**—p. 164—from age 8) and take a guided tour of Paimpol. The train makes a stop in the heart of the forest, at the Maison de l'Estuaire de Traou Nez, to let you enjoy Breton music, look at an exhibition on the surroundings, and taste local cider and crêpes. Please note that pre-booking is essential.

Time 5hrs. Open May–Sept; see calendar on website for days and times. Fare return trip 22€ adult, 11€ child 4–16, 60€ family (2+2). Advance booking required. Amenities 🅿

Village Gaulois ★ ★ ★ AGE 3 & UP

Cosmopolis, Pleumeur-Bodou; ☎02 96 91 83 95; http://levillagegaulois. free.fr. 7.5km (4.5 miles) northwest of Lannion on D21.

Vapeur du Trieux, Paimpol

In the Swim

Known as 'petit pingouins' in French because of their resemblance to penguins, razorbills are so adept in the water that they can actually swim before they can fly, and in late summer they moult so much that they can't take to the air at all for a while. You may see some of these elegant birds on the cliffs of Brittany, or on the water, where they often bob up and down together in 'rafts'. They spend so much time at sea, far from land, that sadly they're some of the most common victims of oil slicks.

A themepark with a heart, the 'Gallic Village' is run by MEEM (Monde des Enfants pour les Enfants du Monde), a humanitarian association that channels the profits into schools in Togo. The 20 Celtic-themed games, in a setting right out of an Astérix book, complete with thatched huts and wooden boats you can take out on the lake, offer fun with an educational bent. Have a try at the catapult, a giant puzzle, swing boats, a cairn maze, and fishing with wooden fish. There are also displays, demos and videos about Gallic life, including salt production and menhir building. At the traditional oven, youngsters get to mill grain and make flour to cook their own galettes. Don't miss the African zone overlooking the Village, with a thought-provoking display on the schools built by MEEM, and a mock schoolroom.

Time half a day. **Open** Apr–June and Sept Sun–Fri 2–6pm; July and Aug daily 10.30am–7pm. **Admission** 4.50€ adult, 3.50€ child 5–16. **Amenities** 🅿 🎪 ∥∥ ♿

INSIDER TIP ⟩⟩

Note that the Village Gaulois is on the same leisure site as the Cité des Télécoms (p. 174) and Planétarium de Bretagne (p. 174), making for an all-round excellent—and very educational—day out.

Animal Attractions

Aquarium Marin ★ ALL AGES

Bd du Coz-Pors, Trégastel-Plage; ☎02 96 23 48 58; www.aquarium-tregastel.com. 8km (5 miles) west of Perros-Guirec on D788.

Visits to this small aquarium—set amidst a mass of huge pink-granite boulders, in caves that once served as a chapel and as a World War II weapons store—begin outside, in the Zone des Embruns ('Seaspray Zone'). A combination of rain, wind and salt make the terrain inhospitable for all but lichens (life forms halfway between seaweed and mushrooms, sea snails and sea roaches), which you can see amongst the rocks or in the touching pool. Inside, the Zone des Marées (notice its 5,500-tonne ceiling consisting of a single slab of rock) is full of hardy types who can survive the constant movement of the tides, including lobsters, scallops, sea-horses, sea bream and abalone. Interactive displays help you to understand the tides, especially the links with the stars and planets. Last comes the Deep Zone, with its anemones, sponges and sea-fans, plus fish such as rays, conger eels and rock salmon, which have evolved to deal with the lack of light.

Time 1hr 30mins. *Open* Apr–June and Sept Tues–Fri 10am–6pm, Sat–Mon 2–6pm; July and Aug daily 10am–7pm; Mar and Oct Tues–Sun 2–5pm. *Admission* 7.50€ adult, 5€ children 4–16, 20€ family. *Amenities*
P 🛈 ♿

Ecomusée de la Ferme d'Antan ★ ALL AGES

St. Esprit-des-Bois, Plédéliac; 📞02 96 34 80 77; www.ferme-dantan22. com. 34km (21 miles) southeast of St. Brieuc on D55.

The 'Farm of Yesteryear' is an old farm reincarnated as a museum of rural life, with guides in period costume escorting you around the restored farmhouse, cowshed, stables, pigsty and henhouse, complete with resident animals. It's chastening to see how three generations would have lived together in the one main room of the farmhouse. You can also explore the storeroom where cider was made, with a 1750 apple press, and the barn full of early agricultural machinery. The garden is planted with old crops, including flax, Jerusalem artichokes

and *blé noir* or buckwheat, the chief ingredient of Breton galettes. At the end of the tour, opt to watch a short film on daily life on the farm in 1925. The lively programme of events includes summer-holiday workshops and activities for families and a chestnut festival.

Time 1hr–1hr 30mins. *Open* Sept and Nov hols Tues–Sun 2–6pm; June–Aug Tues–Sat 10am–6pm, Sun and Mon 2–6pm. *Admission* 5€ adult, 3€ child 6–16. *Amenities*
P ♿

Haras de Lamballe ★ AGE 4 & UP

Place du Champ de Foire, Lamballe; 📞02 96 50 06 98; www.haras patrimoine.com. 22km (13.5 miles) southeast of St. Brieuc off N12.

This stud farm—once France's biggest, and still one of Brittany's most important—runs guided tours (in English regularly in July and Aug, or rest of year by arrangement) of its 12 impressive stables, built in 1825 under Charles X and home to about 50 Breton stallions. These powerful, hardy but good-natured horses divide into *chevaux de trait*, which were employed for farm tasks, and *postiers*, a cross between *traits* and Norfolk horses; these are lighter and were used for pulling carriages, including postal carts and cannons in WWI. There are also French trotters, English thoroughbreds, Arabians, French saddle horses and ponies, Connemaras and a lone black donkey, though be aware that in the breeding season (mid-Mar–mid-July) all but about

Haras de Lamballe

20 of the residents are 'out visiting'. Special events include Les Jeudis du Haras horse shows on Thursday evenings (mid-July–mid-Aug), when horse-and-trap rides are offered, and Christmas, when the Haras is turned into Santa Claus's Stables, with kids' workshops and a festive market.

For the **Mille Sabots** in the Haras grounds, see p. 158.

Time 1hr 30mins. *Open* July–mid-Sept for several guided tours delay (call for details), rest of year guided tours Tues–Sun 3pm. *Tickets* 5.50€ adult, 3€ child 6–12. *Amenities* P ♿

Maison de la Baie ★ AGE 2 & UP

Site de l'Etoile, Hillion; ☎02 96 32 27 98; www.saintbrieuc-agglo.fr. 14km (8.5 miles) east of St. Brieuc on D80.

At the time of writing, this small local-environment museum perched on a windswept bluff (with superb views over the Baie de St. Brieuc), was still closed for renovation work. Usually, the small interactive Galerie des Oiseaux showcases the 40,000 or so birds that winter in this immense bay, where the tide can retreat by more than 7km (4 miles). The main attraction here has always been the French-language nature outings run by the Maison, from storytelling walks to sea-kayaking, for a variety of ages; some are free. There's also an outside children's play area on site as well as an 'interpretation path' (part of the GR34 route) round this part of the coast, which is a *réserve naturelle* out of bounds to horseriders and mountain bikers. The wild **Dunes de Bonabri** where you can spot amphibians, orchids and other species are worth visiting, as is the **Plage de la Granville,** though signs alert you to the dangers of sudden flooding. Take note that **Hillion** itself is on the site of an ancient Celtic settlement and has the remains of a Roman path.

Time 1hr for visit, up to half a day for site. *Open* June and Sept Wed–Fri and Sun 2–6pm; July and Aug Mon–Fri 10.30am–6.30pm, Sat and Sun 1.30–6.30pm; Oct–May Wed, Fri and Sun 2–6pm. *Tickets* 3€ adult, 2€ child 6–12; joint tickets available with La Briqueterie (p. 173). *Amenities* P ∧ ♿

> **INSIDER TIP** »
>
> If you want to spend more time in this calm, untouristy spot, ask about the Maison de la Baie's basic, keenly priced **studios** with kitchenettes.

Terrarium de Kerdanet

ALL AGES

Plouagat; ☎02 96 32 64 49; http://terrariumdekerdanet.over-blog.com. 12km (7.5 miles) east of Guingamp off N12.

This junglesque reptile and amphibian discovery centre, run by a man who's been a passionate collector since boyhood, is home to all manner of creatures, from affable plodding tortoises to some of the world's deadliest snakes. Visits are by guided tour, in French; this leads you through the outside space with its mainly native species then inside to the vivarium, where more exotic specimens are found. At the end comes a touching session for the brave, with pythons, boa constrictors and adders. Families can book private tours in high summer.

Time 1hr 30mins. Open May, June and Sept Wed, Sat, Sun and hols 2–5pm; July and Aug Tues, Wed, Sat, Sun and hols 10–11.30am and 2–5.30pm, but call or email ahead. Admission 5.80€ adult, 4.80€ child 4–12. Amenities ♿ ⛽

Zooparc de Trégomeur

★★ **FIND** **ALL AGES**

Le Moulin Richard, Trégomeur; ☎02 96 79 01 07; www.zoo-tregomeur.com. 16km (10 miles) northwest of St. Brieuc on D47.

Established on the site of a previous zoo and opened in 2007, **Trégomeur** (sister to La Bourbansais in the Ille-et-Vilaine; p. 49) has a unique selling point in that its animals are all Asian in origin—a choice based on the fact that Auguste Pavie, an explorer and diplomat to the Far East, came from the Côte d'Armor. Hence, the zoo's inhabitants—including tigers, snow leopards, a Malay bear— live amidst reconstructions of Asian landscapes, including a rice field, a bamboo plantation, and Vietnamese farm (new in 2010), plus plenty of exotic plant life. There's even a pan-Asian restaurant, as well as a snack kiosk. The emphasis here, as at all responsible zoos these days, is on conservation and educating the public on environmental issues. There's plenty of fun to be had too, with frequent special events and play areas with inflatables for the kids to let off steam.

Open Apr–Sept daily 10am–7pm; Oct and Feb half-terms (Zone A) daily 10.30am–5.30pm; rest of year Wed, Sat, Sun and hols 1.30–5.30pm. Admission 12€–13.50€ adult, 8€–9.50€ child 3–12. Time 3–4hrs. Amenities 🍷 🍽 ♿ ⛺ ▪ 🍴 ⛽

Best Beaches

Aside St. Cast le Guildo and Erquy on the Côte d'Emeraude, Binic and Perros-Guirec (for all, see below), the Côtes d'Armor's designated 'Stations Familles' (p. 57) are St. Quay Portrieux and Trébeurden.

Binic ★★

For tourist office, see p. 154.

Part of the rocky Goëlo coast sweeping up from St. Brieuc to Paimpol, this charming resort— dubbed the Côte d'Armor's 'beauty spot'—has three sheltered

One of many beaches around St. Cast le Guildo

sandy beaches, including Plage de la Banche near the centre, with seawater and paddling pools, trampolines and donkey rides. During high-season take a 'seaside safari' (a guided tour of the shore at low tide, offered every other month or so from March to August), or an eco-themed treasure hunt (*jeu de piste*) for ages 7 to12 (you pick up a booklet for 1€ from the tourist office). Alternatively, enjoy classic Punch and Judy shows and various festivals including the Festival Place aux Mômes (p. 57), a puppet festival in late Apr/early May and (also in May) the **La Morue en Fête,** a 'cod festival' with sailors' songs, trips on old fishing boats, a children's area and fireworks. When it rains, there's a superb indoor waterpark (p. 175).

Côte d'Emeraude ★★

For tourist offices, see p. 154.

This easternmost coast of the Côtes d'Armor, the lovely 'Emerald Coast' that began in the Ille-et-Vilaine (p. 49), is studded with family-friendly resorts and fine wide sands. They include **Lancieux,** famous for its red-streaked rocks said to be stained by the blood of St. Siog; **St. Cast le Guildo,** a 'Station Famille' (p. 57) offering seven beaches and boat trips around the Cap Fréhel (p. 163) or to St. Malo (p. 61); **Sables d'Or les Pins,** with its wonderful beach; **Erquy,** another 'Station Famille', and a place that may have inspired the creators of Astérix (p. 172); and **Le Val-André,** with its expansive flat central beach that is great for kids, plus some wilder stretches popular with surfers, yachters and paragliders. Le Val-André also has great views over towards St. Brieuc, some stylish little shops selling everything from trendy home decor to buckets and spades, and a very good fish restaurant (p. 179).

The Elusive Gaul: in Search of Astérix

Astérix the Gaul and his companion Obélix first appeared in the comic *Pilote* in 1959 and went on to star in more than 50 adventures of their own, which sold more than 280 million copies round the world. There's long been debate among fans about the location of the name-less village in which the Gaulois heroes form a stronghold against the Roman invaders, with many people pointing to the similarities between the Cap d'Erquy on the Côte d'Emeraude and the terrain of the fictional village, especially the three rocks out to sea at the Anse de Port-Blanc.

In an interview, one of the creators of the *bande dessinée*, Albert Uderzo, said that though he didn't consciously choose to base Asté-rix's village on Erquy, he realised that he'd been greatly inspired by the coast of the Côtes d'Armor, and especially the Cap d'Erquy, to which he'd been sent with his brother as a child during World War II, and where he'd subsequently spent family holidays. It's more likely than not, however, that the cape *did* succumb to the Roman invaders: in 1979 the domestic baths of a Gallo-Roman villa were found here.

INSIDER TIP ❯❯

Be sure to check in at local tour-ist offices; some, including Le Val-André, have kids' trails/trea-sure hunts (*jeux de piste*) around town.

Lac de Guerlédan ★★

For tourist office (Mûr-de-Bretagne), see p. 154.

With its safe artificial beaches, this lovely lake on the southern boundary of the *département* is a brilliant place to spend a day or two *en famille*. The lake is long—12km (7.5 miles)—and narrow, with resorts dotted round its shore, notably **Beau Rivage** near Caurel, popular for watersports and boat trips, and **L'Anse de Sordan** near St. Aig-nan (actually in the Morbihan), with a campsite offering a res-taurant alongside canoe and pedalo hire, the **Merlin Les**

Pieds dans l'Eau (☎*02 97 27 52 36, www.restaurant-merlin.fr*). Other activities include wind-surfing, waterskiing and fishing, plus *boules* for those who would prefer to stay on dry land. Bring a picnic to walk off in the lovely pine forest to the south.

INSIDER TIP ❯❯

If you're at the lake in high sum-mer, head for the **Abbaye de Bon-Repos** (☎*02 96 24 82 20, www.bon-repos.com*) at the western tip of the lake, overlook-ing the Nantes–Brest canal (p. 223). In August the ruined abbey hosts spectacular *son-et-lumière* shows recounting the history of the region from Neo-lithic times to the Revolution and culminating in a fireworks dis-play. Visit the farmer's market on Sunday mornings (10am–1pm; Mar–Oct) in the abbey grounds, and there's a restaurant and a crêperie on site.

Perros-Guirec ★

For tourist office, see p. 155.

Though not the best family resort in Brittany—its size can make it feel a bit impersonal—Perros-Guirec's position on the Côte du Granit Rose (p. 161) and outstanding range of activities make it a good bet for families. The main beaches, **Trestignel** and the larger and more commercialised **Trestraou,** are very toddler friendly; the **Centre Nautique** (☏ 02 96 49 81 21) on the latter run a high-season **Jardin des Mers** of sailing-themed activities for 4- to 8-year-olds plus tuition for kids of various ages, including sea-kayaking for ages 9 to 14. Both beaches host children's **Clubs de Plage,** and there's an old-fashioned **carousel** (Feb–Oct) on the square near Trestraou beach. For beach gear and other toys, head for **L'Ile aux Jouets** (☏ 02 96 23 16 02) on Place de l'Hôtel de Ville near the tourist office. Since Perros-Guirec is a 'Station Famille', **high summer sees Festival Place aux Mômes (p. 57) events, plus Les Estivales,** a programme of free activities that might include a football-themed day.

For yet more fun, there's a skate park and, at the Bassin du Linkin marina on the east side of town, a **Miniature Port** (☏ 02 96 91 06 11) where kids 3 and up (plus adults) can steer model ferries and other boats (Apr–Aug). If you fancy a real boat trip, you can sail out to the **Sept Iles** archipelago (see p. 165) to see the puffin colony, perhaps glimpsing seals en route. For those who can read French, be sure to ask at the tourist office (or download from its website) for *Le P'tit Perrosien*, a free magazine with info on Perros-Guirec for kids, plus comic strips and quizzes.

Museums

See also **Towns & Cities** and **Fun Days Out,** p. 159.

La Briqueterie
★ ★ **FIND** ALL AGES

Parc de Boutdeville, Langueux; ☏ 02 96 63 36 66, www.saint brieuc-agglo.fr/fr/la_briqueterie. php. 5km (3 miles) southeast of St. Brieuc off N12.

Located in an old brick and slate factory on the Baie de St. Brieuc, this museum explores the bay's history and industry. Housing a model railway and lively programme of events, (among them various creative workshops for kids), this is a surprise hit with families. A French-language trail for ages 6 to 12, takes them inside the 30m-long (98ft) brick oven and around the rest of the museum, including an old train wagon where you can watch a film about the last train that ran on this coast. Outside, take a *petit train* ride in the shady grounds, taking in stunning views over the bay. Note that you can get joint tickets with the Maison de la Baie (p. 169).

Time about 1hr 30mins. Open Feb and Nov half-terms, Easter and Christmas school hols Tues–Sun 2–6pm; June and Sept Wed and Fri–Sun 2–6pm; July and Aug Mon–Fri 10.30am–6.30pm, Sat and Sun

1.30–6.30pm; Oct–May Wed, Fri and Sun 2–6pm. **Admission** *4€ adult, €2.50 child 6–12.* **Amenities** 🅿 🏕 🧗 ♿

Cité des Télécoms
★ ★ AGE 5 & UP

Cosmopolis, Pleumeur-Bodou; 📞 *02 96 46 63 80, www.leradome.com. 7.5km (4.5 miles) northwest of Lannion on D21.*

Set up by France Télécom and occupying, in part, a huge dome used for the first satellite broadcast of images between France and the United States, in 1962, this telecommunications museum should occupy budding young tech-heads. The main attractions are a GPS-based orienteering game—a mystery trail with codes to crack, handhelds to navigate the displays, an interactive quiz, workshops, and perhaps best of all, a virtual reality zone where you can snowboard and play beach volleyball, among other things. The Râdome itself hosts a show that allows spectators to relive that first broadcast of TV and a further video, laser and sound show on telecommunications in general. Do note that some of the above are only available in school holidays, and just about everything is in French only, though shows and guided tours can be given in English and some other languages by prior arrangement. The exhibition takes you from the first undersea cables to the Internet and beyond, with interactive exhibits, most notably in the Jardin des Sciences for ages 6 to 12;

you can, for instance, save the Earth from a hail of meteorites or steer a satellite. A café is open in the height of summer, otherwise there are picnic areas. The souvenir shop is full of wacky gifts, gizmos and knick-knacks ideal for keeping kids occupied—at least for a while, on the car journey home.

Time 2–3hrs. **Open** *Apr–June and Sept daily 10am–6pm (with some variations in Apr and Sept); July and Aug daily 10am–7pm; for rest of year see website.* **Admission** *museum and one show in Râdome: 7€ adult, 5.60€ child 5–17, 19.60€ family.* **Amenities** ☕ 🅿 🏕 🛍 ♿

▶ INSIDER TIP ▶

On the same site as the Cité des Télécoms, the **Planétarium de Bretagne** (📞 *02 96 15 80 30, www.planetarium-bretagne.fr*) hosts 3D shows on astronomical themes (in French), with some shows aimed at children as young as three. New in 2010, La Petite Planète is the tale of three animals who pollute their planet so badly they have to leave it. Older children (from 10 years) may prefer watching a virtual visit of local chateaux and abbeys. Shows cost 7€ for adults, 5.60€ for ages 5–17.

Musée du Rail AGE 2 & UP

Train station, Dinan; 📞 *02 96 39 53 48; www.museedurail-dinan.com.*

Occupying part of the eastern wing of Dinan's train station, this railway buff's dream has scale models of trains and a vast track on which to watch them operate, with scale models of local buildings alongside displays

Rainy Days in the Côtes d'Armor

In addition to museums, the following are handy standbys for days when sunshine isn't forthcoming. Note that there's also an indoor aquatic centre at **Armoripark** (p. 161).

Aquabaie (Espace Brézillet, St. Brieuc, ☎*02 96 75 67 56*, *www.saint brieuc-agglo.fr/fr/aquabaie.php*), a large sports and health complex with excellent slides, water games and a paddling pool.

Aquatides (Les Livaudières, Loudéac, ☎*02 96 66 09 09*, *www.cideral. fr*), is not as flashy as St. Brieuc's Aquabaie, but is a handy inland option with plenty of classes and facilities for babies and children.

Cinéma Club 6 (40 Bd Clémenceau, St. Brieuc, ☎*02 96 33 83 26*, *www.cineland.fr*), a six-screen cinema in the centre of town, shows kids' films dubbed into French. There's a sister cinema, Cinéland, just outside St. Brieuc at Trégueux, together with a bowling hall, **Le Strike** (☎*02 96 75 14 01*).

Espace Aqualudique Goëlys (Rue Pierre de Coubertin, Binic, ☎*02 96 69 20 10*, *www.piscinegoelys.fr*) is a fabulous indoor swimming complex two minutes from the beach, with a whopping 65m (213ft) main slide, a wild rapids feature, a paddling pool and more.

Forum de Trégastel (Plage du Coz-Pors, Trégastel, ☎*02 96 15 30 44*, *www.forumdetregastel.com*) yet another excellent indoor water-park, reopened after substantial renovation work in 2010, with a pad-dling pools and kids' games, wild rapids and other features.

Loisirsland (Parc des Expos, Brézillet, St. Brieuc, ☎*02 96 79 96 11*, *www.loisirsland.com*) is part of a chain of indoor soft-play centres across northern France, with inflatables but also wooden and board games.

La Patinoire (Espace Commercial, 24 Rue du Pont Léon, ☎*02 96 33 03 08*, *www.saintbrieuc-agglo.fr/fr/patinoire.php*) offers a small but decent ice-rink, with lessons for children and teenagers, plus evening sessions with music and lights.

of old station clocks, signs, plat-form lanterns, and scales. If trains aren't your bag, you may still appreciate the wonderful collection of old French railway posters from various eras, most showing Breton landmarks of the region, including Carnac (p. 107), the Mont-St. Michel (p. 65) and the Côte d'Emeraude (p. 171), plus some old movie posters with a railway connection.

Time 1hr. *Open* Easter hols daily 2–5.30pm; June–mid-Sept 2–6pm; Nov half term 2–5pm. *Admission* 4€ adult, 3.25€ child under 12. *Amenities* 🅿 ♿

Côtes d'Armor Shopping

The Coopérative Maritime—a fishermen's society set up in the late 1900s—now owns almost 60 **Comptoir de la Mer** shops in ports on France's northern and Atlantic Coast. In the Côtes d'Armor, venues include Erquy and St. Cast Le Guildo on the Côte d'Emeraude (p. 171) and Paimpol; for all addresses, see *www.comptoirdelamer.net*. Catering to adults and children, to expert sailors and to people who just love the sea, they stock everything from fishing and sailing gear to nautically inspired clothing, decorative items such as ships' models, books and comic-strips, soft toys and seaweed-based cosmetics. Whatever you busy, make sure you pick up a free Horaire des Marées booklet, which as well as the tide tables, contains handy advice on how to catch and cook various shellfish.

St. Brieuc is blessed with good independent toyshops; **Le Blé en Herbe** (13 Rue Saint Gouéno, ℃*02 96 61 95 55*, *www.ble-en-herbe.com*; there's a second branch in Lannion) with its motto 'Adventure makes us big' is perhaps its best. It's not huge, but within its four colourful walls it crams a vast array of toys, games and books for all ages. All stock has been selected lovingly, whether it's high-quality wooden toys for tots (including the French Vilac range of pull-alongs), fantasy models and figurines for older children, or Czech hand puppets. The range of both model animals and books are especially impressive. This is also a good place to pick up cards and postcards, and CDs with classic stories such as *Le Petit Prince*—handy for road trips.

Just around the corner, on Rue Charbonnerie, you'll find the fantastic children's shoe shop **Patt'ine** (℃*02 96 77 03 31*), with brands including Geox trainers and sandals (designed not to absorb sweat and thus to remain odour-free), plus a large play area at the rear.

Parks & Gardens

Parc des Promenades

Rue des Promenades, St. Brieuc; contact tourist office (p. 155) for information.

St. Brieuc's huge public 'Park of Walks', surrounding the Palais de Justice, offers the pleasures of an open-air sculpture park, with works in granite by local artists, against a backdrop of rare trees and plants, including Lebanese cedars, and views over the Goudéc valley. The latter, a 'greenway' into the town from the port, is a good spot for games (there's a big lawn for ball sports and a basketball court), sunbathing and picnics, and also links up with the pleasant **Parc des Eaux Minérales,** with its stream crossed by several wooden bridges.

The Elle Est Ou La Mer? collection of nautically inspired kidswear (p. 64), can be found at the Boutique Coudémail at Rue St. Guillaume (☎02 96 87 05 10; there's a second branch in Dinan).

Like the rest of Brittany, the Côtes d'Armor is mad for biscuits; if you are too, then head for the **Biscuiterie des Iles** at Belle-Isle-en-Terre west of Guingamp (☎*02 96 43 30 03*, *www.biscuiterie-des-iles.com*), and join a tour (daily in summer at 11pm), presenting traditional methods of biscuit making. There's also a shop at Trégastel-Plage on the Côte du Granit Rose (p. 161).

The Côte d'Armor's main **markets** are:

Binic	Tues morning
Dinan	Thurs morning
Erquy	Sat morning
Guingamp	Tues and Fri mornings, plus a smaller one Sat mornings
Lamballe	Thurs morning
Lancieux	Tues morning
Lannion	Thurs morning
Matignon	Wed morning
Paimpol	Tues afternoon
Perros-Guirec	Fri morning
Pléneuf–Le Val-André	Tues and Fri mornings
Plestin-les-Grèves	Sun morning
St. Brieuc	Sun morning (two markets; main one on Place Martray)
St. Cast le Guildo	Mon morning
Trébeurden	Tues morning
Trégastel	Mon morning

Open *daily 8am–nightfall.* **Admission** *free.* **Amenities** 🅿 🏕 🈳 ♿

Jardin du Val Cocherel FIND

Dinan (behind castle); ☎*02 96 87 69 76.*

This public park behind the chateau in Dinan (p. 158), alongside the old town walls, though nothing exceptional, is still worth a visit; young ones will enjoy seeing the deer, peacocks, rabbits and other small animals whilst families can challenge each other on the mini-golf course or ping pong tables. The rose garden has picnic tables (some covered). Fittingly, perhaps, locals call this park Le Jardin des Petits-Diables—Little Devils' Garden.

Open *daily 8am–7.30pm.* **Admission** *free.* **Amenities** 🅿 🏕 🈳 ♿

For Active Families

See also **Best Beaches,** p. 170. For diving tuition from age 8, head for the highly regarded **Centre Activités Plongée de Trébeurden** (✆02 96 23 66 71; *www.plongeecap.com*) on the Côte du Granit Rose (p. 161).

Ecurie du Gallais
★ **FIND** AGE 2 & UP

Le Logis du Gallais, Rue du Bois-es-Lucas, St. Cast le Guildo; ✆*02 96 41 04 90; www.ecurie-du-gallais.com.*

These stables a few minutes from the coast can take you out on guided horse rides lasting from an hour to 4 days—destinations include the Cap Fréhel and Fort La Latte (p. 162) and the Ile des Ebihens, which is reached across the sands at low tide. Tots are also catered for, with pony rides around the farm, and there are riding courses throughout the year. You can even stay on-site, in simple B&B rooms, including a family room for four; kids then have the run of the pretty garden with its play equipment.

Time half an hour to 4 days. *Open* all year; booking required. *Cost* varies by ride. *Amenities* 👪 ⚲

Pêche en Mer ★ AGE 6 & UP

Gare Maritime, Plage de Trestraou, Perros-Guirec; ✆*02 96 91 10 00; www.armor-decouverte.fr.*

A great opportunity for a father–son bonding session, these sea-fishing excursions run by the same folks as the trips to the Sept Iles (p. 165) are open to anyone aged 3 and up but are better for those with older kids, both for enjoyment and safety's sake. Fishing rods and bait are provided if you need them, but you can bring your own equipment. Your catch might include mackerel, pollock, sea bream, trout or red mullet—perfect to toss on the BBQ back at your gîte or campsite.

Time 3hrs. *Sailings* 2–4 times a week in July and Aug 7.30–10.30am. *Tickets* 29€ for fishers, 19€ for non-fishers.

Station VTT Arguenon-Hunaudaye ★★
FIND **GREEN** ALL AGES

Chalet Sports Nature, Jugon Les Lacs; ✆*02 96 31 67 04 (or outside July and Aug contact tourist office); www.jugon-les-lacs.com/en/ sn_vtt.php.*

The Côte d'Armor doesn't have any Voies Vertes except that beginning at Dinard and ending at Dinan (p. 82), but this mountain-bike resort at Jugon Les Lacs (p. 159) is an exceptional place to come cycling as a family, with 200km (124 miles) of signposted paths through natural settings, divided into 10 trails of varying length and levels of difficulty. The centre dispenses maps and has bike-washing facilities; you can also hire bikes (plus baby seats), and staff offer tuition to both beginners and the more experienced who want advice on specific trails.

Time from half a day. *Cycle hire* 11€ half day–70€ week; children's bikes 7€–45€; for supervised rides, see website. *Amenities* 🚲 ⚲ 🌲 Ⓥ

Vivons Perché

★ GREEN AGE 2 & UP

Crec'h Ar Beg, Pleumeur-Bodou;
📞 *06 22 53 46 45; www.vivons-perches.com. 7.5km (4.5 miles) northwest of Lannion on D21.*

This treetop adventure course in a forest setting handy for the Station LPO (p. 165) and the Village Gaulois (p. 166) and other attractions at Cosmopolis is unusual in that its eight courses of varying difficulty include a 'mini forest' for ages 2 and up. There's also a pedestrian trail with benches for those just watching, plus picnic tables. Note that those who come by bike get a discount.

Time *courses vary from 30mins to 2hrs 30mins.* **Open** *Apr–June, Oct and Nov Wed, Sat, Sun and school and public hols 10.30am–7pm; July and Aug daily 9.30am–8pm; Sept Wed–Sun 1–7pm.* **Admission** *prices vary by course: Mini Fôret and Petite Fôret 5€ and 11€pp.* **Amenities** 🅿️ 🏕️

FAMILY-FRIENDLY DINING

The Côtes d'Armor is famed for its large, nutty-flavoured scallops (from the Baie de St. Brieuc; p. 159), its oysters (from Paimpol and the Tréguier estuary) and its seaweed. Non-marine produce to look out for in markets and on restaurant menus are apples from the Dinan area (the Vallée de la Rance), the unappetisingly named BF15 potatoes, and the *coco de Paimpol*, a semi-dry white haricot bean that goes well with smoked sausage, chorizo or local lobster.

Dinan & Around, & Côte d'Emeraude

With its string of unpretentious family resorts, the Côte d'Emeraude offers plenty of good child-friendly dining at friendly prices, with the emphasis on seafood, but inland Dinan can also be a fine place for a family meal.

EXPENSIVE

Au Biniou ★★

121 Rue Clémenceau, Le Val-André;
📞 *02 96 72 24 35.*

With its minimalist facade and dining room, this fish restaurant a minute's walk from the seafront of the family resort of Le Val-André (p. 171) doesn't look an obvious family choice. Yet the children's menu (12€) is top-notch, offering the likes of roast pollock with creamy rice, and roast chicken breast with tagliatelle, followed by chocolate mousse or ice cream. Staff, though somewhat reserved, are unusually attentive to safety issues, moving knives and glasses away from grabbing little fingers, for instance. The main menu offers everything from the classic (*moules marinières* using mussels from the bay of Hillion down the road) to the highly creative (perhaps John Dory with coriander and chive noodles and Vietnamese fish sauce).

Desserts are too tempting to pass up on—old-fashioned (very thick) *crème brûlée* with Bourban vanilla, or pear crumble with caramel sauce and *crème fraîche*. This is a favourite with locals, so book ahead, especially at weekends. On the other hand, it's not at all touristy, so don't expect English-language menus or English-speaking staff.

Open *Mon, Thurs–Sun noon–midnight, Tues noon–3pm; open Tues eve and Wed all day during July–Aug. Closed Feb.* **Main courses** *17.50€– 32.50€.* **Amenities** ⬜ 耳 ✆

Chez la Mère Pourcel ★★

3 Place des Merciers, Dinan; ☎ *02 96 39 03 80.*

Another very busy spot, prized by both locals and visitors (try to book ahead), 'Mother Pourcel's' charms first and foremost by its setting in a medieval merchant's dwelling in the historic heart of Dinan (p. 158), with a cosy wood-beamed interior. Food is an appealing combination of the rustic and the inventive—think scallop carpaccio with crab and a lime marinade, tartare of salmon with chive oil, and *magret* of duck with gooseberry sauce. Children are welcomed with a rather less sophisticated menu (10€) of fish filet or *steak haché* with chips or vegetables, a drink, and a surprise dessert. If they're quite adventurous they can get a half-price version of the much more interesting Menu Terroir (26€/13€), which includes rabbit terrine with onion jam, fish choucroute, and strawberry

gratin. In high season the restaurant doubles as a daytime brasserie serving crêpes, ice cream, local beers and ciders, and more.

Open *early May–late Sept daily noon–2.30pm and 7–10pm; rest of year Mon and Thurs–Sat noon– 2.30pm and 7–10pm, Tues and Sun noon–2.30pm.* **Main courses** *13€– 17€.* **Amenities** 耳 ✆

MODERATE

La Moulerie de la Baie ★ FIND

Jospinet, Planguenoual; ☎ *02 96 32 82 22. 7km (4 miles) southwest of Le Val-André on D34.*

A well-deserved reputation for its mussels (which can been seen growing on their bouchots— wooden posts—nearby) keep locals coming back to this cheerful beach-side spot. Although there are a couple of other choices (steak and cheese), it's a shame not to enjoy a generous plate of *moules frites*—seafood 'don't come any fresher than this'. The kids' menu (€7.50) features a small dish of *moules marinières* followed by ice cream. Staff are charming; it's only the rather limited dessert choice (mainly ice creams) that lets the place down. Try to time your visit with sunset on a fine day— and to bag a table on the terrace.

Open *late Apr–Nov Tues–Sun noon– 2pm and 7–9.30pm.* **Main courses** *8€–12€.* **Amenities** ⬜ ✆

La Stalla

48 Rue du Port, Erquy; ☎ *02 96 72 01 03.*

Come early evening to this welcoming seafront Italian and you may walk in on the chef still eating with his own kids, which inspires confidence from the start. Expect no-nonsense, good-value renditions of the basics in an unpretentious decor of wood and red-checked tablecloths, with cheerful service. There is a *menu bambino* for under-12s (7.50€)—pizza, spaghetti bolognaise, or nuggets and chips, plus a soft drink, and ice cream or chocolate mousse—but, as in most Italians, there's plenty on the main menu for junior palates, including a huge selection of pizzas (available to takeaway), pasta dishes and substantial omelettes.

Open *Tues–Sun 12.30–2.30pm, 7.30–10pm.* **Main courses** *6.90€– 14.60€.* **Amenities** 🎿 ☕

The most highly rated crêperie in Dinan is the **Ahna,** at 7 Rue de la Poissonnerie (☎02 96 39 09 13)—book ahead to be sure of a table.

Le Bonheur est dans Le Blé ★ FIND

17 Rue du Duc d'Aiguillon, St. Cast le Guildo; ☎02 96 81 03 99.

With its red, flower-embellished façade and its setting (and terrace) on a pedestrian street five minutes' from the main beach at child-friendly St. Cast (p. 155), this cosy crêperie is a magnet to families, who come for the freshly made sweet and savoury pancakes and the home-made ice creams and sorbets (made without flavourings or aromas and hence particularly delicious). Under-10s get an 8.50€ menu of ham and cheese galette, a crêpe or ice cream, and a *sirop* drink, but can of course choose from the wider menu, highlights of which include La Bretonne, a galette with local sausage, cheese, creamy mushrooms and egg, and L'Orange Noire, a crêpe with bitter-orange marmalade, candied oranges and hot chocolate.

Open *daily noon–3pm and 7–10pm.* **Main courses** *2.60–15.80.* **Amenities** ☐ 🎿 ☕

St. Brieuc & Around

Though St. Brieuc is not as alluring an option as you might imagine given that it's the *départemental* capital, there are plenty of tempting family options around its magnificent bay, especially on the Goëlo coast leading up to Paimpol. If you like scallops, don't miss those from St. Quay Portrieux.

Via Costa ★ ★

Plage du Moulin, Etables sur Mer; ☎02 96 70 79 57. 3.5km (2 miles) north of Binic on D1.

The beach itself is nothing out of the ordinary, but this camp Brazilian-themed 'lounge restaurant' down by the sands provides a blast of originality in a sea of crêperies and seafood joints. Inside, it's all fairy lights, funky lightshades and exotic flowers; for summertime dining, there are tables outside, plus loungers where you can enjoy a moonlit cocktail to the cheesy jazz soundtrack (try the tequila and aloe vera based Via Costa, for two to share!). Food-wise, the place runs the gamut from pizzas, steaks, beef carpaccio and seafood classics (including platters) to the likes of chicken tagine with preserved lemons and Asian dishes such as cod in curry and coconut milk or wok-fried pork with noodles. The kids' menu (10€; under-10s) is surprisingly basic (steak or ham with chips, or *pizza bambino*). Even out of season, on a weekday lunch, this place gets busy—recommendation indeed for somewhere off-the-beaten track—but if it's full (or you're in a hurry), tapas and ice creams are served in the bar.

Open *noon–2.30pm and 7–11pm (bar 11am–2am) Mar–Sept and school hols daily, Oct–Feb Fri–Mon only.* ***Main courses*** *9€–44€.* ***Amenities*** 📋 🎧 ☎

MODERATE

Don't miss the wonderful **Le Char à Bancs** inn on the same site as La Maison des Lamour (p. 186).

La Moana ★

32 Rue Joffre, Binic; 📞 *02 96 73 65 89.*

There's no arguing with the genuine Italian fare at this cosy restaurant one street back from Binic's marina. Dine on home-made pasta, pizzas (including takeaways) and grown-up dishes such as *osso bucco à la milanaise*. There's no children's menu, and portions can be almost terrifyingly

huge, so with younger kids it's a good idea to pick two or three dishes to share between four—perhaps a Ronde des Dieux ravioli sampler plate, a Dolce Vita pasta sampler plate, and a pizza. As is typical of a seaside eatery, there's a decent choice of fish-based pasta dishes, plus *moules-frites* and some interesting seafood salads. Everyone will be happy with the dessert menu, which includes strawberries and cream, frozen nougat, chocolate-and-banana or fruit pizza and—naturally—plenty of ice cream concoctions.

Open *daily 11.45am–2pm and 6.45– midnight (closed Wed Oct–Mar).* ***Main courses*** *9€–17.90 €.* ***Amenities*** 🎧 ☎

INEXPENSIVE

Crêperie des Grèves ★★★

23 Rue des Grèves, Langueux; 📞 *02 96 72 56 96. 5km (3 miles) southeast of St. Brieuc off N12.*

Immensely welcoming, this Crêperie Gourmande occupies the former home and bistro of the owner's great-grandparents. You have to fight your way past a bustling front counter providing locals with takeaway galettes to reach the appealing dining room with its touches of nautical décor. Celtic music plays unobtrusively as you browse the menu of galettes (made using mainly local farm produce) and organic crêpes, while younger visitors look at the children's books piled by the hearth or even wander out to the adjacent seaside play area (you can keep an eye from the window). The kids' menu

Wooden play fort at Le Char á Bancs, part of La Maison des Lamour (see p. 186)

(9.50€) offers various basic galettes, a sugar/butter, caramel or chocolate crêpe, and a drink. But children might also like the speciality Coquinette (scallops with *julienne* of vegetables), Ouessant, with goats' cheese, blue cheese, Gruyère and salad, or Hillionaise, with local mussels, leeks and shallot. Some of the dessert crêpes contain honey from the restaurant's own hive, or homemade caramel or you can enjoy one of the hand-made ice creams.

Open *July and Aug Tues–Sat noon–2.30pm, Sun and Mon 7–11pm; rest of year Wed, Thurs and Fri noon–2.30pm and Sat and Sun 7–11pm.* **Main courses** *2.50€–13.50€.* **Amenities**

Côte du Granit Rose

The Pink Granite Coast with its family-friendly resorts is a great place for seaside dining.

Tréguier, at the gateway to the Côte du Granit Rose and home to the Hôtel Aigue Marine (p. 187),

is a good place for all-day eating options, with a central square full of useful all-day brasseries and crêperies, including **Le Martray** (☎02 96 92 20 71) and **Resto Bar les Vieilles Poutres** (☎02 96 92 45 73). On the quays, the **Crêperie la Dînette** (☎02 96 92 93 22) is a decent, untouristy spot with a courtyard kids' play area.

INEXPENSIVE–MODERATE

Digor Kalon ★

89 Rue du Maréchal Joffre, Perros-Guirec; ☎*02 96 49 03 63.*

This Breton tapas bar with its bold façade, bizarre knick-knacks and old furniture is a lively venue for offbeat musical performances, which you can enjoy while eating a suitably eclectic range of sharing dishes. The menu varies according to the season and the mood of the chef, but might include *pissaladière* (a kind of French pizza with anchovies and onions), dips, *empanadas* (Latin American filled pastries), *patatas bravas* (fried potato chunks), prawns, squid, Serrano ham and chorizo. The mussels come served with rice or *patatas*, and are cooked in a variety of interesting ways, including with Dremmwel Rousse (an amber Breton beer). It's perfect snacky fare if you had a full lunch and want a bite to eat and a drink in an informal setting.

Open daily 5pm–2am. **Main courses** 8.50€–15.90€. **Amenities** ✆⚲

Le Ker Bleu ★

17 Bd Joseph Le Bihan, Perros-Guirec; ✆*02 96 91 14 69.*

This handy option on Perros-Guirec's busiest beach (p. 173) serves galettes, crêpes and drinks all day, plus, at standard restaurant opening times (or all day in July and August), almost 30 kinds of hand-made pizza, pasta dishes, Italian classics such as beef carpaccio and *osso bucco*, fish of the day, seafood platters, and main-course salads containing the likes of scallops and langoustines. The kids' menu 8€ is wide ranging, offering pizza, pasta, steak, ham or mussels with chips, or a galette, plus a crêpe or an ice cream. The bright and breezy dining room with its old comic-strip images on the walls is air-conditioned in sweltering weather, but the decked terrace with its view of the Sept Iles bird reserve (p. 165) is the place to be.

Open July and Aug daily noon–11pm; Sept–Nov and Feb–June Thurs–Mon noon-11pm. **Main courses** 2€–35€. **Amenities** 🛜📶🎵

FAMILY-FRIENDLY ACCOMMODATION

The Côtes d'Armor is an interesting place to stay, with few places to splurge but lots of characterful, often quirky family accommodation, whether inland or by the sea.

Dinan & Around, & Côte d'Emeraude

It's the Côte du Granit Rose that draws the crowds, so canny families might do well to look in this less touristy area for good-value accommodation.

Best Picnic Spots

If you're not picnicking amidst the weird rocks of the Côte du Granit Rose, try one of the following great alfresco eating spots:

At the end of the 'magic pathway' at the **Centre du Découverte du Son,** p. 160.

At the **Village Gaulois,** p. 166.

In the pine forest by the **Lac de Guerlédan,** p. 172.

At **La Briqueterie,** over looking the Baie de St. Brieuc, p. 173.

At **Vivons Perché** forest adventure course, p. 179.

Hôtel Le D'Avagour ★ FIND

1 Place du Champ, Dinan; ☎02 96 39 07 49; www.avaugourhotel.com.

This is the perfect hotel for exploring the historical town of Dinan (p. 158) and surrounds, offering sparkling-clean if plain, rather outmoded rooms. The public areas are newly renovated, and the bathrooms are modern too, so perhaps the guestrooms will be overhauled before too long. The staff are genuinely charming and very helpful, and there are lovely gardens backing onto the old town walls. Families are directed toward one of the three garden-view suites, which have one large room with a double and two single beds, plus space for an extra bed or cot, a small dressing room, plus a bathroom and separate shower-room. Kids up to 10 get breakfast free, otherwise it's 13.50€. If you want more privacy, there's also an interconnecting double and twin facing the square.

24 units. **Rates** *87€–145€; suite 220€–240€ (except during Fête des Remparts in July). Extra bed 16€.* **Amenities** 🚲 📶 **In room** 🛏 ☐

Among the handful of campsites in this area recommended by Camping Qualité (p. 93) is the four-star **Camping Caravaning Château de Galinée** (☎02 96 41 10 56, **www.chateaudegalinee. com**) in the grounds of an elegant château near St. Cast le Guildo, with a mini-farm for kids and accommodation that includes mobile homes styled as roulettes (Romany caravans). Camping

Qualité also recommends an inland site, **Camping au Bocage du Lac** (☎02 96 31 60 16, **www. campinglacbretagne.com**) on the lake at Jugon Les Lacs (p. 159).

The **Ecurie du Gallais** (p. 178) at St. Cast le Guildo offers inexpensive B&B on its farm.

Ferme de Malido ★

St. Alban; ☎02 96 32 94 74, www. malido.com. 5.5km (3.5 miles) south of Le Val-André on D786.

Four kilometres (2.5 miles) from the sea, this working farm offering six basic but comfy B&B rooms (two for families) and two large gîtes (for up to 10 and 14, including a baby each) is a great summer base. During July to August (and some weekends in September) a mystery maze is dotted with playful artworks. This is best experienced on a night tour so bring a torch and, if you like, meat to cook on the campfire; crêpes, galettes, ribs and drinks are also available. In summer, the farm grounds are used for wooden and traditional Breton games, a bouncy castle, a pedal-cart track, a '*pied-nus*' trail with different surfaces to experience with bare feet, special events as *fest noz* (p. 16) and treasure hunts, so there's no way you can be bored here.

8 units. **Rates** *43€–55€, family room for four 73€–85€; gîtes POA.* **Amenities** ❌ 📷 🎵 **In room** *(gîtes only)* ❌ ☐

La Julerie ★

Corseul; ☎02 96 27 24 23; www. lajulerie-gites.com. 13km (8 miles) northwest of Dinan on D794.

These English-run **gîtes,** renovated to retain their traditional Breton style, are a great find given that they share the use of a heated indoor pool—a blessing on wet days when the beaches 20km (12.5 miles) away lose their appeal. Next to the pool is a games room with table tennis; outside are sun loungers, grassy play areas, a swing, a slide and a sandpit. The setting is peaceful—at night you'll hear little except owls—and the main roads are far away. The four gîtes, one with space for up to eight people, are all part of the same long building but have their own patio/lawn areas. The biggest, Le Grenier, boasts terracotta tiled floors, a wood-burning stove and a clawfoot bath; children get a lovely attic floor to themselves, with twin beds and a sofabed for two, and a private bathroom.

4 units. **Rates** *435€–1290€ per week (weekend rates available).* **Amenities** ▨ ▨ *In room* ▭ ✕ ◪ ▯

St. Brieuc & Around

You're unlikely to base yourself in the *départementale* capital itself, though if you're passing through, it does have a branch of the **All Seasons** budget chain.

La Maison des Lamour
★ ★ ★ GREEN

La Ville Guerfault, Plélo; ☎ *02 96 79 51 25; www.lamaisondeslamour. com. 22km (13.5 miles) northwest of St. Brieuc on D79.*

Having undergone a name change and expansion since the first edition of this guide, this eccentric venue is no less extraordinary. The Lamour family in question have embraced eco-tourism since the 1970s, as a means to bring new life to the working farm that passed down to them—most famously in their charming on-site inn, **Le Char à Bancs,** which combines rustic period details with funky modern touches. Local families flock to it both for the *pot au porc* and divine caramelised rhubarb crêpes, and for the incredible grounds with their large wooden play fort, little hill crisscrossed by tunnels to climb through, slide and swings, wooden horse, field full of real ponies they can pet (and ride in summer), and pedalo hire on the river in summer. Accommodation is up a winding lane, in the old ancestors' farm buildings, where five shabbychic B&B rooms for two to four people have been supplemented by four equally charming gîtes, one fitting two people and a baby, two fitting four and a baby, and one for up to six and a baby. All have a private terrace, and one even has its own vegetable garden.

9 units. **Rates** *69€–79€; room for four 117€–130€; gîte for four to five 460€–1600€.* **Amenities** ◪ ⛰ ⋀ ▥▮ ▯ *In room (gîtes)* ▭ ✕ ▯

INSIDER TIP ›

If La Maison is booked up, the owner's Irish sister-in-law has similarly stylish gîtes and B&B rooms at Les Petites Maisons dans la Prairie (☎ *02 96 79 52 39,* ***www.chambres-gites-bretagne. fr***), 3km (2 miles) to the north.

See **Camping Qualité** (p. 93) for its handful of selected Goëlo coast campsites with incredible bay views. For camping inland of St. Brieuc, see **Lac de Guerlédan** (p. 172).

Côte du Granit Rose

This is prime beach territory, so expect prices to be a little higher than elsewhere in the *département*.

MODERATE

Hôtel Aigue Marine

Port de Plaisance, Tréguier; ☎ *02 96 92 97 00; www.aiguemarine.fr.*

Situated on the marina of a pretty cathedral town, this is a decent if slightly old-fashioned family hotel with outdoor pool and a gourmet restaurant, complete with a family area overlooking the garden. Three kids' menus are offered—one basic, for younger children (10€), and two more sophisticated, featuring choices from the main menu (14€–18€). Aigue Marine's good-value (if blandly furnished) family rooms consist of a small room with bunkbeds, a large double bedroom, a seating area with table and chairs, a fridge, a terrace or balcony, and a bathroom with tub. There are also a number of L-shaped triples without a fridge or seating area, so if there are three of you, you may prefer to get a large double with these extras plus an extra bed.

48 rooms. **Rates** *91€–128€, family room for four 118€–126€. Cot 10€, extra bed 20€.* **Amenities** ⛱ 🏃 ⛵
🖼 🍴 📺 *In room* 🖥 🛁 🍼

Château de Kermezen ★

Pommerit-Jaudy; ☎ *02 96 91 35 75; www.chateaux-france.com. 8km (5 miles) south of Tréguier on D8.*

A gorgeous little château at the end of a sweeping driveway lined by oaks, surrounded by splendid grounds, Kermezen is owned by a real-life count and countess yet is remarkably laidback and unstuffy. The genial hosts embrace families with open arms, dispensing coffee or home-made cider to parents and providing them with all sorts of practical facilities—highchairs, changing mats, bottle warmers and even a babysitting service. The five rooms here are spacious and very flowery with the requisite period furniture; the twin has a cosy sleeping alcove that might appeal to older children and the two triples come with single beds on a separate mezzanine. Downstairs, an unassuming, beamed dining room with a large table is set up for the copious Continental breakfasts and a comfy *salon* in which to relax and admire the family portraits. You're just a five-minute drive from the coast, and there's plenty else to do nearby, including cycling and riding.

5 rooms. **Rates** *90€–110€, family room for three 110€.* **Amenities** 🖼 🔍 📺 🎏

A five-minute walk from Perros-Guirec's toddler-friendly beaches (p. 173) **Camping Claire Fontaine** (☎ *02 96 23 03 55, www. camping-claire-fontaine.com*), is a low-key site based around an old Breton farmhouse with tents and caravan pitches, a gîte for four, comfy bungalows for up to six, and some attractive (given the rock-bottom prices) double and triple rooms with use of a self-catering kitchens. Though lacking the bells-and-whistles facilities of the four-star campsites, it does have a play area and all the basics. For more recommendations on this coast, see **Camping Qualite** (p. 93).

If you want to really get away from it all, Swiss Family Robinson style, the **Ile Milliau** just off Trébeurden, accessible by foot at low tide, has three basic walkers' gîtes in an old farmhouse, sleeping three, five and seven in single beds, and available by the night (contact the tourist board for details; see p. 155).

Auberge de Jeunesse Les Korrigans ★

6 Rue du 73eme territorial, Lannion; *02 96 37 91 28; www.fuaj.org.*

This remarkable youth hostel in a handsome blue-shuttered stone building in the centre of Lannion, next to the train station, is named after the mischievous fairies said to populate the area (p. 2). All rooms contain two brightly painted bunkbeds, private bathroom and a table and chairs, and have doors adorned with little fairy paintings. Breakfast is included in the rates, picnics are available at a charge, or you can prepare your own meals in the shared kitchen. Other communal facilities include a bustling 'tavern' with Internet access, a pool table and occasional events, such as concerts and exhibitions. Guests can hire mountain bikes, and coastal hiking packages are offered.

12 rooms. **Rates** *17.30€ pp.* **Amenities** 🍸 🚲 ✕ ▨ @ 🛄

6 Finistère

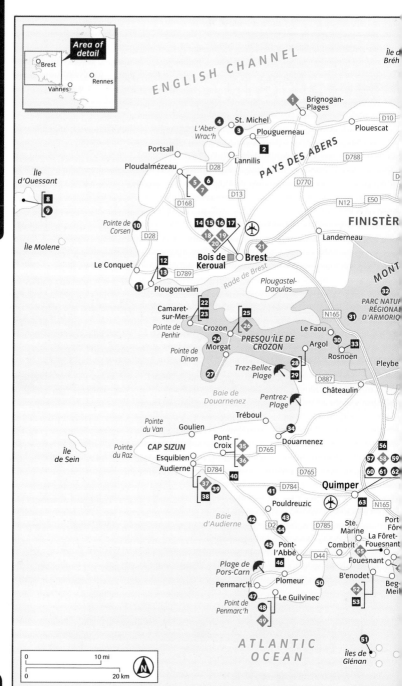

Attractions ●
Arbreizh Aventure **15**
Bigoud'Anes **44**
Capitaine Némo **50**
Celtic'Train **61**
Centre de Découverte des Algues **85**
Centre International de Plongée
  des Glénan/Les Glénans **51**
Château du Taureau **82**
Domaine de Ménez-Meur **31**
Fort de Bertheaume **13**
Haliotika II—La Cité de la Pêche **48**
Iliz-Koz **3**
Jardin du Moulin Neuf **6**
L'Aquashow **39**
Maison de l'Amiral **42**
Maison de la Réserve Naturelle
  et des Castors **71**
Maison des Jeux Bretons **45**
Maison des Johnnies et
  de l'Oignon Rosé **83**
Maison des Minéraux **27**
Maison des Vieux Métiers Vivants **28**
Marinarium **64**
Musée de l'Ecole Rurale
  en Bretagne **30**
Musée de la Faïence **60**
Musée de la Pêche **65**
Musée Départmental Breton **59**

Musée des Beaux Arts **57**
Musée des Phares et Balises/
  Ecomusée de l'Ile d'Ouessant **9**
Musée du Loup **76**
Océanopolis **16**
Parc Animalier de la Pommeraie **43**
Parc Botanique de Suscinio **78**
Parc d'Attractions Odet Loisirs **68**
Parc de Loisirs de Bel Air **41**
Parc Naturel Régional d'Armorique **32**
Peninsula Le Labyrinthe **24**
Phare d'Eckmühl **47**
Phare de l'Ile Vierge **4**
Phare de Trézien **10**
Pointe Saint Mathieu **11**
Port-Musée **34**
Roche Tremblante **73**
Ti-ar-Gouren **75**
Zone de Créac'h Gwen **62**

Dining ◆
A L'Aise Breizh Café **18**
Crêperie Blé Noir **20**
Crêperie Chez Annick **55**
Crêperie des Myrtilles **74**
Crêperie du Ménez-Gorre **26**
Crêperie L'Epoké **35**
Crêperie Le Salamandre **5**
Hippopotamus **21**
L'Ilot Jardin **54**
L'Iroise **37**
La Brocéliande **52**
La Chaumine **7**
La Corniche **1**
La Couscousserie **58**
Latitude Crêperie **19**
Le Petit Relais **81**
Le Porte au Vin **67**
Le Pub **36**
Le Rabelais **49**
Restaurant Patrick Jeffroy **80**

Accommodation ■
Aire Naturelle de Keraluic **46**
All Seasons **56**
Auberge de Jeunesse de Brest **14**
Auberge du Youdig **72**
Auberge Saint Thégonnec **77**
Camping du Goulet **17**
Camping du Vougot **2**
Camping Le Grand Large **23**
Camping Le Ty Nadan **69**
Camping Les Hortensias/
  Gîtes de Kermen **79**
Camping Les Pins **25**
Camping-gîte de Loquéran **40**
Carré d'Etoiles **12**
Domaine Ker-Moor/Villa de l'Océan **53**
Ferme Apicole de Térenez **33**
Hôtel de l'Océan **66**
Hôtel Le Temps de Vivre **84**
Hôtel Thalassa **22**
Hôtel-Restaurant Le Goyen **38**
L'Orangerie de Lanniron **63**
Le Keo **8**
Le Rhun **29**
Roulottes des Korrigans **70**

We end our tour of Brittany 'Where the earth (terre) finishes'— literally, the end of the world, the place from which Druids seem to have believed they could depart for the afterlife. For many people, Finistère is synonymous with Breton beach holidays and stunning shorelines, yet the interior of this *département*, much of which is subsumed by the vast Parc Naturel Régional d'Armorique, more than repays exploration. The Monts d'Arrée especially has much to offer active families, as well as those who want to experience some authentic Breton culture—this is a fiercely Breton region where pride in local traditions can be seen in the many *fest noz* (p. 16) and other celebrations, some attracting Celts from around the world.

This is also a region of tall things—soaring lighthouses that count among the world's highest and most powerful, and towering *coiffes*: lacy headgear that you now really only see at traditional festivals and other cultural gatherings, or in museums. Lace is not just one of the country's finest products; it inspired some of its famous biscuits, *crêpes dentelles* ('lace crêpes'). Those who don't have a sweet tooth will find plenty to tempt them in the local seafood and seaweed specialities, sold in markets in towns all over the region, or even direct from the boats.

But back to that famous coastline, which dips in and out in a series of sweeping bays and dramatic headlands that are home to splendid beaches and beautiful unspoilt resorts well-geared towards families in terms of hotels, restaurants and facilities, including beach and watersports clubs. As for larger towns and cities, Roscoff is more than just a ferry port, and the naval port of Brest has some real gems amidst its sprawling, modern bulk. The capital Quimper positively drips with attractions for families, while further south, Concarneau is a fascinating tuna fishing port with many visitor attractions.

VISITOR INFORMATION

Information Centres

The very good CDT website, *www.finisteretourisme.com*, has a links page (under 'Useful Tips') to all the tourist information offices within the region. It also has a dedicated (but French-only) family holidays website, *www.finistere-enfamille.com*.

Audierne: 8 Rue Victor Hugo, ☎ 02 98 70 12 20, *www.audierne-tourisme.com*.

Bénodet: Avenue de la Mer, ☎ 02 98 57 00 14, *www.benodet.fr*.

Brest: Place de la Liberté, ☎ 02 98 44 24 96, *www.brest-metropole-tourisme.fr*.

Camaret-sur-Mer: 15 Quai Kléber, ☎ 02 98 27 93 60, *www.camaret-sur-mer.com*.

Carantec: 4 Rue Louis Pasteur, *02 98 67 00 43, www.ville-carantec.com.*

Concarneau: Quai d'Aiguillon, *02 98 97 01 44, www.tourisme concarneau.fr.*

Douarnenez: 2 Rue du Docteur Mével, *02 98 92 13 35, www. douarnenez-tourisme.com.*

Huelgoat: 18 Place Aristide Briand, *02 98 99 72 32, http:// lesmontsdarree.fr/.*

Ile d'Ouessant: Place de l'Eglise, Lampaul, *02 98 48 85 83, www.ot-ouessant.fr.*

Morgat: Place d'Ys, *02 98 27 07 92.*

Pay des Abers: 1 Place de l'Eglise, Lannilis, *02 98 04 05 43, www.abers-tourisme.com.*

Penmarc'h: Place du Maréchal Davout, *02 98 58 81 44, www. penmarch.fr.*

Pont-L'Abbé'Lesconil: Square de l'Europe, Pont-L'Abbé, *02 98 82 37 99, www.pontlabbe-lesconil.com.*

Quimper: Place de la Résistance, *02 98 53 04 05, www.quimper-tourisme.com.*

Roscoff: Quai d'Auxerre, *02 98 61 12 13, www.roscoff-tourisme. com.*

Orientation

The **N165** *route nationale* which begins down in Nantes in the Loire Atlantique, slices up through the region via Vannes and Lorient in the Morbihan (p. 106). From Lorient, it's a fast 70km (43 miles) to **Quimper** and 135km (84 miles) to **Brest**.

From Brest running east, the **N12** takes you round **Morlaix** (58km/36 miles) and into the Côtes d'Armor (p. 151), to St. Brieuc (146km/91 miles). Then it goes on to Rennes (242km/150miles) in the Ille-et-Vilaine and ultimately right on to Paris (595km/370 miles) via the Mayenne and Normandy, becoming a motorway for some of the way.

Off these roads, including north of Brest towards Roscoff, you're confined to *routes départementales* and rural roads so allow more time for journeys.

Arriving

By Boat If you're bringing your car to France and staying exclusively on the west coast, it's worth coming into **Roscoff** because it's the only port west of St. Malo back over in the Ille-et-Vilaine (p. 49). **Brittany Ferries** (p. 37) sail there from **Plymouth** up to three times a day, with daytime trips lasting from 5 hours 30 minutes to 6 hours and night sailings of 8 hours. You may want to check for crossings on the *Pont-Aven*, the company's luxurious flagship ferry, which as well as providing standard facilities such as children's play areas and entertainment, has a small swimming pool and a cinema.

The *Pont-Aven* also makes one night-sailing a week between Roscoff and **Cork** in **Ireland,** taking 13 hours. Alternatively, you can sail from **Rosslare** with **Irish Ferries** (p. 24) in 17 to 18 hours; the ship, the *Oscar Wilde*, has a children's play area and a cinema.

By Train TGVs from **Paris** (via Rennes in the Ille-et-Vilaine) to **Brest** and to **Quimper** each take about 4 hours 20 minutes; see p. 30 for SNCF details. Some trains to Brest also stop at **Morlaix** and **Landerneau**; some to Quimper also stop at **Quimperlé** and **Rosporden**.

By Air **Ryanair** (p. 25) runs budget flights between **London-Luton** and **Brest** airport, 10km (6 miles) east of the city, taking 1 hour 10 minutes, and also from Dublin (summer only). **Flybe** (p. 25) flies there (summer only) from **Southampton** (65 minutes), **Birmingham** (1 hour 20 minutes) and **Manchester** (about 1hr 30mins); its website gives other flights but these are non-direct. For up-to-the-minute schedules, see the Brest airport website, *www.brest.aeroport.fr*.

For those coming from Paris, **Air France** (p. 25) flies between Brest from both Charles de Gaulle and Orly airports, taking about 1 hour 15 minutes, while **easyJet**, (*www.easyjet.com*) also serves the CDG route. Flights from other French cities are also available.

Air France also flies to **Quimper** airport (☎02 98 94 30 30, *www.quimper.aeroport.fr*)

from Paris Orly in roughly the same time.

Getting Around

Finistère, perhaps more than any other area of Brittany, is very difficult to explore by **public transport,** and any holiday will be severely limited if you attempt to use the scant local buses and even scanter train services, though local tourist offices always do their best to provide details.

If you don't bring your own vehicle, there are five **car-hire** firms at **Brest airport** and four at **Quimper airport;** see airport websites (p. 25) for details. For those coming by train, **Easycar** (p. 103) (*www.easyCar.fr*) offers pick-up at **Brest** and **Quimper train stations**. Or for those arriving by ferry at **Roscoff,** Europcar (p. 199) has an office at the Gare Maritime. Note that there is no longer motorhome pick-up at Brest; Rennes is now the Breton base (p. 29).

WHAT TO SEE & DO

Children's Top 10 Attractions

❶ **Observing** the penguin colony or experiencing a multi-screen helicopter ride over Antarctica at Brest's **Océanopolis**. See p. 210.

❷ **Braving** the wind-lashed island of **Ouessant,** with the world's most powerful lighthouse and a unique light-house museum. See p. 203.

❸ Exploring the **Glénan isles** by family canoe or glass-bot-tomed catamaran. See p. 200.

❹ Following a nocturnal story-telling and music walk run by the **Musée du Loup**, a wolf museum. See p. 217.

❺ Discovering the animals, marshes and forests of the Monts d'Arrée at the **Domaine de Ménez-Meur** animal park. See p. 209.

❻ Seeing the crazy boulders and legend-shrouded ponds and grottoes of **Huelgoat** and its valley. See p. 202.

❼ Wondering at the cliffs, headlands and sea caves of the **Crozon peninsula**, with its fam-ily resorts. See p. 207.

❽ Learning about mazes through human civilization and getting lost in one at **Peninsula Le Labyrinthe**. See p. 206.

❾ Falling asleep to the waves lapping against your wall at Roscoff's **Hôtel le Temps de Vivre**. See p. 233.

❿ Riding a zipwire over the waves to the ruined island-fort of the **Fort de Bertheaume**. See p. 201.

Children-Friendly Events & Entertainment

For Breizh Sable Tour, **Festival Place aux Mômes**, and Cou-leurs de Bretagne events, see p. 104, p. 57 and p. 55.

For events at the **Fort de Bertheaume,** see p. 201.

Festival de Cornouaille ★★★

This major Breton festival, started in the 1920s and lasting a week, attracts performers as high profile as Youssou N'Dour. Wander the 'village' on the banks of the Odet, lined with stalls selling Breton crafts, tex-tiles, culinary specialities and more, it offers nightly *fest noz* (p. 16), Breton dance workshops for kids and adults, children's shows, and two grand proces-sions—one of 550 children in traditional costume, the other of more than 3,500 people, also in their Breton finery.

Date mid–late July. **Admission** free; tickets for concerts and some events, prices vary.

Fête des Brodeuses

Pont-l'Abbé; ☏ 02 98 82 37 99 (tourist office); www.fetedesbrodeuses. com. 20km (12 miles) southwest of Quimper on D785.

The family highlight of this four-day 'embroiderers' festival is the street parade of 200 chil-dren in traditional regional costume, looking very cute, followed by a dance show involving them all and then various group performances. Expect lots of music, including bagpipe bands, Breton dance lessons and competitions, *son-et-lumière* galas and a firework spectacular over Pont-l'Abbé's small lake.

Date early–mid-July. **Admission** free.

INSIDER TIP ≫

Lesconil near Pont-l'Abbé has an interesting and free **Fête de la Langoustine** ('prawn festival') in August, with trips in old fishing boats, sailing tuition, lifesaving demonstrations, seafood and crêpe stalls and tastings, kids' rides, concerts and late-night fireworks. Contact the tourist office for details (p. 192).

Fête des Cabanes ★ FIND

Iles de Kerévennou, Nizon; ☏*02 98 06 13 03; www.pontaven.com. 19km (12 miles) southeast of Concarneau on D24.*

At this wonderfully quirky one-day festival, a countryside picnic meets modern art as visitors come to eat alfresco and admire huts that have been made from leaves, branches and other natural materials, then filled with installation pieces by modern artists and hung in the trees beside the river. Everyone is welcome to make a hut beforehand, but you do need to register in advance. You're advised to bring wellies to best enjoy the wooded setting.

Date *June.* **Admission** *free.*

Fête du Nautisme ★ FIND

www.fetedunautisme.com

France's countryside sailing festival, part of its Journées de la Mer, involves venues and sailing schools all over Brittany's coast but also inland too. Brest (below) is the main focal point of the event, with free tuition and demonstrations on four sites, plus entertainment and competitions.

Date *9 days in late May and early June.* **Admission** *mainly free.*

Towns & Cities

Brest ★

For tourist office, see p. 192.

This naval port (Finistère's biggest city by far, though not its capital) isn't an obvious destination—it's sprawling and in parts very ugly (it was totally rebuilt after World War II, when the Allied forces bombed the German U-boat base here). Nor is it blessed with any outstanding family eating or sleeping options (see p. 225 and p. 233 for my recommendations). On the positive, there are still plenty of reasons to spare a day or two to see the city; head here for the wonderful **Océanopolis** (p. 210), and the **Rade de Brest,** its breathtaking natural bay, which you can experience in its full glory on a boat trip from the marina (☏*02 98 41 46 23, www.azenor.com*; lunch and dinner cruises available). The most dramatic bit is the narrow Goulet ('throat'), through which massive cargo and military ships squeeze into the bay; you get right up close to them.

Otherwise, Brest has a botanical park, the **Conservatoire National,** in the Stang Ar valley north of Océanopolis, just east of the city, and beside it a good public park with playgrounds and **Le Blé Noir** crêperie (☏*02 98 41 84 66*). For culture/history lovers, there's a **fine-arts museum** (Rue Traverse, ☏*02 98 00 87 96*), an

Graffiti in Brest

outpost of the national maritime museum within the medieval castle (℡02 98 22 12 39), and opposite the castle the **Tour Tanguy** (℡02 98 00 87 93) housing displays on the city on the eve of World War II.

INSIDER TIP

Brest's Port de Commerce is one of the city's liveliest spots, especially on Thursdays in July and August, when the **Jeudis au Port** programme (*www.brest.fr*) features free shows, concerts, cabaret and street art from 7pm until the small hours.

Brest's impressive commercial docks, between the Port de Commerce and Océanopolis (p. 196), are surrounded by an urban wasteland of derelict buildings. On no account cross this by foot, but on your way to or from Océanopolis, don't miss the incredible **graffiti** of gangsters, superheroes and more, bearing witness to a vast store of artistic talent among the city's youth.

Concarneau ★★

For tourist office, see p. 192.

One of France's biggest working fishing ports, Concarneau has a touristy heart in the form of its **Ville Close**—a little walled island in its river estuary, accessed via a bridge and enclosed by ramparts you can stroll around. Some might find it too twee, with its gift shops and seafood restaurants (most of which have highchairs and kids' menus, see p. 230 for my eating picks), but explore beyond its main street and you'll find some gems, including 'the world's shortest sea cruise'—a two-minute **ferry service** that has run since the 17th century. If you take this rickety little *bac* across to the other shore, you can link up with the GR4 long-distance footpath to get wonderful views back over Concarneau and its bay. This is also the way to the **Le Porzou** city sports complex

Entrance to Ville Close, Concarneau

(📞02 98 50 14 50), with tennis courts, an indoor pool and a large seaside park with children's play areas and picnic areas. Five kilometres (3 miles) from the beach there's also the **Parc Kersimonou** (📞02 98 97 81 44, *http://parc.kersimonou.free.fr*), with a pirate ship, comedy bikes, bouncy castles, a mini-golf course and more, amidst lots of sculptures and trees.

Back near the ferry point in the Ville Close is the **Carré des Larrons,** a little open-air amphitheatre hosting free shows all summer. The Ville Close is also home to the interesting **Musée de la Pêche** (p. 218). The best beach, the beautiful Sables Blancs, has a good, unpretentious family hotel (p. 239).

Quimper ★★

For tourist office, see p. 192.

The Finistère capital—most famous for its pottery, and perhaps as host for its **Festival de**

Cornouaille (p. 195)—was once the capital of the traditional region of La Cornouaille and has a suitably Celtic ambiance in its Old Town with its cobbled streets, gabled houses and quaint footbridges. It also has an impressive Gothic cathedral with a bend in the middle (to compensate for its being built on swampy ground), plus a great fine arts museum (p. 217) the **Musée Départmental Breton** (Rue du Roi Gradlon, 📞02 98 95 21 60), home to mainly archaeological finds from the area, and the **Musée de la Faïence** pottery museum (14 Rue Jean-Baptiste Bousquet, 📞02 98 90 12 72). The little **Celtic'Train** (📞02 98 97 25 82) does the round of the old town and the quays in 35–40mins, with guided commentary. Quimper is also a good stand by for rainy-day options (p. 221).

For accommodation and eating, see p. 230 and p. 238.

▶ INSIDER TIP ▶▶

Quimper's 'green lung' is the **Zone de Créac'h Gwen** beside the Odet, 5 minutes from the city centre, with a variety of open-air activities for kids, including a skatepark, a miniature port, a sailing and watersports club, a tennis club, play areas, a treetop adventure course, Bonobo (p. 222), and the Aquarive swimming complex (p. 221). There are also a number of shops here, including an organic and Fair Trade supermarket, **Brin d'Avoine** (📞02 98 10 13 50), and an outpost of the family-friendly budget hotel chain **All Seasons** (p. 239).

Roscoff

For tourist office, see p. 192.

Best known to Brits and the Irish from the shipping forecast and as a ferry port, Roscoff is also famous for its 'Johnnies'—local onion-sellers who, in the 19th century, began to cross the Channel every August to ply their wares in Britain (leading to the British stereotype of a Frenchman with a string of onions around his neck or the handlebars of his bike). The **Maison des Johnnies et de l'Oignon Rosé** (48 Rue Brizieux, *02 98 61 25 48*) is a suitably eccentric museum where, among other things, you'll learn about the 15 'Johnnies' carrying on the profession today (the pink Roscoff onion is in demand for its flavour and its nutritional benefits). Try to come on a Thursday from mid-June to mid-Sept, when the tour of the Maison is followed by a trip to a local onion producer in a *petit train*. Whenever you come, you need to book one day in advance at the tourist office (see below).

A *petit train touristique* putters around town in summer, and in August the town hosts a Pink Onion Festival, with music, dance, exhibitions and stalls selling onion products. Since Roscoff is a peninsula, there are also plenty of sheltered beaches, with decent kids' amenities and activities. Kids will love the **Jardin Louis Kerdilès** for the ducks, geese, ponies, Ouessant sheep (p. 204) and kangaroos, and also the **Jardin Exotique** botanical garden (*02 98 61 29 19*) complete with waterfalls, ponds with turtles and fish, fountains, cacti and more.

Lastly, don't miss the **Centre de Découverte des Algues** (5 Avenue Victor Hugo, *02 98 69 77 05*, *www.algopole.fr*), set up by a firm that makes health products and cosmetics from the more than 800 species of algae that live in this area. As well as free 45-minute screenings on

An onion seller's bike in Roscoff

seaweed-related topics (some specially for kids 6 and up; French only), it runs fascinating scientist-led, 2- and 3-hour excursions and walks along the shore at low tide, during which you'll learn about such oddities as sea lettuce and find out about old and new uses of seaweed.

For eating and accommodation recommendations, see p. 225 and 233.

INSIDER TIP ≫

From Roscoff, three companies offer 15-minute sailings to the **Ile de Batz** with its untouristy beaches, lighthouses (including one you can climb) residential sailing centre and cycle-hire. For more on the island, see *www.iledebatz.com*.

Fun Days Out

Capitaine Némo
★ ★ ★ ALL AGES

Departures from Loctudy; ☎ *02 98 57 00 58; www.vedettes-odet.com. 18km (11 miles) southwest of Bénodet.*

Among its various boat trips along the Odet estuary (p. 212) and to the Glénan islands (p. 222), Vedettes de l'Odet run day trips in this catamaran with submarine viewing 'salons'. Only the claustrophobic can fail to love the novelty of getting so close to all varieties of marine life, including starfish and mermaid's-hair seaweed. The outing includes free time to explore St. Nicolas and a guided tour of the archipelago by a marine expert.

Time 1 day (10.15am–5.45pm). Open phone to check. Admission 42€ adult, 22€ child 4–12, 5€ child under 4. Amenities **P**

INSIDER TIP ≫

Vedettes de l'Odet also offers return sailings to the Glénans combined with hire of **double** or **family canoes,** the latter for two adults and one to two children under 10/1.2m in height (who must be able to swim). A nature guide can accompany you if you like. Cost is around 140€ for a family of four.

Cap Sizun/Pointe du Raz
★ AGE 5 & UP

For Audierne tourist office, see p. 192. www.pointe-du-raz.com.

Squeezed out between the bays of Douarnenez (p. 212) and Audierne (p. 213) like a tongue, Cap Sizun is the French equivalent of Britain's Land's End. The shorter and less touristy of the promontories is the **Pointe du Van,** a good place from which to view the more famous **Pointe du Raz** to the south, from which Celtic Druids may have believed they could depart for the afterlife. To get from one to the other, you cross the **Baie des Trépassés** or 'Bay of the Dead', shrouded in many a legend. This bay has some charming caves to explore at low tide.

The Pointe du Raz can get inundated by visitors—there are nearby paying car parks with a shuttle bus to the headland itself, from which you gain amazing views of the wild waves, the coastline and a pair of iconic

Pointe du Raz

lighthouses, plus, in the distance on a clear day, the Ile-de-Sein. The heritage centre has displays on the natural environment, shops and restaurants.

As well as coastal paths along the northern and southern shores, there are some fine beaches on the mainly rocky Cap, especially in the **Anse de Cabestan** and at **Ste. Evette** near the fishing port of **Audierne** with its aquarium (p. 213). The nearby **Réserve du Cap Sizun** (☎ 02 98 70 13 53, *www. bretagne-vivante.org*) is a sea-bird sanctuary; ask for a '*sac à falaise*' with binoculars and a magnifying class, an interpretation booklet, and colouring materials.

Time half a day to 1 day. **Amenities**

Fort de Bertheaume
★★ AGE 4 & UP

Plougonvelin; ☎ 02 98 48 30 18 *(tourist office). 21km (13 miles) west of Brest on D789.*

Just along the coast from Brest and overlooking its glorious Rade (p. 196), this ruined island-fort designed by the famous military architect Vauban is accessed by a footbridge over the waves. Come by day to admire the structure and learn about its history, freely or by guided tour, and with kids from age 10 to experience **Bertheaume Aventure** (☎ 06 64 24 06 41, *www.arbreizh.com*)— two hair-raising zipwires over the sea and a *via ferrata* (a sort of rock-climbing course involving both hiking and climbing), taking you 2hrs to complete. Summer sees theatrical tours led by a costumed guide, with dressed-up kids acting out parts, plus evening tours that families also enjoy. There's an open-air theatre here too, hosting plays, dance and concerts by artists as internationally renowned as Sonic Youth, plus a little kids' theatre—while they're watching, you can enjoy a bite and some cider in the crêperie.

Time half a day. **Open** *July and Aug daily 1.30–7pm; rest of year Wed only for guided tours at 10am.* **Admission** *island 2€, free to kids under 11; Wed guided tour 3€, free to kids under 11; tickets for other tours, performances and concerts vary.* **Amenities**

> **INSIDER TIP** »
>
> Plougonvelin, home to the Fort de Bertheaume, is a Sensation Bretagne 'Station Famille' (p. 57). Aside the fort, it's worth visiting for the **Pointe Saint Mathieu** headland with its 10th-century ruined abbey and 50m

(164ft) lighthouse, accessible by guided tour June–Sept and in school holidays (☏02 98 89 00 17), and for its four fine-sand beaches. Among the latter, Trez-Hir has a sailing centre and watersports.

Huelgoat ★★ AGE 3 & UP

For tourist office, see p. 193.

Part of the Monts d'Arrée, a sweep of hills that forms one of inland Finistère's main attractions (p. 209), the valley of Huelgoat is strewn with as many legends (some of them Arthurian) as it is strangely shaped rocks—it seems no one was content with the natural explanation for them (river erosion). The most famous is the **Roche Tremblante** or 'trembling rock', which is huge (around 100 tonnes) but so precariously balanced that even a child can make it move if they touch it in the right spot. Twice as big but immovable is the mushroom-like 'Champignon', and some people claim to make out wild boars' heads in the rocks of the **Mare aux Sangliers,** where film director Roger Vadim came to shoot in the 1960s, while his then-wife Jane Fonda learnt to make crêpes in the **Crêperie des Myrtilles** (☏*02 98 99 72 66*) in the centre of Huelgoat. By moonlight visit the **Mare aux Fées** to see if you can glimpse fairies bathing here, preening themselves with golden combs.

Explore the Arthurian legends of the Huelgoat Valley

All these sights are accessed via the signposted *sentier pittoresque*. More prosaically, you can visit the vestiges of a Gallo-Roman camp later occupied by Julius Caesar's armies, or feed the ducks and swans on Huelgoat's town lake.

Time half a day to 1 day.

INSIDER TIP »

On your way to the Monts d'Arrée from Brest, be sure to stop off at Landerneau, to see the **Pont de Rohan**. One of the rare surviving bridges in Europe to hold inhabited houses, it celebrated its 500th birthday in 2010.

Ile d'Ouessant ★ ALL AGES

For tourist office, see p. 193. Boats: ☎ *02 98 80 80 80; www.pennarbed. fr; flights:* ☎ *02 98 84 64 87; www. finistair.fr.*

The windlashed, treeless island of Ouessant in the Atlantic Ocean, 20km (12 miles) from the French coast has wild landscapes, a romantic 'end-of-the-world' atmosphere and is shaped a little like a crab's claw. Countless ships have been wrecked on the rocks surrounding it, despite its five soaring lighthouses (including the **Phare du Créac'h**, the world's most powerful; p. 215) It's well worth the 75-minute boat-trip from Le Conquet (or longer trip from Camaret on the Crozon peninsula—p. 207—or Brest; you can also fly from the latter in 15 minutes). Some boats allow you to bring your bikes but there is cycle-hire at the quay where you disembark.

As well as Ouessant's lighthouse museum (p. 219), you might visit the **Ecomusée/Maisons du Niou-Huella** (☎ *02 98 48 86 37*), two traditional houses where you can learn about the life of the island's womenfolk (the men were more or less constantly at sea, often failing to return) through displays of costumes, tools and furniture made from shipwrecked wood. The islands are a bird reserve, and the **Centre d'Etude du Milieu de l'Ile d'Ouessant** (☎ *02 98 48 82 65, www.cemo-ouessant.fr*), an ornithological centre, runs nature outings in French. Ouessant is perhaps best known for its dwarf black sheep (p. 204), but there aren't many left on the island (don't worry—you'll see plenty in animal parks across Brittany). You might, however, be lucky and spot seals off the north coast. **Kalon Eusa** (☎ *06 07 06 29 02, www.kalon-eusa.com*) runs (also in French only) guided tours, hikes and cultural visits, including evening storytelling walks and family outings.

The only settlement of any size, **Lampaul,** is your best bet for sleeping (p. 234) and eating, although there are few very interesting lunch or dinner options on the island—try the windswept-looking (and indeed, leaning) **Crêperie Ty à Dreuz** (☎ *02 98 48 83 01*) with marine-inspired decor and lovingly prepared galettes and crêpes (don't miss the Ouessantine with potato and smoked sausage).

Time 1 day or more. **Sailings** to/from Le Conquet at least one daily, subject to weather; times vary. **Fare** 18€– 30.20€ adult return, 16.80€–24.20€ teen 12–16, 15.20€–18.25€ child

The Black Sheep of the Family

Ouessant's famous black dwarf sheep are Europe's smallest breed and perhaps the world's smallest natural breed, reaching just 45–50cm (18–20ins) at the shoulder. Until the early 20th century they were only seen on Ouessant itself, providing islanders with wool, but now you can see them in farm parks around France—you may even spot rare white or caramel-coloured ('red') ones.

Ouessants are descended from two breeds: the Morbihan, from southern Brittany, and the Vendéen from further south. The first was small and black, brown or white; the latter larger, purely black and endowed with quite spectacular horns—Ouessant rams still have impressive curly horns. The two lines merged, but the new breed nearly died out in the mid-1900s due to the barrenness of the island (which contributed to their small size). They were saved from extinction by rich locals, who let them graze on their land. Today, ironically, they're nicknamed *tondeuses ecologiques* ('eco-lawnmowers') because they can subsist on small plots and are resistant to many modern sheep diseases.

4–11. **Flights** *to and from Brest twice-daily; for times see website.* **Fare** *93€ adult return, 57€ child 2–12.*

INSIDER TIP »

Ouessant is surrounded by some even smaller islands; the largest is **Molène,** to which you can also sail from Le Conquet, Brest and Camaret with Penn Ar Bed. Its main sight is the **Musée du Drummond Castle** (℡ 02 98 07 38 41, *www.vacances-en-iroise. com*), which tells of the shipwreck of an English cruise liner en route from South Africa in 1886. The British flag on display was presented to the island by the Queen in 1996 in thanks for the islanders' work in recovering and burying the bodies. **La Maison de l'Environnement Insulaire** (℡ 02 98 07 38 92) is a small natural heritage museum that organises guided visits and sea trips with fishermen, to spot seals and dolphins.

Maison des Jeux Bretons
★ ★ ★ **FIND** **VALUE** AGE 2 & UP

Saint Jean Trolimon; ℡ *02 98 82 13 45, www.saintjeantrolimon.fr. 24km (15 miles) southwest of Quimper on D57.*

The 'house of Breton games' offers fun for families, in the form of about 15 traditional games from the region, which you can come and play freely (staff are on hand to give out information and advice). Some of the games, such as the *galoche bigoudène*, are in danger of disappearing unless places like this keep up the tradition; the Maison aims to show children how much enjoyment can be had playing with simple wooden toys and encourages different generations to play together, though there are some games strictly for adults and others just for kids (a colour coding system tells you which). In summer, outdoor games and activities such as archery, sack-racing and horse-shoe hurling are organised. Don't leave without raiding the shop for interesting wooden toys and games to take home.

Time 2–3hrs. **Open** *July and Aug Mon–Sat 2–6pm (plus occasional eve sessions); other school hols (all zones) Tues–Sat 2–6pm; rest of year Wed and Sat 2–6pm.* **Admission** *2€pp inc raffle ticket, family membership inc unlimited access for one year 20€.* **Amenities** 🅿 🔒 ♿

Parc de Loisirs de Bel Air FIND VALUE ALL AGES

Landudec; 📞*02 98 91 50 27,* *www. parc-loisirs-belair.com. 23km (14 miles) west of Quimper on D784.*

This leisure park set in large, leafy grounds offers lots of low-tech, rather old-fashioned entertainments for kids of all ages, including an aqua-complex with water-slides, bouncy castles, pedal cars, trampolines and playground equipment, giant chess and other games, and a land train. There's a snack bar but also an area where you can eat your own picnic fare. Watch out for deals at the neighbouring campsite, the Domaine de Bel Air, offering free park access.

Time half a day. **Open** *Apr, May, June and Sept Wed and Sat 11am–7pm; July and Aug daily (phone to confirm other dates).* **Admission** *6.50€ adult, free to children under 1m tall.* **Amenities** 🍸 🅿 🧺 🔒 👤 ♿

INSIDER TIP ≫

Not far from Quimper, the **Parc d'Attractions Odet Loisirs** at Elliant, (📞*02 98 59 18 25,* *www. odet-loisirs.fr*) has a ropebridge, zipwire over a lake and suchlike, plus a botanic garden with 600-plus species of trees and shrubs.

Parc Naturel Régional d'Armorique ★ ★ ★ ALL AGES

Information centre: 15 Place aux Foires, Le Faou; 📞*02 98 81 90 08);* *www.pnr-armorique.fr. 31km (19 miles) southeast of Brest on N165.*

One of 43 Regional Natural Parks in France, designated such to protect their fragile ecosystems and rich cultural heritage, the **Parc Naturel Régional d'Armorique** covers a hefty 172,000 hectares (around 660 square miles), of which 60,000 (around 230 square miles) are part of the ocean. The area is split across the islands of Ouessant and Molène (p. 204) and Sein (off the Pointe du Raz; p. 200), the Crozon peninsula (p. 207), the Aulne estuary, and the Monts d'Arrée (p. 209), and comprises a huge range of nature and culture themed attractions that could fill a book of their own. Venues include the **Domaine de Ménez-Meur** (p. 209), **Musée du Loup** (p. 217), **Musée des Phares et Balises** (p. 219), **Maisons du Niou-Huella** (p. 203), **Centre d'Etudes du Milieu de l'Ile d'Ouessant** (p. 203) and **Musée des Vieux Métiers Vivants** (p. 216). A slightly smaller-scale museum is the **Maison de la**

Réserve Naturelle et des Castors ($02 98 79 71 98$) in the old station at Brennilis, which takes as its main topic the local beaver population and runs walks out to find traces of them.

Those interested in traditional Breton games and sports, especially *gouren* (a form of wrestling once practised by local warriors and nobles, then by peasants), can take a course (or simply play) at **Ti-ar-Gouren** ($02 98 99 03 80, *www.tiargouren. fr*), the 'Maison de la Lutte et des Sports Bretons', at Berrien.

Time 1 day or more.

Pays des Abers ★ ALL AGES

For tourist office, see p. 193.

The stretch of coast northwest of Brest is named for the river estuaries that cut into its shoreline, forming deep, narrow inlets. In many ways it's a rather inhospitable place, home to mighty lighthouses that warn ships away from the rocks, or try to—they weren't successful in preventing the sinking of the *Amoco Cadiz* oil tanker off Portsall in 1978, causing an ecological disaster of epic proportions. Yet, it has some splendid wide beaches popular with sand-yachters, especially north of **Plouguerneau** where you'll also find the unique **Ecomusée/Musée des Goémoniers et de l'Algue** ($02 98 37 13 35) or 'seaweed-gatherers' museum devoted to the algae trade prevalent along this coast. On the coast near St. Michel is the medieval necropolis of **Iliz-Koz** (p. 207), while

Les Amis de Jeudi-Dimanche ($02 98 04 90 92, *www.bel-espoir. com*) runs boat trips from L'Aber-Wrac'h (or 'Fairy's Estuary') between Plouguerneau and Lannilis, to Ouessant (p. 203), Belle-Ile (p. 110) and other destinations.

Further south, past Aber Ildut, at Plouarzel, summer visitors can tour the 37m (120ft) **Phare de Trézien** ($02 98 89 69 46), an automated lighthouse with amazing views of the Ile d'Ouessant (p. 203) from the top of its 182 steps. Next you'll come to the **Pointe de Corsen,** a headland with a signpost to New York 5,080km (3,156 miles) away—this is apparently the nearest point on the French mainland to North America (there's also a sign to London 430km (267 miles) away). South of it lies the vast, quite wild, curving beach of the **Anse des Blancs Sablons,** a protected site where you may see dolphins leaping (note: it has a naturist section).

Time 1 day.

Peninsula Le Labyrinthe ★★ FIND ALL AGES

Menez Kerbasguen, Route de la Pointe de Dinan, Crozon; $02 98 26 25 34; www.peninsulabyrinthe. com.

This unique location mixing fun and culture deep in woods on the Crozon peninsula (p. 207) is focused on a giant open-air wooden maze along which visitors can discover elements of a different local legend every year, serving as clues as to which way

Village Under the Dunes

A veritable medieval necropolis, Iliz-Koz or 'The Old Church' (📞 *02 98 04 71 84, www.iliz-koz.fr/*) near St. Michel in the Pays des Abers consists of the substantial vestiges of the parish church of Tremenac'h, which—together with its village on Finistère's north coast—became buried by rising sands in the early 18th century and lay forgotten until the 1960s, when it was uncovered by building work. A signposted circuit takes you to the churchyard, where you can see more than 100 extraordinary, elaborately carved tombs of local nobles, cavaliers, merchants, priests and sailors. Onwards, visit the remains of the nobles' chapel, the ossuary, a medieval alleyway and, a tiny museum, housing 13th–15th-century murals from the church's north wall. It's all the more spooky when you know that the rest of the village is still under the surrounding dunes.

to go next (if you're worried about losing family members, there's a central look-out tower to help you find those who've gone astray). Afterwards you can find out all about mazes throughout human civilisation in the permanent exhibition. A stand sells Fair Trade drinks in summer.

Time 2hrs. Open Apr, May, June and Sept daily 2–6pm; July and Aug daily 10am–7pm; other school hols (all zones) daily 2–5pm; rest of year, Wed, Sat, Sun and public hols 2–6pm. Admission 7€, 6€ child 5–16, 6€pp family. Amenities 🍴 🏞

Presqu'île de Crozon ★★
ALL AGES

For tourist offices, see p. 192 and 193.

This spectacular portion of coast with its awesome headlands and cliffs is one of Brittany's highlights, and with some good family accommodation (p. 234) makes a great base for a seaside holiday. Its main resort is

Morgat, in a sheltered bay on the south side of the peninsula, with fine-sand beaches hosting kids' clubs in summer, plus some famous **sea caves** (*grottes marines*) you can visit by guided boat-trip (Vedettes Rosmeur, 📞 *06 85 95 55 49, www.grottes-morgat.com*), including the 80m (250 ft) long 'cave of the altar' and the funnel-shaped 'devil's chimney'. The *Peugeot* car family founded this resort in 1884, building the strange white metal villa, Ker Ar Bruck, that you can still see by the sea (it was falsely attributed to Gustav Eiffel), and the clan still holidays here today.

Another scenic spot is **Camaret-sur-Mer** with its natural jetty of pebbles ballooning out into the bay, dotted with old fishing boats and a decapitated chapel; see p. 234 for accommodation. From Camaret it's a short trip to the dramatic **Pointe du Toulinguet** to the north and the **Pointe de Penhir** to the

Camaret-sur-Mer

south, with the huge rocks of the Tas de Pois ('pile of peas') speckling the Atlantic. Still further south, the Anse de Dinan is a vast bay from which you can see the **Pointe de Dinan,** dubbed the 'Château' because it resembles a castle with a drawbridge. Nearby is a mineral museum (p. 216).

Time *1 day or more.*

Animal Attractions

L'Aquashow ★ ALL AGES

Rue du Goyen, Audierne; 📞 *02 98 70 03 03; www.aquarium.fr. 40km (25 miles) west of Quimper on D784.*

This smallish but very good aquarium overlooking the estuary at Audierne (p. 213) focuses on sealife from around the Breton coast. It houses more than 180 species including sharks, giant lobsters, octopuses, hermit crabs and sea urchins, and in the discovery zone touchpool, you can stroke

starfish, sea-snails and rays. Oddly, however, the place is best known for its Cité des Oiseaux, which hosts seabird and falconry displays in an outdoor arena at 4pm (featuring cormorants hunting underwater). The adjoining crêperie, built on stilts over the water, serves seafood, crêpes, snacks and ice cream, and there's a little gift shop.

Time *2hrs.* ***Open*** *Apr–Sept daily 10am–6.30pm; Oct–Mar school hols daily 2–6pm.* ***Admission*** *13.80€ adult, 10.80€ child 4–14, 2€ child 2–3, 50€ family (2+3).* ***Amenities*** 🅿 🍴 ♿ &

> **INSIDER TIP** ⟩⟩
> You can save money by coming to L'Aquashow before noon, when kids under 12 get free entry.

Bigoud'Anes FIND ALL AGES

Ferme de Kerbenoc'h, Ploénour-Lanvern; 📞 *02 98 87 72 16; http://bigoud anes.canalblog.com. 25km (15.5 miles) southwest of Quimper on D2.*

This friendly (French-speaking) farm welcomes families to walk and feed the donkeys (bring your own carrots or dry bread) and also to feed geese, ducks, hens, sheep, goats and pigs. Smaller kids can ride donkeys, led by an older child or adult, around a reservoir close to the farm. If that's not enough, ask about occasional longer walks, lasting from several hours to a couple of days (including camping). There are no facilities on site, so bring your own picnic.

Time 2hrs–2 days. *Open* call for times and to book. *Admission* 7€ adult, €4 child 4–12. *Amenities* 🅿 ⛱

Domaine de Ménez-Meur
★ ★ ALL AGES

Near Hanvec; 📞 *02 98 68 81 71; www.pnr-armorique.fr. 32km (20 miles) southeast of Brest off D18.*

The 520 hectare (1,300 acre) 'Big Mountain' park, set up by a gold prospector who made a fortune in America to preserve the local countryside and animal species, forms the heart of the Monts d'Arrée and indeed the **Parc Naturel Régional d'Armorique** (p. 205) as a whole. Visitors have a choice of circuits, the most obvious one for children being the 3.3km (2-mile) 'animal circuit' around a renovated farm, with spacious enclosures housing wild animals such as wolves, boar and deer, and mainly Breton endangered farm breeds such as Armorican and piebald Breton cows. The ox-like auroch species (extinct since the Bronze Age) has been reproduced by breeding domestic cattle strains and can be found here. Check out the permanent exhibition on the Parc Naturel Régional d'Armorique and the background behind France's regional natural parks.

Time half a day or more. *Open* Mar, Apr and Oct Wed, Sun, public and school hols 1–5.30pm; May, June and Sept daily noon–6pm; July and Aug daily 10am–7pm; Nov–Feb school hols 1–5pm. *Admission* free. *Amenities* 🅿 ⛱ ♿

Bird of prey at Cité des Oiseaux, part of L'Aquashow

Maison de l'Amiral AGE 3 & UP

Penhors Plage, Pouldreuzic; 📞 *02 98 51 52 52; www.maison-de-l-amiral. com. 32km (20 miles) west of Quimper on D40.*

This old-fashioned seaside museum of shells and seabirds lacks the modern hands-on touch, but most children find something to interest them. The 10,000-odd shells of all shapes and sizes from both local beaches and those around the world include a giant clam nearly 1m long. The bird collection is smaller, but among the 200 specimens are rarities such as a great bittern and grey heron. French-language display boards and a booklet give you the low-down. Dotted throughout the room are minerals, fossils, corals and some impressive sharks' heads, and you can watch a loop of short videos on themes such as fishing, seaweed gathering and the treatment of birds damaged by oil slicks. On the shore of the Baie d'Audierne—which can be bleak but is alive with birdlife—the museum has a garden with play equipment and deckchairs, picnic tables, a duckpond and views of the famous Pointe du Raz (p. 200). Seashells and local produce can be bought in the shop.

Time 1hr. *Open* Feb–June and Sept–Dec Tues–Fri 10am–noon and 2–6pm, Sat and Sun 2–6pm; July and Aug daily 10am–8pm. *Admission* 5.60€ adult, 2.90€ child 5–15. *Amenities* 🅿 🏕 ⛺ 🗑 ♿

Marinarium ★ FIND AGE 3 & UP

Place de la Croix, Concarneau; 📞02 98 97 06 59; www.mnhn.fr/concarneau/.

Part of France's mighty natural history museum, this working research lab in the world's oldest marine biology station, dating back to 1859 (when it was a breeding centre) allows fans of the deep a close-up view of science in action. Many important discoveries have taken place in this seafront building, as the displays point out. Permanent exhibitions focus on the biodiversity of the oceans; the role of plankton; tides and the coast; ecology; the Glénan islands (p. 222); and the laboratory's history and current scientific work. Temporary exhibitions look at the latest in marine biotechnology. There are also fish tanks and a large pool with local fish such as pollock, a 'nursery' with lobsters, prawns, squid and other creatures bred here, occasional kids' workshops and free outings to discover the life of the seashore at low tide.

Time 1–2hrs. *Open* Apr–June and Sept daily 10am–noon and 2–6pm; July and Aug daily 10am–7pm; Oct–Dec, Feb and Mar 2–6pm. *Admission* 5€ adult, 3€ child 6–14.
Amenities 🅿 ♿

Océanopolis ★★★ ALL AGES

Port de Plaisance du Moulin Blanc, Brest; 📞02 98 34 40 40; www.oceanopolis.com.

Brittany has many aquaria, but Brest's sealife centre—which celebrated its 20th anniversary in 2010—is in a league of its own, with large, beautifully designed habitats housed in a huge space station-like building. The most awesome of the three huge 'pavilions' is the Polaire, where you can observe a colony of penguins swimming through vast tanks and watch the multiscreen film *Antarctica*, taking you on a tummy-tickling helicopter flight over the icy continent (worth the relatively hefty entry fee alone). The Temperate Pavilion, meanwhile, has masses of hands-on displays that can teach kids about the tides, currents and so on, plus touching pools where

Sharks at Océanopolis

they can get up-close to marine life. The two daily seal shows, designed to train the animals (rather than to entertain the audience) to accept examinations by vets, should be on everyone's list, as should a ride in the glass lift down the side of the shark tank, giving you 'submarine vision'. Don't rush your visit, or you'll miss the interactive gizmos dotted throughout, such as the periscope viewers and the quotes from *20,000 Leagues under the Sea* painted on the walls. Each area has its own flashy multimedia space where you can deepen your knowledge should you wish. Younger kids can head for the indoor model boats, and the nautically themed outside play area. Everyone will find something pleasing in the huge gift shop or bookshop, and there are several eating options on-site.

Time at least half a day. **Open** daily 10am–5pm; see website for detailed calendar and closure days.

Admission 16.50€ adult, 11€ child 4–17, 61€ family (2+3). **Amenities** 🍷📷🥤 ⚡🎣⛰🍴🛍♿

INSIDER TIP ▶

At busy periods, save time by pre-buying Océanopolis tickets on the website or at a local tourist office (p. 192), so you don't have to queue. In high summer it's best to arrive as soon as Océanopolis opens its doors, at 9am. Note that your ticket gives you discounts on the boat-trips run by Vedettes de l'Odet (p. 200) and Penn Ar Bed (p. 204).

Parc Animalier de la Pommeraie FIND   ALL AGES

Peumérit; 📞 *02 98 82 91 52. 26km (16 miles) west of Quimper off D57.*

This little animal park is home to animals from all over the world—including llamas, zebus, black pigs and free-roaming goats—that visitors can get up close to and pet. There are also donkey rides on offer, a 'talking tree' where children can listen to tall tales, and—for stressed out parents—an outdoor Zen space.

Time 2hrs. **Open** July and Aug daily 10am–7pm; rest of year Sat, Sun and school hols 2–7pm. **Admission** 4€ adult, 2€ child up to 16. **Amenities** ⚡♿

Best Beaches

Finistère resorts bearing the Sensation Bretagne 'Station Famille' label (p. 57) for their family-friendliness are **Carantec** (p. 213), **Roscoff** (p. 199), nearby **Plouescat, Plougonvelin** (p. 201), and to the south,

Fouesnant Les Glénan, La Fôret Fouesnant'Port la Fôret, and Névez'Port Manec'h. In the last, the tourist office (☎02 98 06 87 90) organises half-day or day-long French-language nature excursions for families.

Baie de Douarnenez ★

For tourist office, see p. 193.

Cutting back into the land south of the Crozon peninsula (p. 207), the bay of Douarnenez is made up of several lovely untouristy beaches in an area rich in legends (the waters themselves are supposed to be the home of the mythical drowned citadel of Ys). On the northern side of the bay, eastwards from Morgat, are huge unspoilt beaches with dunes and areas of pebbles that local families use to build walls to demarcate their 'patch', including the open, tranquil **Plage de l'Aber, Trez-Bellec Plage** and **Pentrez-Plage**. The southern side, dominated by the fishing town of **Douarnenez** with its port-museum (p. 219) is speckled with less accessible sandy beaches and is best appreciated by walking along the coastal path from **Tréboul** (check out the **Pointe du Millier** a viewing post with a squat lighthouse jutting oddly from the façade of its keeper's house).

Bénodet and Sainte Marine ★★

For tourist office, see p. 192.

The gentle **Anse de Bénodet** is home to two gorgeous resorts facing each other across the **Odet estuary** with its charming creeks that you can explore aboard little cruisers (☎02 98 57 00 58, *www.vedettes-odet.com*; see also p. 200). Bounded to the west by a superb beach leading from Ile-Tudy, **Ste. Marine** consists of a handful of restaurants and cafés nestled around a little port. Across the Pont de Cornouaille with its stunning views, **Bénodet** is much larger, with a bustling marina and four beaches, including the central **Plage du Trez** with pedaloes, sea canoes and other sporting equipment for hire and kids' clubs in high summer, and the smaller **Plage St. Gilles,** popular with youngsters for its rockpools full of crabs and shrimps. There's also a summer-only 'seaside museum' with model boats (☎02 98 57 00 14), a petit train (☎02 98 73 37 92) and two lighthouses (one pyramid-shaped). Rounding the Pointe de Mousterlin, you'll come to **Cap-Coz,** a serene spot with an island atmosphere and pine-fringed beaches. For eating and sleeping, see p. 225 and p. 233.

INSIDER TIP ►►

Don't miss Bénodet's **Atelier des Saveurs** (5 Rue du Letty, ☎02 98 57 01 27), for award-winning Breton caramels, jams, chutneys, spices and other gastronomic treats. For fish at its freshest meanwhile, head for nearby **Beg-Meil** to buy seafood straight off the boats.

Carantec ★★

For tourist office, see p. 193.

On its own peninsula reaching up the western side of the Rade de Morlaix near the ferry port of Roscoff (p. 199), this relaxed family resort is reminiscent of Perros-Guirec on the Côte du Granit Rose (p. 161) but is more compact and generally smarter. Like Perros-Guirec, it erupts with children's activities in summer, including a beach club for ages 3 and up (offering swimming lessons in a heated pool), and a Jardin des Mers sailing-and-sealife themed activity programme for ages 4 to 6, run in partnership with the sailing club. Festival Place aux Mômes events take place here (p. 57), and at other times you can take advantage of the mini-tennis, a skate park, a nature trail for ages 6 and up in the Parc Claude-Goude arboretum, open-air painting lessons and the small **maritime museum** (📞 02 98 67 01 46). Among the seven beaches, the **Plage du Kélenn** has a sailing centre (see below), a volleyball pitch, cafés with terraces, plus pretty blue-and-white and red-and-white striped bathing huts in high season. You can walk out from it—at low tide—to the fine-sand beaches and protected creeks of the Ile Callot. For accommodation and eating, see p. 233 and p. 227.

> **INSIDER TIP ▸▸**
> From its base on Kélenn beach, **Carantec Nautisme** (📞 02 98 67 01 12) offers sea-kayak tuition

for all ages and guided trips out into the Baie de Morlaix, with canoes suitable for kids aged 8 and up or '*kayaks-polo*' for one child and one adult. You might choose to stop off to tour the **Château du Taureau,** the bay's sea fort and former prison, which reopened to visitors in 2010. The latter can also be accessed by boat trip (📞 02 98 62 29 73; tickets also sold on the Plage du Kélenn), as can the bay as a whole, which is a bird reserve housing puffins, terns and more.

Pointe de la Torche/Plage de Pors-Carn ★★

For tourist office (Penmarc'h), see p. 193.

The immense, wild **Baie d'Audierne** south of the Cap Sizun (p. 213) is most famous—at least among the French—for the grim autobiography *Le Cheval d'orgueil*, in which Pierre Jakez Hélias writes about peasant life around **Pouldreuzic** (now home to a shell and seabird museum; p. 209) in the early 20th century, when children slept on seaweed-stuffed bedding. You can get a lighter view of the area south of **Pouldreuzic,** at the wind and wave pounded **Pointe de la Torche,** a location for the World Windsurfing Championships and also a great spot for funboarding, sand-yachting, surfing and fly-surfing. The lovely crescent-shaped **beach of Pors-Carn** leading south of the headland can also be excellent for surfing, while

Centre de Découverte Maritime and Phare d'Eckmuhl

the aptly named **Plage de la Joie** is better for young children, especially if they like hunting for crabs, prawns and winkles.

INSIDER TIP ➤➤

Your kids will find it fascinating that **Penmarc'h** close to the Pointe de la Torche is the starting point for transatlantic telephone cables that link it with Rhode Island and New York in the USA via Land's End in the UK—a distance of 6,321km (3,928 miles). Almost as interestingly, it has France's second-tallest lighthouse, which you can climb if you've got the stamina (see p. 215), together with a museum on local prehistoric finds (℡ 02 98 58 60 35).

Museums

For small-scale museums, see also **Towns & Cities.**

Haliotika Il'La Cité de la Pêche ★★ AGE 4 & UP

Le Port, Le Guilvinec; ℡ *02 98 58 28 38;* **www.haliotika.com**. *32km (20 miles) southwest of Quimper on D57.*

Set in France's third-largest fishing port, this 'Fishing City'—massively revamped for 2010—is both an exhibition space about the industry and a very busy activity centre, offering workshops on various subjects, from seafood cookery to tastings (some especially for kids—great for those who've convinced themselves they don't like fish), tours of the port, of Le Guilvinec's raucous fish auctions (*criée*) and of the foreshore, treasure hunts and trips out to sea in trawlers. A visit will teach you all kinds of things you didn't know about fishing techniques, identifying different species, life at the port, recognising the various types of boat and the challenges

Phare Out: Brittany's Lighthouses

Its vicious coastline means that Brittany is dotted with some of the world's most majestic lighthouses, among them the **Phare de l'Ile Vierge** in the Pays des Abers (p. 206). Constructed in 1897 to 1902 and attaining a height of 82.5m (270ft), this is Europe's tallest lighthouse, and the world's tallest stone lighthouse. Still standing next to it, the island's previous lighthouse looks comically small. You can travel out to the island (1.5km or less than 1 mile from the coast) with **Vedettes des Abers** (02 98 04 74 94); trips sometimes include a guided tour of the lighthouse. Otherwise, from parts of the coast north of Plouguerneau you can watch its light ease the passage from the Atlantic Ocean into the Channel every five seconds, carrying a distance of 52km (32 miles). The horn of the smaller lighthouse, which now houses the two lighthouse-keepers (it's one of only five lighthouses in France to still have keepers), emits a 1,200-watt, 3-second sound every minute.

Built in 1859 to 1863, the striped **Phare du Créac'h** at the north-west tip of the shipwreck-plagued island of Ouessant (p. 203) may not reach the heights of the Ile Vierge, at 55m (180ft), but its scope of 63km (39 miles) makes it the world's most powerful. To ensure safe passage into the Channel, though, it has also had a variety of sirens, including an underwater one. A system of lights at its summit stops migrating birds crashing into it. You can't go inside, but you can visit the **Musée des Phares et Balises** (p. 219) in the old electrical station.

As for the second-tallest lighthouse, that's the **Phare d'Eckmühl** (02 98 58 60 19; open July–Sept daily 10.30am–6.30pm if weather allows) built at Penmarc'h at the southern end of the Baie d'Audierne (p. 213) in 1897, with a range of 30km (19 miles). You can climb its 307 steps, to a height of 65m (213ft). Beside it, the old lighthouse now contains the **Centre de Découverte Maritime** (02 98 58 72 87), with changing displays on maritime themes in the old lighthouse-keeper's quarters.

Outside Finistère, Brittany's third-highest lighthouse, the 58m (190ft) **Phare des Roches-Douves** off the Sillon de Talbert (p. 162) on the Côtes d'Armor, is the furthest lighthouse in Europe from a coast (it's more than 40km/25 miles out to sea, towards Guernsey). Built in 1867 to 1869 but reconstructed after being destroyed in World War II, it was manned until as recently as 2000, with one keeper spending 20 years there.

for fishing in the modern world; kids are encouraged to take an interest through games dotted throughout the space and the awarding of a certificate at the end of their visit. There'll be much to contemplate and talk about as you relax on the museum's terrace, which from about 4pm affords views of the colourful fishing fleet returning with the day's catch.

For eating in Le Guilvinec, see p. 229.

Time exhibition 1hr; activities vary. *Open* Mon–Fri 10am–12.30pm and 2.30–6pm, with weekend openings in high summer; check website for long annual closures (half of Dec, all Jan and most of March). *Admission* exhibition 5.80€ adult, 3.80€ children 4–16; workshops, tours and other activities vary. *Amenities* ♿ ⚒

Maison des Minéraux AGE 5 & UP

Route du Cap de la Chèvre, Saint Hernot; ☎ 02 98 27 19 73; www. maison-des-mineraux.org. 6.5km (4 miles) south of Crozon on D887.

The highlight of this geology museum in an old rural school is the darkened room with Europe's largest collection of fluorescent rocks, including quartz and manganese—red, yellow, orange, mauve and green rocks twinkle at you from every corner like fireflies. The items on display come from a variety of sources across Brittany; from the Crozon peninsula (an area rich in marine fossils), and Finistère to the Armorican Massif—a vast plain covering much of Brittany, parts of Normandy and a few *départements* outside them. As well as viewing display cases full of rocks, visitors can go on geology and nature walks (Apr–Sept) and sign up for 'interactive conferences' and science workshops in the laboratory of Professor Kaolin, an expert on the peninsula. The shop has interesting souvenirs, including geological maps of French regions.

Time 1hr for visit; walks and 'conferences' vary. *Open* July and Aug daily 10am–7pm; rest of year Mon–Fri 10am–noon and 2–5pm, Sun 2–5pm. *Admission* 4.80€ adult, 3€ child to young adult 8–18; activities and workshops vary. *Amenities* ♿ 🏠 ⚒

Maison des Vieux Métiers Vivants ★★ AGE 4 & UP

Argol; ☎ 02 98 27 79 30; www.argol. fr.st. 14km (9 miles) east of Crozon on D60.

This 'living museum' at the entrance to the Crozon peninsula (p. 207) consists of about 15 workshops in which volunteers demonstrate various trades of yesteryear: you simply wander from one to another to watch (and talk to, if you so desire) the artisans, who include a cobbler, basket-maker, wool spinner and rope maker. Check the website ahead of your visit for details of the busy programme of events— the likes of a horse festival with wheel-waxing, a bread festival with butter-making, Breton dance lessons, and days featuring pony-and-cart rides, sheepshearing, honey-gathering or crêpe-making over an open fire. The grounds hold a selection of old Breton games to try, and there's space for picnics. This is great fun for both kids and parents—and an opportunity to immerse your family in Breton culture.

Time half a day. *Open* Easter–June and Sept Tues, Thurs and Sun 2–5.30pm; July and Aug daily 2–6pm. *Admission* 4€ adult, 2.30€ child 6–14. *Amenities* ♿ 🏠 ⚒

Musée des Beaux Arts

★ AGE 4 & UP

40 Place Saint Corentin, Quimper;
02 98 95 45 20; www.musee-
beauxarts.quimper.fr.

Quimper's fine-arts museum has a colourful collection that consists of works by Breton artists or paintings inspired by Brittany, including city-born painter and poet Max Jacob, many of whose drawings, oil paintings, letters and manuscripts are on display, alongside works by friends such as Pablo Picasso and Jean Cocteau. The free creative **workshops** (in French; 3.20€), designed to make the collections accessible to children aged 7 to 12 through learning painting, drawing, engraving, modelling and collage techniques, begin with a themed tour of the museum, during which kids are encouraged to share ideas that come to them. Held in school holidays except at Christmas, they last 2hrs 30mins and have space for just 12 participants, so book well ahead (02 98 95 52 48).

Time 1–2hrs. Open July and Aug daily 10am–7pm, rest of year Wed–Mon 10am–noon and 2–6pm. Admission 4.50€ adult, 2.50€ under-26s, free under-12s. Amenities 🅿 🛍 ♿

Musée de l'Ecole Rurale en Bretagne AGE 5 & UP

Trégarvan; 02 98 26 04 72, www.musee-ecole.fr. 23km (14 miles) east of Crozon off D60.

Opened around 1910 for more than 100 local children and closed in the 1970s when the total had shrunk to just five due to rural depopulation, this school was restored as a museum with a reconstructed 1920s classroom hosting rather dry permanent and temporary exhibitions on the history of rural schooling in France. Come in summer, though, and your children (and sometimes you too) can join in with a host of imaginative activities, all free with museum entrance—they change from year to year but might sessions with home-made countryside toys, including marbles, skipping ropes and whirligigs; traditional games such as hopscotch; science experiments; and drawing and poetry competitions for kids and adults. It's a lovely way to taste some Breton culture if you speak good French.

Time half an hour for visit, activities vary. Open mid-Feb–June Sun–Fri 2–6pm; July and Aug daily 10.30am–7pm; Sept daily 2–6pm; Oct and Nov Sun–Fri 2–5pm; Dec–mid-Feb Mon–Fri 2–5pm. Admission 4.50€ adult, 2.50€ child. Amenities 🅿 ♿

Musée du Loup ★★ AGE 5 & UP

Le Bourg, Le Cloître—Saint Thégonnec; 02 98 79 73 45; www.museeduloup.fr. 35km (22 miles) south of Roscoff on D111.

Another fascinating nature site within the Parc Naturel Régional d'Armorique (p. 205), this unique 'wolf museum' tells the story of the wolves who roamed this area just over a century ago, striking fear into the hearts of locals, who received rewards for killing them. Ironically, today they're a protected species, and at this museum you learn about modern-day

The Height of Fashion

You're very unlikely to see any worn in the street, but the tall *coiffe* lace headdresses that form such an iconic image of Brittany are often sported by women or girls at one of the region's festivals or celebrations (p. 218). The town of **Pont-l'Abbé,** famous as the home of a particularly skyscraping and richly embroidered variation of the *coiffe* that attained a height of 32cm (13ins), has lots of them on display in its **Musée Bigouden** (℡ *02 98 66 09 03, www.museebigouden.fr*), housed in the medieval dungeons of its Château des Barons. You can also see peasant furniture, seaside crafts and other local costumes in the museum, and there are French-language children's workshops on the likes of art, jewellery making and the Breton language. Nearby, the 1930s granite **Monument aux Bigoudens** shows five local women and a little girl in traditional costume, all thinking of a father, son, husband or grandson fighting for survival on the high seas.

preservation measures, as well as about wolves from a biological viewpoint and in legends, stories, superstition and art, including 'Le Petit Chaperon Rouge' ('Little Red Riding Hood') and cave paintings in the Dordogne. There are stuffed wolves aplenty, multimedia terminals, an art gallery and a slide show with commentary by a storyteller. It's good to time your visit with an event, especially a Nuit du Loup nocturnal visit to the museum followed by a walk in the nearby former wolf-habitat of the Landes du Cragou with a storyteller and musician (prebooking is essential). There are also 'wolf days' combining a visit here with the chance to see live wolves at the Domaine de Ménez-Meur (p. 209). Don't miss the striking fountain covered with carved wolves in the Le Cloître St. Thégonnec's Place de la Mairie.

Time 1–2hrs. **Open** *July and Aug daily 2–6pm; mid-Feb–June and Sept–mid-Dec Sun 2–6pm.* **Admission** *3.50€ adult, 2.50€ child 5–12.* **Amenities** 🅿 ♿

Musée de la Pêche
★ AGE 2 & UP

3 Rue Vauban, Concarneau; ℡ *02 98 97 10 20.*

A highlight of the fishing (and fish canning) port of Concarneau (p. 197), set at the entrance to the touristy Ville Close, this museum looks at maritime traditions and techniques locally and around the world. As well as diverse items such as the frighteningly huge wall-mounted Japanese spider crab (with a leg span of almost 2m, or 6ft), lobster cages, a reconstructed ship's cabin with radar equipment, tanks with local fish, scale models of the town showing the Ville Close protruding into the bay like an island, and an amazing array of sardine tins, children love the *Hémérica*—a 34m (112ft) fishing boat permanently moored outside the museum, where the sea sloshes against the rampart. Clambering aboard to see its engine room, bunkrooms, kitchen and more really gives you a feel of the ardours of life at sea (you need to be fairly agile to navigate its warren of decks linked by steep steps and ladders). July sees French-language workshops and activities for kids 4–8 and 7–12 (4€); pre-booking is advisable. The small shop sells shrimping nets, colouring books, models and other crafts, and candle-powered 'Pop Pop' boats (p. 64).

Time 2hrs. **Open** Apr–June, Sept and Oct daily 10am–6pm; July and Aug 9.30am–8pm; Nov hols and Christmas hols 10am–noon and 2–6pm. **Admission** 6€ adult, 4€ child 5–15, 20€ family (2+3). **Amenities** 🛍 ♿

Musée des Phares et Balises/ Ecomusée de l'Ile d'Ouessant
★★ AGE 5 & UP

Phare du Créac'h, Ouessant; ☎ 02 98 48 80 70; *www.pnr-armorique.fr.*

In a machine room of the Phare du Creac'h's old electrical station (p. 215), this museum—the only one of its kind in the world—traces the history of lighthouses and maritime signals on the island that saw the world's first automatic lighthouse and the testing of many optical and auditory signals. The navigation lights, beacons and buoys on display date from the early 1800s to the present day;

there are models that throw into sharp relief the complicated and often dangerous process of building lighthouses, plus maps, objects from shipwrecks (including the British *Drummond Castle*; p. 204) and displays about lighthouse-keepers' harsh lives. In summer there are 2-hour tours of the island's signalling system, which includes five lighthouses (not all of them accessible), foghorns, turrets and sea marks.

Time 2hrs. **Open** Apr–June and Sept daily 11am–5pm; July and Aug daily 10.30am–6pm (plus 9–11pm two nights a week); rest of year Tues-Sun 1.30–5.30pm outside school hols, daily 11am–5pm in school hols. **Admission** 4.50€ adult, 3€ child 8–14. **Amenities** ♿

INSIDER TIP ❯❯

Before visiting the lighthouse museum, download the educational French-language booklet from the website—it's intended for school groups but is very useful for parents looking to get their kids engaged in what they see.

Port-Musée AGE 4 & UP

Place de l'Enfer, Douarnenez; ☎ 02 98 92 65 20; *www.port-musee.org.* 26km (16 miles) northwest of Quimper on D765.

This small museum of traditional boats (with a focus on those from the region), has entered the modern era in the past few years and now presents visitors with image and sound installations and hands-on elements to liven the displays about boats and the local fish-canning industry. The best bit is outside, however, where a few boats afloat in the Port-Rhu estuary can be boarded and explored: a sand barge and a Thames barge, a lobster boat, and a British steam-tug.

Time *2hrs.* **Open** *July and Aug daily 10am–7pm; rest of year Tues–Sun 10am–12.30pm and 2–6pm.* **Admission** *(low to high season) 5.50€– 7.50€ adult, 3.50€–4.50€ child 6–16, 15€–20€ family (2+2 or more).* **Amenities** 🅿️ ♿

INSIDER TIP ›

While in the fish-canning town of Douranenez, pop into **Penn Sardin** (7 rue Le Breton, 📞02 98 92 70 83) to choose from more than 100 types of canned sardines, all beautifully packaged.

Parks & Gardens

The pleasant **Parc Botanique de Cornouaille** (📞02 98 56 44 93. *www.parcbotanique.com*) is at Combrit, between Bénodet (p. 212) and Pont l'Abbé. For the Parc Naturel Régional d'Armorique, see p. 205.

Jardin du Moulin Neuf FIND
ALL AGES

Route de Lannilis, Ploudalmézeau; http://parcdumoulinneuf.free.fr. 25km (16 miles) northwest of Brest on D26.

Inhabitants of the small inland town of Ploudalmézeau must thank their lucky stars every day to have such a wonderful municipal park, encompassing koi carp-filled pond, streams and water gardens, an animal enclosure (home to white llamas, Ouessant sheep—p. 204—and more) and two playgrounds for kids of different age ranges, all set amidst an abundance of trees and plant life both exotic and domestic. A huge picnic area lies just opposite— handy for takeaway crêpes from Le Salamandre (p. 227).

Time *2–3hrs.* **Open** *Apr–Sept daily 8.30am–9.30pm; rest of year daily 8.30am–6pm.* **Admission** *free (donations appreciated).* **Amenities** 🅿️ 🍽️ ⛺ ♿

Parc Botanique de Suscinio
★ FIND **ALL AGES**

Ploujean; 📞02 98 72 05 86. 4km (2.5 miles) north of Morlaix on D46.

If you're passing through Morlaix, make time for a detour to this 3 hectare (7.5 acre) botanical garden set around a 16th-century turreted manor. Its 1,100-plus species are divided into imaginative areas such as the lush 'Valley of Lost Worlds'; the 'Corsaire's Garden', where famous pirate Charles Croisic used to walk (he owned the manor); the 'Garden of the Round Table' with its ring of lime trees; and a terraced kitchen garden. It's a great place to just amble, discovering secret corners, but children will want to make for their very own area, the 'Village des Enfants', where they'll find rush cabins, a rope-bridge and a fantastic treehouse (the gardens have received awards for their remarkable trees). The aviary and small animal enclosure are also worth a visit. Ask about summer events and workshops, including hunts for ladybirds or other inhabitants of the park.

Rainy Days in Finistère

The weather can change quickly in Finistère so it's a good idea to have a list of indoor entertainment options to hand.

Aquacap, Esquibien, *www.aquacap.fr*. The Cap Sizun's aquatic complex, which only opened in 2007, includes a 'fun pool', a giant slide, a paddling pool with jets, and outdoor space for sunbathing and picnicking. Activities include 'Jardin Aquatique' play sessions for ages 3–5 and 6–10.

Aquarive, Route de Kerogan, Quimper, ☎ *02 98 52 00 15*, *www.quimper-communaute.fr*. An outstanding pool complex on Quimper's riverside (in the Zone de Créac'h Gwen; p. 198), with one of Brittany's rare wave pools, excellent slides, a kids' pool with games, and activities including 'Aqua-bébé' play sessions for ages 6 months to 5½.

Les Balnéides, Allée de Loc'Hilaire, Fouesnant Les Glénan, ☎ *02 98 56 18 19*, *www.balneides.fr*. A brilliant aquatic centre in a 'Station Famille' (p. 57), with tropical décor, a giant slide, a waterfall, water canons and more, plus 'Baby Dolphins' tuition for ages 6 months and up and other activities. There's another aquatic centre, Aquasud (☎ *02 98 66 00 00*) not far away at Pont-l'Abbé.

Bowling le Master, Rue du Président Sadate, Quimper, ☎ *02 98 53 09 59*, *http://quimper.lemasterbowling.fr/*. Bowling for all the family at Quimper's Zone de Créac'h Gwen (p. 198).

Cinéma Celtic, Rue de Colguen, Concarneau, ☎ *02 98 97 02 46*, *www.cineceltic.com*. A bog-standard cinema showing the latest kids' films, dubbed into French.

Cinéville Bretagne, 5 Allée François Truffaut, Quimper, ☎ *08 92 70 21 31*, *http://quimper.cineville.fr*. A multi-screen cinema with a Ciné Bambino programme for kids (in French), with tickets just 3.90€ for kids and adults.

L'Ile aux Mômes, Rue Aimé Cesaire Colguen, Concarneau, ☎ *02 98 97 10 28*, *www.lileauxmomes.fr*. Indoor softplay for ages up to 12, including a secure area for kids aged 1–3, a café and Wi-Fi access. It's best to call ahead in case of party bookings or special sessions.

Les Petits Monstres, ZA de Troyalac'h, 3 Rue Gustave Eiffel, Saint Evarzec, Quimper, ☎ *02 98 56 29 29*, *www.lespetitsmonstres.com*. An indoor softplay with electric karts, plus an outdoor play area with a terrace. There's a lunchtime café and a Wi-Fi zone. See the website for details of creative workshops and shows (clowns, puppets, balloon sculptors).

Ty Marmouz, ZA de Ty Boutic, Plomeur, ☎ *02 98 87 30 19*, *www.tymarmouz.fr*—a big indoor softplay venue for kids aged 1–12.

Zone del Hippo, 5 Rue du Docteur Picquenard, Quimper, ☎ *02 53 08 65*, *www.zonedelhippo.com*. Another indoor play venue at Quimper, open to children aged 0–12.

Time 3hrs. *Open* May and June Sun 2–6pm; July and Aug daily 2–6pm. *Admission* free in May and June; July and Aug: 3€ adult, 2€ child 12–16. *Amenities* 🅿 ⋀ ♿

For Active Families

See also **'Fun Days Out'**, p. 200, and **'Best Beaches'**, p. 211. For family canoeing in the Glénans or the Baie de Morlaix, see p. 200 and p. 213.

Arbreizh Aventure ★ AGE 4 & UP

Bois de Keroual, Brest; 📞06 64 24 06 41; www.arbreizh.com.

A ropebridge, a zipwire and nets are just part of the fun at this treetop adventure course on the western outskirts of Brest, a children's course suitable for ages 4 and up. English is spoken by the instructors. There's a sister course, plus a zipwire over the ocean, at Fort Bertheaume (p. 201).

Time 3hrs. *Open* Easter–Nov school hols Sat, Sun, and school and public hols 10am–6pm. *Admission* adult course 10€, children's course 7€. *Amenities* 🅿

INSIDER TIP

There are further treetop adventure courses at Quimper, where **Bonobo Parc** (📞02 98 53 09 59, *www.bonoboparc.com*) in the Zone de Créac'h Gwen (p. 198) caters to ages 4 and up, and **Karaez Adrenaline** (📞06 50 19 15 98, *www.karaez adrenaline.com*), at Carhaix, for ages 5 and up.

Centre International de Plongée des Glénan/Les Glénans
★ AGE 13 & UP

Centre International de Plongée: 📞06 81 20 62 32; www.cip-glenans.org; Centre Nautique des Glénans: 📞01 53 92 86 00; www.glenans.asso.fr.

Famous for their shipwrecks (more than 50 boats have come to grief here since the 18th century), the Iles de Glénan, an archipelago of 13 islands and lots of islets and rocks 20km (13 miles) off Concarneau, are some of Europe's best places to learn to sail and dive, although there are no hotels or campsites and only two restaurants—the latter on **St. Nicolas,** the only one of the islands to be officially inhabited (by one person). This is the landing point for cruisers from Concarneau, Port-la-Forêt and Bénodet and the site of the **Centre International de Plongée,** running residential courses for divers aged 14 and up, plus initiation for ages 10 and up, mid-April–mid-October. St. Nicolas also has good beaches, a sandy spit linking it with the Ile de Bananec at low tide, and a protected area where the Glénan narcissus, unique to these islands, grows.

Meanwhile, **Penfret,** the second-largest island (after the Ile du Loch) has, in addition to a lighthouse, several bases belonging to **Les Glénans,** a world-renowned residential sailing school that rents some of the other Glénan islands for activities and runs courses in other locations. Courses here cater for ages 13 and up, and unusually there are a few courses run in English, though these are for adults.

For boat-trips to and family canoeing in the Glénans, see p. 200.

Initiation aux Danses Bretonnes ★ AGE 5 & UP

Penmarc'h; 📞 *02 98 58 81 44 (tourist office). 31km (19 miles) southwest of Quimper on D785.*

Here's something that's bound to end up among everyone's most embarrassing holiday memories—lessons in the traditional Breton dances performed at *fest noz* (p. 16), including the *an dro, anter dro, laridé* and *gavotte.* They're only offered in French, but even if yours is basic you should be able to keep up and enjoy yourself. Best of all, they're followed by a free *fest noz.*

Penmarc'h tourist board also offers Breton-language lessons, though to learn the basic vocabulary, place names, names of boats and so on, and to appreciate the humour of many Breton expressions, you need good French.

Time 1hr 30mins. **Classes** *July and Aug Wed 7.30pm.* **Admission** *3.50€ adult, free under 8.* **Amenities** 🅿

Nantes–Brest Canal ALL AGES

www.smatah.fr

Though this 385km (239 mile) canal across Brittany begins (or ends) in Finistere, the best sections are in the Morbihan (p. 99). The main town on the *branche finistèrienne* is tranquil **Châteaulin,** where you can fish for salmon and trout (permits are available at fishing shops and most bars in town). On the *Quai Charles de Gaulle,* the 'aquatic observatory' allows you to see the canal bed and watch fish swim through a *passe à poisons,* or you might just stroll along the town's towpaths with their friendly squirrels and rabbits.

Time 2–3hrs.

Voie Verte Quimper–Douarnenez ALL AGES

www.voiesvertes.com

Finistère's 'greenway' (p. 54) takes cyclists and walkers a distance of 26km (16 miles), including 16km (10 miles) of recently renovated track. Note that to get from the centre of Quimper to the actual start of

Idyllic lock-keeper's cottage near Cadoret, Nantes-Brest Canal

Shopping & Producer Tours

Food shopping is where Finistère truly excels. In Pleyben near Châteaulin (p. 223), **Chocolatier Chatillon** (02 98 26 63 77, *www.chatillon-chocolat.com*), a prizewinning producer of fine chocs, Florentines (almond and chocolate cookies with mint or orange) and Breton biscuits, offers short guided tours of its workshops, where you can see hand-production of specialities such as pink or grey Granit de Bretagne—a white-chocolate confection that doesn't melt up to a temperature of 45°C (handy for picnics!).

Not far away, the Miellerie de Fouesnant (02 98 56 59 66, *www.mielleriedefouesnant.fr*), a small-scale producer of honey and related products (obvious things such as pollen and royal jelly but also jams, honey vinegar and *chouchenn*) offers summer tours when you can watch bees going about their business in the hives and see honey being extracted in the pollen-drying room.

Brittany takes its biscuits very seriously indeed, as you'll see from the number of *biscuiteries* (factories) and shops dotted around. Specialities range from light *crêpes-dentelles* ('lacy crêpes', a sort of wafer) to butter biscuits called, confusingly, *galettes*. One of the best places to buy Breton biscuits and cakes, and see them being made and taste some for free, is **Biscuiterie François Garrec** at Bénodet (p. 212; 02 98 57 17 17, *www.garrec.com*). Meanwhile, **Larnicol** in Concarneau's Ville Close (p. 197; 02 98 60 46 87, *www.larnicol.com*; other stores in Quimper, Locronan and Pont-Aven) lures you in with its *torchettes* (big round biscuits made without fat, containing almonds, hazelnuts, raisons and Breton seaweed) together with its huge decorative chocolate dolphins and other animals and its luscious specialities such as *kouignettes* (moist little cakes in around 20 flavours), including salted-butter caramel made with *fleur de sel* (seasalt), and riotously colourful *moumettes*—mini meringues in lots of alluring flavours.

Concarneau's Ville Close is also a great place for children's shopping: **La Perle Rare** (02 98 97 53 08) sells lots of *jouets*

the Voie, you have to go along a secondary road, so it's best to start at Ty Planche (which has a car park). See the website for bike-hire and repairs, places to stay and eat en route, and sights to see along the way.

INSIDER TIP »

For more on 'Vélo Promenades' (including Voies Vertes) in Finistère, see *www.randobreizh.org*, which has four downloadable circuits in the Pays d'Iroise (the northwestern corner of Finistère), taking 1hr 30mins to 5hrs.

d'hier ('toys of yesteryear'), such as clockwork mice, clowns, elephants and penguins, tin 'Pop Pop boats' (p. 64), wooden sailboats and fishing games, spinning tops and compasses. On the same street (Rue Saint Guénolé), **Le Bois d'Angèle** (02 98 97 46 17) is a wooden games and toys specialist that also stocks quality soft toys.

Close by, on adjoining Rue Vauban, **Mille et Une Bagues** (02 98 50 71 82) is a slightly schlocky shop with interesting figurines of *korrigans* (p. 2) and Breton witch dolls, plus carved wooden animals, porcelain snails and lots of grungy jewellery. Outside the Ville Close you'll find a branch of **Comptoir de la Mer** (p. 176); others in the département include Carantec, Roscoff, Audierne and Brest (at the Port du Moulin Blanc).

Brest is quite a good place to shop overall, with a **Fnac** book and multimedia store at 65 Rue Jean-Jaurès (08 25 02 00 20) and a branch of the **Atelier de Courcelles** designer kidswear shop on Rue Rue Etienne Dolet (02 98 80 56 09).

Finistère's **main markets** are as follows:

Audierne	Wed and Sat morning
Bénodet	Mon morning
Brest	Sun morning
Camaret-sur-Mer	Tues, Thurs and Sat morning
Carantec	Thurs morning
Châteaulin	Thurs morning (and Sun morning in high summer)
Concarneau	Mon and Fri morning
La Forêt-Fouesnant	Sun morning, plus Tues eve in summer
Huelgoat	Thurs morning
Pont-l'Abbé	Thurs morning
Quimper	Wed, Sat and Sun morning, and Fri afternoon
Roscoff	Wed

FAMILY-FRIENDLY DINING

North Coast & Ile d'Ouessant

With the exception of Ouessant this area can be a really exciting area to eat *en famille*—unsurprisingly, perhaps, for somewhere where pink onions, artichokes and seaweed are local specialities, complementing wonderfully fresh seafood.

Restaurant Patrick Jeffroy ★★

L'Hôtel de Carantec, 20 Rue de Kélenn, Carantec; ☎02 98 67 00 47; www.hoteldecarantec.com. 18km (11 miles) southeast of Roscoff via D173.

Views don't come much better than from the panoramic dining room of the Hôtel de Carantec, the resort's poshest restaurant, with the Baie de Morlaix at your feet. Chef Patrick Jeffroy, a sort of French Heston Blumenthal, specialises in 'mischievous associations' such as fried porridge, pork brawn and roast whelk, with buckwheat pancake, local pink onions and sour cream. That might make the place sound daunting for families, but for older, more adventurous kids there's a 20€ children's menu that changes with the seasons and the market's offerings but might feature hermit crab and avocado salad, local pollock with new potatoes, and chocolate cake with strawberry sorbet. To top it off, the staff are very welcoming towards younger diners since, as the chef himself explained to me, they're future customers! Various set menus makes for a more affordable special-occasion treat than it might at first appear.

Open mid-June–mid-Sept Wed and Fri–Sun noon–2.30pm and 7.30–10pm, Mon, Tues and Thurs 7.30–10pm; rest of year daily noon–2.30pm and 7.30–10pm. Main courses 35€–75€. Amenities ⬚ 🎎 ↻

La Corniche ★★ FIND

Rue de la Corniche, Brignogan-Plages; ☎02 98 85 81 99. 37km (23 miles) west of Roscoff on D770.

Part raucous locals' and sailors' bar, part top-notch seafood restaurant, this is one of only a couple of eateries in an untouristy little seaside town and can get fiendishly busy on a weekend night, while on holiday weekends staff turn people away in droves (though if you come very early with kids and don't look as if you're going to spend all night here, they might squeeze you in). The dining room's gorgeous panoramic views of Brignogan's bay (shaped like a figure eight) are more than matched by the food. The menus, written up (in French only) on large chalkboards that are hefted to your table, change daily but might include an exquisite skate wing with capers, sauté potatoes, courgettes and cherry tomatoes, and 'fisherman's stew' (*cotriade du pêcheur*) with tuna, scallops, monkfish, prawns and more in a dark, buttery sauce, and there'll certainly be a large choice of other fish dishes, mussel specialities, and some meats. You'll need to prompt the somewhat cool staff for the good 9€ kids' menu of *steak haché* or creamy white monkfish with the most delicious chips, tagliatelle or rice, followed by ice cream. It's hard to resist the desserts, but your curiosity about ice cream flavours such as *chouchenn* (p. 236) or seaweed may be outweighed by the desire for a home-made *fondant au chocolat* (half-mousse, half-cake) with strawberries.

Open *Mar–June and Sept Tues–Sun noon–2pm and 7–11pm; Aug and July daily noon–2pm and 7–11pm; Oct–Easter Fri–Sun noon–2pm and 7–11pm.* **Main courses** *9.50€–34€.* **Amenities** 🍽 🎱 ✎

INEXPENSIVE–MODERATE

Le Petit Relais ★★★

Plage du Kélenn, Carantec; 📞 *02 98 78 30 03. 18km (11 miles) southeast of Roscoff via D173.*

Located on Carantec's busy Plage du Kélenn (p. 213) and boasting a wonderful terrace, this brasserie/pub/bar/*glacier* tries to be everything to everyone, at just about all hours of the day—which makes it a handy family option. If you want to eat between regular mealtimes, there are baguette sandwiches, ice creams and pastries, and children are warmly welcomed with games, books and colouring sheets (you, in the meantime, could be checking your emails for free at the computer terminal). You can also come for a relaxed late family breakfast if you're fed up with the ubiquitous Continental variety—choices include fried eggs and ham and smoked salmon with scrambled eggs on toast. 'Proper meals', French and otherwise, range from *chilli con salsa* and various tartares to pasta dishes, oysters and *moules breton* (with cider and artichokes). Of the two under-12s menus (6€/9€), the cheapest comprises

ham and sausage with chips followed by Smarties ice cream, *fromage blanc* or apple compôte; the second offers mussels or *steak haché* with chips, vegetables, pasta or rice, then ice cream, a lolly, or a mini chocolate mousse.

Open *May–Sept daily 10.30am–1am, plus certain other times of year (call for details).* **Main courses** *5€–24€.* **Amenities** 📶 🍽 📶 🎱 ✎

INEXPENSIVE

Crêperie Le Salamandre ★★

Place du Général de Gaulle, Ploudalmézeau; 📞 *02 98 48 14 00. 25km (16 miles) northwest of Brest on D26.*

A pretty crêperie with blue shutters and a sunny terrace, The Salamander was set up by the present owner's parents and has a real family atmosphere—kids get colouring materials and a genuinely warm welcome. Alongside more sophisticated offerings such as galette with scallops and baby vegetables, you'll find eggs and ham for kids who like to stick with what they know, plus omelettes and main-course salads. The dessert crêpes are predictably good, but there's also a big choice of ice creams and *coupes*, available in handy half-price mini-portions. Note that you're only two minutes' walk from Ploudalmézeau's Jardin du Moulin Neuf (p. 220) for blowing off some steam before or after your meal, or for a picnic of takeaway crêpes should you prefer.

Open *Apr–June and Sept Thurs–Mon noon–2pm and 7–10pm; July and*

Aug daily noon–2pm and 7–10pm; Oct–mid-Nov and mid-Dec–Mar Sat, Sun and school hols noon–2pm and 7–10pm. **Main courses** *4.50€– 10.50€.* **Amenities** 📶 🧃 ☎

> **INSIDER TIP** ▶
>
> If Le Salamandre is full or closed, head to the adjoining port village of Portsall, where La Chaumine (4 Square de l'Abéric, ☎02 98 48 65 55), a holder of the Crêperies Gourmandes label (p. 39), offers creative galettes and crêpes, two terraces (heated in cooler weather), and baby changing facilities and a highchair.

Brest, Monts d'Arrée & Presqu'île de Crozon

Brest's size makes it a good bet for family eating, but if you're only heading in for Océanopolis (p. 210), there are several eating options on-site. The inland Monts d'Arrée, being largely rural, can be trickier, while the Crozon peninsula is rather disappointing in terms of good child-friendly restaurants.

MODERATE

On the Crozon peninsula; the Thalassa hotel (p. 234) in Camaret-sur-Mer is a reliable moderately priced bet.

A L'Aise Breizh Café ★ FIND

Port de Plaisance du Moulin Blanc, Brest; ☎02 98 42 49 21.

This second branch of a minichain, originating from Vannes (p. 107) has a great waterside setting, cheerful modern décor and a buzzy vibe in which to enjoy Breton classics, sometimes given an exotic twist. Most tastes are covered, with options ranging from healthy salads and seafood to burgers, steaks and duck dishes, together with the odd main-course sandwich. For 7.50€, kids can get the Menu Moutik of salmon and pasta or steak haché and chips, followed by ice cream or fresh fruit salad. Whatever you do, leave room for one of the knock-em-dead traditional Breton desserts—*kouign amann* with apple sorbet, 'honeymoon rice' with salted-butter caramel, or pancake-cake with orange butter.

Open *daily 9am–1am (meals served Mon–Fri noon–2pm and 7–10pm, Sat and Sun noon–2.30pm and 7–10.30pm).* **Main courses** *6€–18€.* **Amenities** 🗔 🧃 ☎

> **INSIDER TIP** ▶
>
> If you're flying into or out of Brest (or driving into or out of the city), there's a branch of the Francewide grill specialist Hippopotamus at the Les Portes de Brest—Guipavas shopping centre (105 Rue Jazek Helias, ☎02 98 34 44 10, *www.hippopotamus.fr*) close to the airport.

INEXPENSIVE

For the Crêperie des Myrtilles in Huelgoat, see p. 202. A trio of decent child-friendly crêperies can be found in Brest—two called Blé Noir (one of them by the Conservatoire National, the other handy for Arbreizh Aventure; p. 196 and p. 222), and a sister restaurant called Latitude Crêperie (☎02 98 33 10 70) at the Port de Commerce.

Crêperie du Ménez-Gorre ★

86 Rue de Poulpatré, Crozon; 📞*02 98 27 19 66.*

Just inland, this Crêperie Gourmande (p. 39) is worth knowing about. The garden has an attractive fountain and space for toddlers to play beside the wooden benches and tables, and conveniently, it opens every day. Set in a handsome stone building, it offers more than 150 galettes and crêpes, which means every member of the family will find something pleasing, whether it's a Morgatoise with tuna, baby veg and cream, or a crêpe with blueberries or home-grown blackberries. The staff pride themselves on cooking everything fresh, a fact you can verify by watching preparation in the semi-open kitchen.

Open *daily noon–2.30pm and 7–10pm.* ***Main courses*** *4.50€– 12.50€.* ***Amenities*** 🍴📞

> **INSIDER TIP** ▶
>
> On restaurant menus and in markets, great local produce to look out for includes cérises griottes, famously good cherries from the Fouesnant area, and strawberries from the peninsula of Plougastel-Daoulas near Brest. The latter are even the subject of their own museum (📞*02 98 40 21 18, http://musee-fraise.net*).

Cap Sizun & Baie d'Audierne

This isn't the best place for family-friendly dining, but there are some gems to be found.

L'Iroise ★★

8 Quai Camille-Pelletan, Audierne; 📞*02 98 70 15 80.*

Deemed by some guests to be worthy of a Michelin star, this is the kind of restaurant where the chef comes to chat to you at the end of your meal, but don't let the high culinary standards and chic ambiance put you off—it's very child-friendly too! Younger diners are treated to a 15€ 'taste apprenticeship' featuring a plate of Serrano ham, then fish of the day or chicken escalope with cream, accompanied by fried potatoes, rounded off by a choice of wonderful sorbets and ice creams or fresh fruit salad. Adults, meanwhile, can choose from a variety of menus suited to most budgets, featuring such sophisticated fare as shell-roast langoustines with a *confit* of curried peppers and fennel sauce, lobster ravioli in a vanilla *velouté*, and hot Grand Marnier soufflé. The light-flooded dining room has lovely views onto the port.

Open *Mon noon–3pm, Wed–Sun noon–3pm and 7–9.30pm, daily in July and Aug.* ***Main courses*** *25€– 30.50€.* ***Amenities*** ▢🍴📞

> **INSIDER TIP** ▶
>
> The restaurant at **Hôtel Le Goyen** (p. 237) is a good second-best to L'Iroise.

Le Rabelais ★ **FIND**

51 Rue Raymond Le Corre, Le Guilvinec; 📞*02 98 58 19 86. 32km (20 miles) southwest of Quimper on D57.*

Newly opened since the first edition of this guide, this seaside brasserie flouts convention by specialising in meat and cheese dishes—imagine beef in beer, stone-cooked pork, and Savoy-style fondues, raclettes and tartiflettes, followed by old-school desserts such as chocolate mousse, profiteroles and apple crumble. In short, comfort food, and for those who can't do without, various seafood dishes, from plain oysters to the likes of monkfish brochette with lime and beurre blanc sauce. The kids' menu, featuring mussels, ham or steak with chips and salad and an ice cream and drink, is very well priced at 7.50€. Live jazz takes place on some evenings.

Open *Thurs–Tues noon–2.30pm and 7.30–11pm.* **Main courses** *10.50€–22.90€.* **Amenities** ⬜ 🖥 🎐 ✎

Crêperie L'Epoké ★

1 Rue des Partisans, Pont-Croix; ☎*02 98 70 58 39. 5.5km (3.5 miles) northeast of Audierne on D765.*

This quaint, welcoming Creperie Gourmande (p. 39), set opposite the impressive cathedral, serves up wonderful fishy crêpes with fillings such as sardine butter with lemon and salmon with creamy spinach, but you can also enjoy hearty main-course salads, omelettes, *croques* and fish soup. For fussy children there are simple crêpes with cheese, ham and so on. Desserts run from elaborate crêpe confections (the caramelised apple with cinnamon ice

cream and grilled almonds is recommended) and ice cream *coupes* to *kouigns bigoudens* (buttery Breton yeast cakes served with chocolate and banana). The dining room has a log fire in the colder months but can get a bit crammed; a better bet is the pretty terrace.

Open *Feb, Mar, May, June and Sept Thurs–Mon noon–2pm and 7–9pm; Apr and Nov daily noon–2pm and 7–9pm; Aug and July daily noon–2.30pm and 7–10pm.* **Main courses** *6€–15€.* **Amenities** 🎐 ✎

> **INSIDER TIP** ≫
>
> If L'Epoké is full, Le Pub (☎*02 98 70 42 73*) on Place de la République has great children's *steak haché*.

Quimper & Southern Finistère

The choice is generally wider here than immediately to the north, but you'll need to be wary of over-priced tourist traps in the more established resorts.

La Brocéliande ★

2 Rue de l'Eglise, Bénodet; ☎*02 98 57 25 71.*

This traditional restaurant by Bénodet's port is a handy standby when some of the family fancy a galette or crêpe while others fancy a more substantial seafood meal. The pancakes, excellent by anyone's standards, include the basics (plain with butter, ham and egg and so on) as well as fancier specialities such as Breton sausage with mustard, and home-smoked salmon with *crème fraîche* and lemon, all containing the freshest ingredients, whether from nearby or more distant climes—the salmon is Scottish, but the majority of ingredients are local. Fishy treats include mackerel rillettes with mustard, stuffed Glénan clams, and home-smoked haddock with *ratte* potatoes, spinach and poached egg. On hot days there is also a salad menu. The decor is a bit old-fashioned, but the home-made ice creams or *entremets tout chocolat* (a plate of chocolate desserts), or the roasted figs with *kouign* (butter cake), will put you in a frame of mind to overlook aesthetics.

Open *school hols daily noon–2pm and 7–10pm; rest of year Tues–Sat noon–2pm and 7–9pm.* **Main courses** *4.50€–18€.* **Amenities** 🍴

La Couscousserie ★ FIND

1 Bd de Kerguélen, Quimper; 📞 *02 98 95 46 50.*

When you've overdone it on the seafood, this Moroccan on the river at Quimper, with a refined Middle Eastern decor, red parrots and lush Arab soundtrack, makes for an excellent change of scene. Staff couldn't be more attentive—a welcome that extends to younger diners, who can order smaller portions of anything on the menu of couscous, tagines (the chicken, prunes and almonds is recommended) and *méchoui* (roast leg of lamb). Alternatively, if you have very little ones, think about getting two or three dishes and

sharing them—portions are large, and you can get free refills of vegetables and couscous. Cocktails from the bar are a good way to start your meal; fresh mint tea is an excellent *digestif* at the end.

Open *daily noon–1.30pm and 7pm–midnight. Closed most of Aug.* **Main courses** *12€–20€.* **Amenities** 🍴

Le Porte au Vin ★★

9 Place St. Guénolé, Concarneau; 📞 *02 98 97 38 11.*

In the heart of Concarneau's picturesque but touristy Ville Close (p. 197), this former fishermen's bistro has changed both owner and chef since the first edition of this guide but the cosy rooms are still full of discerning locals tucking into excellent seafood from a very wide menu. The highpoint is a house *choucroute* with cod, salmon and smoked mackerel in cider butter with steamed potatoes—a hearty dish best washed down with a light Britt Blanche from among the good list of Breton beers. Children can choose from the very good and light savoury and sweet pancakes (served all day), or there's an excellent, plentiful, under-12s menu at a bargain 8.50€, which offers *moules marinières* with chips, fresh breaded fish with rice and new potatoes or chips, or a ham, egg and cheese crêpe, followed by a sweet crêpe or ice cream.

Open *daily noon–10.30pm (crêpes served outside main meal times); closed Oct–Feb.* **Main courses** *4.50€–20.50€.* **Amenities** 🖼 🍴

Best Picnic Spots

Aside Finistère's countless wonderful beaches—including Caran-tec's **Plage du Kélenn** (p. 213)—the following are great places to picnic:

Iles de Kerévennou, during the **Fête des Cabanes,** p. 196.

The seaside park at **Le Porzou,** Concarneau, p. 197.

Domaine de Ménez-Meur, p. 209.

Jardin du Moulin Neuf, Ploudalmézeau p. 220.

INEXPENSIVE–MODERATE

L'Ilot Jardin FIND

2 Hent Levern, just outside Fouesnant; ☎*02 98 51 69 03. 9km (6 miles) east of Bénodet on D44.*

This no-frills restaurant is set inside a leisure park of the same name, with tennis, squash courts, mini-golf, and a large terrace situated by an enclosed playground, which means the kids can blow off some steam while you enjoy a beer from the bar (you don't have to eat here). This is a useful stop-off on the way home from the beach, whether you want something snacky such as omelette and chips or pizza (also available for take-away) or proper meals from the *à la carte* menu of steaks and the like. The 7.50€ kids' menu runs to the usual *steak haché* and *jambon blanc* with chips.

Open *Tues–Sun noon–2pm and 6–10pm for food (bar open all day), plus Mon eve in July and Aug.* **Main courses** *5€–15€.* **Amenities** 🍴 ⚠ ☎ ⚡

INEXPENSIVE

Crêperie Chez Annick

9 Hent Lenn, Route de Gouesnac'h, Clohars-Fouesnant; ☎*02 98 57 02 98.*

4.5km northeast of Bénodet on D34 then Route de Nors-Vras.

Just northeast of Bénodet, in a leafy spot outside Fouesnant, this friendly crêperie has a quiet covered terrace and small garden with a swing for kids to play on while you enjoy a *bolée* of cider. Inside, it's all stone walls, checked tablecloths and old Breton furniture. There's plenty to suit all members of the family among the list of galettes, from melted cheese to chitterling sausage, and the crêpes—children love the fresh raspberry *coulis*.

Open *Feb–mid-Sept plus school hols Wed–Sun noon–2pm and 7–10pm, plus Mon eve and Tues July and Aug.* **Main courses** *3.50€–10€.* **Amenities** 🍴 ⚠ ☎

INSIDER TIP »

In Quimper and around, look for the mobile pancake van **A La Crêpe"Rie"** (☎*09 54 88 38 82*), which offers some highly original galettes and crêpes, including lemon curd with meringue pieces, as well as the classics. Locations change but the van can generally be found at Quimper's Wednesday- and Saturday-morning markets (p. 225). There's also a delivery service for four people or more within a radius of 20km (12.5 miles) of Quimper.

FAMILY-FRIENDLY ACCOMMODATION

The North Coast & Ile d'Ouessant

There's no shortage of accommodation in northern Finistère, which is a particularly good place for an inexpensive seaside holiday—in fact, only those looking to splurge will be disappointed.

MODERATE–EXPENSIVE

Hôtel Le Temps de Vivre ★★★ FIND

19 Place Lacaze Duthiers, Roscoff; 02 98 19 33 19; www.tycoz.com/ letempsdevivre.

This lovely little hotel in the old part of Roscoff offers crisp modern rooms with views over either a square with a church or directly over the sea lapping at the walls of the building, towards the Ile de Batz (p. 200). Light-sleepers might want to bring ear-plugs against the noise of seagulls or early-morning church bells. Those with more than one child are best off in one of the *Espaces Familiales*, which combine a double and a twin-bedded room and two bathrooms; those with the stunning sea views ('*Pieds dans l'Eau*') naturally cost more.

The light-flooded, Michelin-starred restaurant in the old stables (this was once a traditional inn) makes bold use of local ingredients such as artichokes, crab and lobster and the flexible menu options, including the 14€ kids' menu, make it an affordable one-off treat. Breakfasts are also dear (14€; less for kids according to age) but do feature wonderful home-made jams, bread and cakes, and you can enjoy them in your room—an amazing experience if you have a sea-view room and the tide is high.

15 rooms. Rates 80€–225€, family suite 196€–317€, extra bed 30€.
Amenities ¶¶ **In room** ▣ ⎕

INEXPENSIVE

Among the low-key campsites recommended by **Camping Qualité** (p. 93) are **Camping du Vougot** at Plouguerneau (*www. campingplageduvougot.com*).

Camping Les Hortensias/ Gîtes de Kermen ★ FIND GREEN

Kermen, Carantec; 02 98 67 08 63, www.leshortensias.fr.

This friendly, eco-friendly alternative to the noisy international campsites in the area is part of an organic vegetable smallholding beside a farm producing organic meat, and you can buy its wares to cook during your stay (or in passing). The relative lack of facilities is reflected in the prices, although there are bouncy castles for youngsters, and you're just 1km (less than a mile) from the sea and 2.5km or 1½ miles from the beaches via direct footpaths (the site is high up so you get amazing views over the bay). For those who don't bring a tent, motorhome or caravan, there are two pleasant gîtes for five or six on site, plus slightly smaller cottages on the farm itself, with private gardens and a shared children's play area.

Rates tent pitch 3€, then 3.50€ per person (under-7s 2.50€); car 1.60€, motorhome 4.60€; gîtes 230€–680€/wk. *Amenities* **Gîtes**

Le Keo ★ FIND

Lampaul, Ouessant; 06 17 88 59 57; *www.lekeo.com.*

Good cheer invades you when you walk into this unpretentious B&B in a characterful old inn 50m (150ft) from the port in Ouessant's main village. There are just three guestrooms, and two connect to form a family suite (with two double beds), all of which are simply furnished with a marine theme. The breakfast room doubles as a crêperie, tea-room, bookshop and art gallery, according to the time of day and you can buy everything from hand-made puppets to Breton beer in the little crafts shop on-site. Be sure to check out the old room with its original 1900 carved wood interior, and ask the kindly owners about their guided taxi tours of the island (or simple taxi shuttle service).

3 rooms. *Rates* 40€–42€, family suite for four 80€. *Amenities*

Brest, Monts d'Arrée & Presqu'île de Crozon

This is a varied area offering everything from eccentric but fun rural B&Bs to seaside options on the Crozon peninsula, and a good choice of campsites.

MODERATE

Hotel Thalassa VALUE

Quai Styvel, Camaret-sur-Mer; 02 98 27 86 44; *www.hotel-thalassa.com.*

Unexciting from the outside, in its bland modern block, this is a classic French seaside hotel and a good family choice given its prices, position 50m (150ft) from the beach and a five-minute walk from the centre of pretty Camaret-sur-Mer (p. 207) and its outdoor heated seawater pool. Family accommodation options include interconnecting rooms sharing a bathroom, and apartments for up to seven, some in a nearby *résidence*, the St. Rémy. All are relatively basic but have tubs; some rooms have enclosed balconies with sea or pool views. If you stay half board, children under 4 get free food and board (one child per room), while those aged 4–11 get 50% off. The breakfast room with its French windows flung open onto the terrace and bay in fine weather turns into a restaurant serving local specialities; a good 10€ children's menu is available. Parents appreciate the sauna, solarium and gym, and the terraced bar, or for all the family, there's a billiards room and the run of the garden.

47 rooms, 34 apartments. *Rates* 62€–120€, interconnecting rooms for four 107€–132€; apartment for four 410€–980€, extra bed 12€.

Amenities *; restaurant:* ***In room***

INEXPENSIVE–MODERATE

Auberge Saint Thégonnec ★

FIND

Place de la Mairie, Saint Thégonnec; 02 98 79 61 18; ***www.aubergesaintthegonnec.com****.*

Whether you're here for the wolf museum (p. 217), are exploring the Huelgoat forest or the Monts d'Arrée as a whole, or are just passing through, this stone inn is a charming place to lay your head and perhaps enjoy a feast of local specialities. Rooms, including triples and family rooms for four, are fairly basic but pretty and clean, with bathtubs. The dining rooms are supplemented by a lovely terrace for fine weather, and there's a spacious garden where kids are free to run around and play.

19 rooms. ***Rates*** *78€–100€, family room for four 100€–140€.* ***Amenities*** ***In room***

Carré d'Etoiles ★★ FIND

Keryel, Plougonvelin; 02 98 48 33 35; ***www.carre-detoiles.com/keryel****. 21km (13 miles) west of Brest on D789.*

Basically a wooden cube plonked in a rural setting, with a transparent dome in the roof that lets you gaze at the stars from your double cabin-bed set at the top of a ladder (there's also sleeping for two at ground level, on a sofabed), the 'Star Box' is best suited to those with slightly older kids for safety and comfort reasons.

There are several such sites around France—this one in the far west of Brittany is in the grounds of a working, family-run farm, by the coast close to the Fort de Bertheaume (p. 201). Star Boxes come with their own 'sky observation kit' including an astronomical telescope, a stellar chart and astronomy-themed games; practically speaking, there's also a kitchen corner, a shower and loo, and even a flat-screen TV, although the board games on loan might be more suited to the sense of calm and quiet here.

The site has a kids' play area and games such as pétanque and ping pong; services include breakfast baskets delivered to your door. There's also a pretty Romany roulotte for four to five people on site.

Rate *90€ per night.* ***Amenities*** ***In room***

Roulottes des Korrigans ★★

FIND GREEN

Goarem Edern, Brasparts; 02 98 81 41 62; ***www.roulottes-des-korrigans.com****. 21km (13 miles) northeast of Châteaulin on D785.*

Adventurous families and fans of 'glamping' (glamorous camping) will love these static Romany caravans with their stunning views over the Monts d'Arrée, available on a B&B basis for up to four people (with bunks for the kids) or in self-catering form for up to five (breakfast is optional for the latter). The welcoming modern reception building has an eco-friendly shop, a play area and other good amenities, including a 'tales and legends' space with books, comic strips and CDs. You can also book a themed stay including storytelling around a campfire and a moonlit stroll. Otherwise, the area is great for cycling and walking (bike hire and hiking excursions are available) as well as conservation-minded (no-kill) fishing.

*13 units. **Rates** self-catering roulotte for four people 59€–110€ per night, with minimum 2- or 3-night stay; for weekly prices and B&B rates, see website. **Amenities** ▦ ▬ ⚲ ▣ ⵜ ◪ ∧ ▣ ☗ ☖ **In room** ('gîte' roulotte). ☒*

For quite adventurous families, Brest has a good modern **Auberge de Jeunesse de Brest** (youth hostel; ☏ *02 98 41 90 41, http://pagesperso-orange.fr/ aj-brest/*) in leafy grounds near Océanopolis (p. 210) and the beaches east of town, with rooms for four with bunkbeds and sinks, a communal kitchen, and a lounge with games such as table football and a piano. Expect to pay less than 20€pp per night.

Among local campsites recommended by Camping Qualité (p. 93) are **Camping du Goulet** in Brest, **Camping Les Pins** at Crozon, and **Camping Le Grand Large** at Camaret-sur-Mer.

Auberge du Youdig ★

Kerveguenet, Brennilis; ☏02 98 99 62 36, www.youdig.fr. 13km (8 miles) northwest of Huelgoat on D764.

The Unique Selling Point of this gloriously rustic establishment comprising four simple B&B rooms for up to three people and a nearby 'village' of five gîtes in the heart of the Monts d'Arrée not far from Huelgoat (p. 202) is a museum containing a scale model of the nearby 17th-century village of Brasparts. Created in 1985 after the collapse of the family farm, requiring 10,000 hours of work and made from discarded roof tiles, it includes a mill, a washhouse, a well, a small lake, a chapel and a cemetery. One of the friendly family members shows visitors around, recounting legends and choice titbits from local history. There's also an inn on site, serving authentic Breton meals such as roast pork in *chouchenn* (weak mead) and *kig ha farz*, buckwheat dumplings with meat and vegetables. On Thursday evenings in high season, and some other times, there are storytelling sessions, in French, on *korrigans* and other local 'characters'.

*****Units** 4 rooms, 5 gîtes. **Rates** 40€ (extra bed 15€), triple 55€; gîte for four 230€–580€ per week. **Amenities** ⵙ ☗ **In room** (gîtes only) ☒ ☐*

Ferme Apicole de Térenez ★★

Rosnoën, just south of Le Faou; ☏02 98 81 06 90; www.ferme-apicole- de-terenez.com. 31km (19 miles) southeast of Brest on N165.

Also home to its own museum, this working honey farm offers fairly spartan B&B rooms for two or four people, plus mountain-bike hire and animals such as black Ouessant sheep (p. 204), hens and geese to pet, in a wooded garden leading down to the river with views of an ancient abbey (from the top you can see the river winding away to the Rade de Brest; p. 196). Beaches with rock pools and the famous fossils of the Crozon peninsula (p. 207) are a 10-minute drive away. If your children are under 6 years old, book a room with a double bed and two singles rather than bunks. Baby equipment (a cot, changing mat, baby bath and highchair for the breakfast room) are all at your disposal. The museum (free to guests) has displays on bees and their habitat plus free tastings, and there's a farm shop selling gingerbread made with honey, cakes, sweets, nougat and more.

Rates 37€–43€, room for four 50€. **Amenities** 🛏 🚲 📺 ♨ 🛍 **In room** ⬜

Le Rhun ★★ FIND

Argol; 📞02 98 17 21 90; www. lerhun.com. 23km (14 miles) west of Châteaulin on D163.

These five tasteful gîtes in a former farmhouse (sleeping up to 14) and its outbuildings (from four to eight people) on the Crozon peninsula are especially good for music-loving families—the British owners are professional musicians and offer crash-courses in saxophone or clarinet to their guests. Otherwise, families can swim, use the sandpit, swings, and swingball and badminton

sets, and discover little surprises such as the living willow tunnel and tree dens. These are especially good gîtes for those with babies—each comes with a stair-gate, baby monitor, travel cot, highchair, baby bath, toddler step, potty and even white towels laundered in non-biological powder. You're 1km (less than a mile) from Argol with its crêperie, bar and bakery, while there are great beaches within a 10-minute drive.

Units 5 gîtes. **Rates** Gîte for four 450€–1250€ per wk; for larger Gîtes see website. **Amenities** 🖼 🅰 🎽 **In room** 🖥 ✏ ❌ ♨ 🛍 ❇ ⬜

Cap Sizun & Baie d'Audierne

As you're not yet in fully blown beach holiday territory, the options here tend to be fairly basic.

INEXPENSIVE–MODERATE

Hôtel-Restaurant Le Goyen

Place Jean-Simon, Audierne; 📞02 98 70 08 88; www.legoyen.com.

This blue-shuttered harbour-front hotel at the northern end of the Baie d'Audierne (p. 213) is another pleasant little traditional seaside option well-suited to families, most of whom stay in the Junior Suites in which the living room converts into a children's room. If your heart's set on a sea view instead (Junior Suites look over the courtyard), ask for an Océanes room over two levels, with extra beds set up in the panoramic living room.

The Continental breakfasts (12€ adult, 6€ ages 3–12) can be taken in your room or in the conservatory restaurant, which offers fancier (and pricier) fare than you'd expect from a hotel of this category, including quite a sophisticated children's menu (10€–12€). Note: the hotel is closed early November to middle of March each year.

26 units. **Rates** *67€–135€, Junior Suite 72€–87€, Océanes duplex suite 149€–181€; extra bed 20€.* **Amenities** 🍸 📷 📶 💼 🍴 *In room* 🛏

Among several campsites recommended by Camping Qualité (p. 93) in this area, the star choice is the **Aire Naturelle de Keraluic** (📞02 98 82 10 22, *www.keraluic.fr*), a 'green' campsite on a renovated Breton farm that also offers B&B accommodation and studios. In the heart of the countryside and surrounded by forests yet only 6km from the coast, it's handy for both Penmarc'h and Bénodet, and the surfer-friendly Pointe de la Torche (p. 213).

Camping-gîte de Loquéran ★★★ FIND GREEN

Rue des Lavandières, Plouhinec; 📞*02 98 74 95 06, http://pointe.raz.free.fr/. 36km (22 miles) west of Quimper on D784.*

Sociable families counting the pennies will love this communal gîte and campsite near Audierne. The gîte, an attractive wooden chalet in lovely flower-filled grounds, houses dorms or single and family rooms with their own bathrooms, and a shared kitchen and dining room—it's a bit like a youth hostel, and very warm and welcoming. The basic 25-pitch campsite is similarly fresh in feel and lovingly maintained. There are no other facilities, but shops and services are a short walk away—including, at the end of the path, a communal *lavoir* or basin where some locals still come to wash their clothes. This a place to enjoy the peace, pet the horses in the surrounding fields, ride donkeys (anything from 10 minutes to a whole day) and wander around the atmospheric nearby boat cemetery. The GR4 footpath runs right nearby, and there are lots of mountain bike and riding trails, as well as some fine beaches.

Gîte: 6 units; 25 pitches. **Rates** *Family room for four 42€–50€; tent pitch 3€, then 3€ adult, 1.50€ child under 13.* **Amenities** *gîte:* 📶 ❌

Quimper & Southern Finistère

This is another great spot for both camping and seaside hotels.

Domaine Ker-Moor/Villa de l'Océan ★★★

Corniche de la Plage, Bénodet; 📞*02 98 57 04 48; www.kermoor.com.*

These smart *résidences* a few minutes' walk from the sea offer the freedom of self-catering accommodation with use of the facilities of Le Ker-Moor hotel just steps away, including a pool, tennis courts, two bars and a restaurant. The latter, with its huge bright paintings and airy sea views, serves superb local seafood and especially good desserts, some featuring local Plougastel strawberries. It also offers a good kids' menu and, on certain summer evenings, themed buffets around the pool. The apartments have one or two bedrooms; both have a sofabed in the living room, so they can sleep four or six respectively, plus a baby. Clean and fresh, they have full kitchens including dishwashers, but no washing machines. Each has a terrace or balcony from which to survey the shady grounds, with a swing and plenty of space to roam. If you like to keep a handle on the chaos, there's maid service at 20€ a day.

15 units. **Rates** *1-bedroom apartment 485€–1105€ per week, 2-bedroom apartment €585–1240.* **Amenities** ▼ ▤ ♻ ⊡ 🖐 🖼 ⏶⏷ ▨ **In room** ☒ ▢ ⊡

Hôtel de l'Océan ★★

2 Rue Plage des Sables-Blancs, Concarneau; 📞 *02 98 50 53 50; www. hotel-ocean.com.*

This is another unassuming, good-value seaside option for families, with plain, slightly outdated décor but 'superior' rooms accommodating up to three people on a double and a single sofabed, and duplexes rooms for up to four, with a double room with a sea or pool view on the lower level and a twin upstairs. The beach is just over the coast road that runs in front of the

hotel, but there's also a heated indoor pool that's a great bonus when the weather isn't being so kind (its walls can be retracted on hot days). The restaurant is good but rather expensive (the kids' menu alone is 15€) so unless you stay half board (including children's reductions) you're best off walking the 1km (less than a mile) into Concarneau centre, which has some good eating options; including seafood restaurant **Le Porte au Vin** (p. 231).

71 units. **Rates** *79€–149€, duplex for four 105€–179€. Extra bed 18€, Cot 12€.* **Amenities** ▼ ▤ ▦ ⊡ 🖐 🖼 ▨ ⏶⏷ **In room** ▢

INEXPENSIVE

There's a branch of the family-friendly **All Seasons** budget chain (p. 95) at Quimper's Zone de Créac'h Gwen (p. 198), offering family suites with connecting rooms from as little as 91€ with no-cancellation advance booking, including an all-you-can-eat breakfast and free Wi-Fi, or about 107€ on a flexible Family Offer with cancellation up to 6pm on the day of arrival.

Among the main local campsites recommended by Camping Qualité (p. 93), a standout is **L'Orangerie de Lanniron** (📞 *02 98 52 15 56. www.lanniron.com*) a huge four-star site within wonderful 17th-century grounds on the outskirts of Quimper. As well as pitches and mobile homes, it offers apartments, gîtes and villas.

Another four-star mega-site well worth checking out,

Wooden chalet at Le Ty Nadan

especially with very active kids, is **Camping Le Ty Nadan** (02 98 71 75 47, *www.camping-ty-nadan.fr*), a 25-minute drive inland at Locunolé near the border with the Morbihan (p. 99). Its first-rate range of activities includes canoeing on the river or the sea, horse and pony-riding, mountain biking, fishing, and wall and rock climbing, and there's also a treetop adventure park with Brittany's biggest zip-wire. As well as pitches and mobile homes, it has ready-set-up tents, wooden chalets and a few apartments. The site is available through several operators, including Eurocamp (p. 38).

Index